The Labor of Extraction in Latin America

LATIN AMERICAN PERSPECTIVES IN THE CLASSROOM

Series Editor: Ronald H. Chilcote

Urban Latin America
  edited by Tom Angotti
Rereading Women in Latin America and the Caribbean: The Political Economy of Gender
  edited by Jennifer Abbassi and Sheryl L. Lutjens
Contemporary Latin American Revolutions, Second Edition
  by Marc Becker
Development in Theory and Practice: Latin American Perspectives
  edited by Ronald H. Chilcote
Latin American Studies and the Cold War
  edited by Ronald H. Chilcote
Latin American Extractivism: Dependency, Resource Nationalism and Resistance in Broad Perspective
  edited by Steve Ellner
Latin America's Pink Tide: Breakthroughs and Shortcomings
  edited by Steve Ellner
Latin America's Radical Left: Challenges and Complexities of Political Power in the Twenty-first Century
  edited by Steve Ellner
Latin American Social Movements and Progressive Governments: Creative Tensions between Resistance and Convergence
  edited by Steve Ellner, Ronaldo Munck, and Kyla Sankey
Venezuela: Hugo Chávez and the Decline of an "Exceptional Democracy"
  edited by Steve Ellner and Miguel Tinker Salas
Contemporary Latin American Social and Political Thought: An Anthology
  edited by Iván Márquez
Mayan Lives, Mayan Utopias: The Indigenous Peoples of Chiapas and the Zapatista Rebellion
  edited by Jan Rus, Rosalva Aída Hernández, and Shannan L. Mattiace
The United States and Cuba: From Closest Enemies to Distant Friends
  by Francisco López Segrera
Rethinking Latin American Social Movements: Radical Action from Below
  edited by Richard Stahler-Sholk, Harry E. Vanden, and Marc Becker
Memory, Truth, and Justice in Contemporary Latin America
  Edited by Roberta Villalón
Latin American Social Movements in the Twenty-first Century: Resistance, Power, and Democracy
  edited by Richard Stahler-Sholk, Harry E. Vanden, and Glen David Kuecker
Transnational Latina/o Communities: Politics, Processes, and Cultures
  edited by Carlos G. Vélez-Ibáñez and Anna Sampaio, with Manolo González-Estay
Latin American Social Movements and Progressive Governments: Creative Tensions between Resistance and Convergence
  edited by Steve Ellner, Ronaldo Munck, and Kyla Sankey

The Labor of Extraction in Latin America

Edited by Kristin Ciupa and
Jeffery R. Webber

ROWMAN & LITTLEFIELD
Lanham • Boulder • New York • London

Published by Rowman & Littlefield
An imprint of The Rowman & Littlefield Publishing Group, Inc.
4501 Forbes Boulevard, Suite 200, Lanham, Maryland 20706
www.rowman.com

86-90 Paul Street, London EC2A 4NE

British Library Cataloguing in Publication Information available

Library of Congress Cataloging-in-Publication Data Available

ISBN 978-1-5381-8754-8 (cloth: alk. paper)
ISBN 978-1-5381-8755-5 (pbk.: alk. paper)
ISBN 978-1-5381-8756-2 (electronic)

♾️™ The paper used in this publication meets the minimum requirements of American National Standard for Information Sciences—Permanence of Paper for Printed Library Materials, ANSI/NISO Z39.48-1992.

Contents

Part I

THEORETICAL FRAMEWORK

Chapter One

Introduction

The Labor of Extraction in Latin America

Kristin Ciupa and Jeffery R. Webber

Natural resource extraction and primary commodity export remain persistent features of Latin American capitalism in the twenty-first century. Since the early 1990s, the Economic Commission for Latin America and the Caribbean (ECLAC) notes that there has been a "systematic year-by-year expansion in primary exports," with their share in total exports between 50 to 60 percent since 2003 (ECLAC 2022a). The most recent iteration of Latin American extractivism was fueled by a primary commodity boom in the early 2000s, driven by demand from emerging economies, particularly China (ECLAC 2011). The price of oil and gas, minerals, and agricultural commodities began rising in 2003, and remained high until 2014, with the exception of a brief drop in 2009 in the context of the global financial crisis (World Bank 2022). Within this general trend, the performance of specific commodities has varied. While nonrenewable natural resource exports (oil, gas, and minerals) were the predominant source of Latin American export growth from 1994 to 2013, renewable natural resources (agriculture) have driven primary commodity export growth since 2013 (ECLAC 2022a). Agricultural prices rose almost 30 percent between July 2020 and July 2021, when oil, gas, and mineral prices declined in the context of COVID-19 in 2020 (ECLAC 2022b). The recovery of primary commodity prices across the board in 2021 indicates that this trend is unlikely to abate any time soon.

The centrality of extractivism to Latin American capital accumulation not only puts permanent pressure on nature, but also ties national economies and social structures to international demand for resources, with Latin America serving as a source of primary commodities in the international division of labor. Extractivism and primary commodity export are thus persistent features of Latin American capitalism across time and space, shaped by the region's role in the global market. While oil, gas, mineral, and agricultural extraction

3

each produce unique economic, geographical, political, and social structures and relations, all have altered nature and peoples' relationship to it, shaping how people live and how work is organized within and outside of extractive sectors. Different political economic periods, characterized by changing conditions in the global market and the political orientations of Latin American governments, have influenced the extent and nature of foreign capital's participation in resource extraction, the role of the state in extractive sectors, the relationship between capital and labor, and the power of labor organizing, all while maintaining systems of extraction. Given the centrality of extractivism to Latin American capitalism, conditions of labor and labor organizing in Latin America should be analyzed within this context. This volume explores the relationship between productive labor and extractive capitalism in Latin America today, situating national variations within the overarching form of extractive accumulation.

This chapter is organized in six parts. First, it distinguishes the category of "productive labor" from "social reproductive labor," and "human labor" in general, and explains the reasoning behind our narrow focus on productive labor. Second, it frames the edited collection as a contribution to a triadic dialectical tradition that focuses on the three interrelated categories of capital, land, and labor, even as it focuses special attention on the third category. Third, it identifies a central methodological problem of existing social scientific literature on extractivism in Latin America as the absence of attention to the question of productive labor that often expresses itself in a dual dialectic between capital and land/nature. Fourth, it suggests a critical reanimation of the analytical framework developed by Charles Bergquist in the late 1980s, to understand workers in Latin American export-production complexes, and offers a useful point of departure for climbing out of the current impasse of extractivist studies in the region. Fifth, it surveys key developments that have transformed extractivist labor markets in Latin America in the decades of neoliberal restructuring since Bergquist formulated his theoretical and historical approach to these questions. Finally, it introduces the architecture of the following chapters of the book.

PRODUCTIVE LABOR AS THE HEART
OF CAPITALIST EXTRACTION

The main objective of this edited collection is to inaugurate a research agenda aimed at filling an enormous gap concerning the question of labor in the extant literature on extractivism in Latin America. It does so by exploring the anatomy of productive labor within contemporary capitalist extraction in Latin

America, a subject matter largely passed over by social scientists in recent years.[1] We depart from the axiomatic premise that productive labor constitutes the "heart" of the matter, as the source of value under capitalism, including capitalism in its extractive form. Following Marx, we understand labor in general to encompass all of the intentional, conscious, creative, and imaginative life activity distinctive to the species-being of humanity in its necessary interaction with non-human nature (Marx 1992, 328). Human life could not go on without biophysical interaction with the natural world—the productive appropriation by humans of aspects of the physical world, including animals, plants, land, and water, among other things—of which humans are also a part. This interaction of humans with nonhuman nature is premised not merely on instinct, but also conscious "awareness of their needs and the ability and intent to design specific ways of meeting these needs," distinguishing humans from most nonhuman animals (Ferguson 2019, 15). As the basis of our species-being, human labor, understood as life-activity, is existential, constituted both by humanity's relations with nonhuman nature, and social relations between humans themselves. As these relationships change, so too does the character of labor and its degrees of freedom and equality (Ferguson 2019, 16–17). The geographically and historically specific social forms assumed by human labor—how it is organized—"matters to how freely, or not, people create their worlds, their societies, their lives. Inquiry into the social organization of work, then, is essential if social theory is to serve freedom" (Ferguson 2019, 17).

With this understanding of general human labor as a backdrop, our analytical remit in the introduction to this book is more restricted. We focus exclusively on capitalistically productive labor in the export-production complex of contemporary Latin American economies.[2] First of all, therefore, we need to distinguish between social reproductive and productive labor, both of which are necessary for capitalism to reproduce itself. By productive labor we refer to labor that directly creates value in the Marxist sense—that is, labor which produces value that can be measured economically from the standpoint of capital, where value is "the surplus (or extra) that returns to capital beyond its expenditure. It is, in other words, the growth of capital after accounting for all expenses in production" (Jaffe 2020, 18). The surplus, or extra, in question is directly traceable to workers (Marx 1997, 301). The worker produces more value than is needed for the reproduction of their own labor-power because they work in excess of the time it takes to create that value. In light of competition with other capitals, the capitalist is driven to expand their business and to "reduce the labor time necessary for the worker's subsistence and increase the rate of exploitation" (Moody 2014, 7).

Capitalism is a socioeconomic system rooted in the production of goods and services for sale on the market in order to make a profit. It is rooted in a principal and exploitative social division of labor between those who own the means of production (capitalists) and those with nothing to sell but their capacity to labor (workers). Both capitalists and workers are market dependent in different ways. Capitalists seek to produce saleable goods and services for profit by mixing the means of production that they own together with labor power that they purchase from the labor market. Workers, in turn, must try to sell their ability to labor to capitalists in exchange for a wage in order to gain access to the means of life, such as rent, clothing, and food, which in capitalist society are commodities (buyable and saleable goods and services) acquirable only through money. Horizontally, there is competition between capitalists which forces each one to try to drive down the costs of production (including wages and health and safety measures) in order to remain profitable. Vertically, there is a conflict of interest between capitalists and workers. For example, at the typical worksite a worker will want higher wages for less intensive work and more autonomy, while a capitalist will want them to have lower wages for more intensive work and managerial oversite to achieve this (Bernstein 2000, 241–70; Wood 2017).

Within the logic of the capitalist system, the entire driving force behind production is the necessity of expanding capitalist value, that is the increase or "valorization" of capital itself (Jaffe 2020, 18). Value is created through the production of goods and services for exchange on the market, that is, when the "product of labor is destined for sale on the market" (Ferguson 2019, 123). This is what we mean when we refer to productive labor in this introduction. This is distinguishable from not-for-profit, social reproductive labor (paid or unpaid), which is explicitly not labor set in motion to produce a commodity for sale on the market.[3] Social reproductive labor is the work involved in maintaining and reproducing human life. Under capitalism, most of this labor has been performed, unpaid, by women within the family unit, but portions have also been carried out, to different degrees in different social formations and in different historical periods, by the welfare state or through the market, with variations traceable in part to the strength or weakness of feminist struggle in distinct settings and circumstances (Arruzza 2015, 11).

Again, social reproductive labor and productive labor are necessary for the reproduction of capitalist society. A full account of labor in any particular historical situation would therefore need to concretely study the interconnections between both kinds of labor and the social struggles surrounding them. A narrowly focused investigation into exclusively value-productive labor, therefore, will necessarily result in "only a partial and incomplete understanding of capitalist society" (Jaffe 2020, 24). We nonetheless proceed on this course for three fundamental reasons. First, no single collection could adequately tackle the entirety of the complex assemblage of labor and its associated struggles that constitutes contemporary extractive capitalism in Latin America. Second, in the extant work on social struggles related to extractivism in Latin America there is an emphasis on social reproductive struggles (around territory, land, bodies, and ecology, for example), even when this angle is not explicitly theorized. Third, and relatedly, the social science literature on Latin American extractivism has paid almost no attention to value-productive labor and its struggles. If the valorization of capital is the driver behind all production under capitalism, it seems a grave analytical miscalculation to ignore the labor directly behind the creation of value.

By extractivism, we mean the matrix of economic, social, ideological, and political processes involved in the capitalist extraction of natural resources in the mining, natural gas and oil, and agroindustrial sectors of the economy, and their transformation into commodities for sale on the market in pursuit of profit.[4] Of course, taking productive labor to be central to extractivism does not exhaust all that needs to be said about the latter topic: "this would be analogous to thinking that the explanation of the anatomy of the heart and its functions would suffice to explain the whole anatomy of the human body" (Arruzza 2014). Even as the overarching analysis of the chapters included in this volume attempts to restore what anthropologist Fernando Coronil called the triadic capital-labor-nature dialectic, our relative emphasis within the triad falls on productive labor, given its systematic neglect in the existing literature compared to the other two parts. Methodologically, this is justified by the dialectical necessity of understanding not just the whole process of capitalist extractivism, but the parts, and not just the connectedness of parts of the whole, but the relative autonomy of the parts themselves (Malm 2018, 188).

THE TRIADIC DIALECTIC OF CAPITAL, LAND, AND LABOR

In his seminal work on the Venezuelan landlord-capitalist state, *The Magical State: Nature, Money, and Modernity in Venezuela*, Fernando Coronil argues in favor of a triadic reading of the Marxist dialectic (involving capital, labor, and land—Marx's "trinity formula"), against the more common Marxist reading of dialectics (at least at the time Coronil was writing) as dual (involving capital and labor) (Coronil 1997, 60–62). For Coronil, such a shift to open dialectics is necessary for a proper understanding of the nature-society relation, in which nature and society are conceived as "distinct but unified," with human beings constituting a part of nature while simultaneously transforming it through their life activities that also transform themselves. Following Marx, this is precisely the "metabolic interaction" between nature and society (Coronil 1997, 26–27). We can describe the properties of nature and society as dialectical insofar as the parts acquire new properties by being part of a whole (in this case, the specific metabolic interaction between humans and extra-human nature characterized by a particular mode of production), and likewise as the parts acquire new properties they transform the properties of the whole: "one thing cannot exist without the other, that one acquires its properties from its relation to the other, that the properties of both evolve as a consequence of their interpenetration" (Levins and Lewontin 1985, 3).

However, as Andreas Malm points out, while the properties of the social are ultimately dependent on natural properties, the inverse is not true. That is, nature is not ultimately dependent on society. The social is made up of material, and the material world is at base natural, with nature having existed long before society's emergence. "Something social," Malm writes, "must have something natural as its substratum. Being material means being bound up with nature. If relations of production are natural, they are also, by definition, built on and maintained through the natural" (Malm 2018, 65–66). While nature can be taken as "given," therefore, it is also true that it is made into a "second nature" through the transformative activities of human beings (Coronil 1997, 26).

Of particular relevance to the framework developed in the present book, Coronil argues that the international division of labor in the world capitalist system should also be conceived as an international division of nature, with the latter providing the material foundation for the former. This dual international division constitutes a unitary process involving both nature and labor, in that labor always exists in space and transforms the nature of particular locations (Coronil 1997, 29). In our warming world, an ever more apparent paradox reveals itself, what Malm calls "the paradox of historicized nature." As human society shapes nature more intensively over time, nature lashes back in equal or excess measure, shaping our own lives all the more decisively in turn (Malm 2018, 76). In Alberto Toscano's complimentary reworking of Jean-Paul Sartre's vignette on peasant labor and deforestation in Chinese history, a similarly paradoxical process is identified, "in which 'we' become our own enemy in the shape of a nature that bears the imprint of our praxis (in ways specific to its material disposition)" (Toscano 2018).

As Coronil reminds us, wealth under capitalism is irreducible to the social creation of value, capitalist wealth being also derivative of the material wealth of nature (Coronil 1997, 31). In contrast to labor, land, for Marx, does not produce value, but rather appropriates it through rents (Coronil 1997, 59). Since value is created by society rather than by nature, rents relate only to the distribution of surplus value and not its generation (Coronil 1997, 47). Crucially, Marx understood land as a social relation, instead of a thing, such that "agricultural or mineral resources [are] not [thought of] as inert objects but as elements of social formations constituted through the socialization of nature" (Coronil 1997, 57). In this way, we arrive at Coronil's "triadic dialectic." The idea of focusing on the commodification of land, labor, and capital together is not simply to add on additional variables, but "to apprehend the relational character of the units included in the making of the modern world" (Coronil 1997, 62).

A DIALECTICS WITHOUT LABOR? THE GAP
IN THE EXISTING LITERATURE

In our view, the problem of dialectics in the twenty-first-century literature on extractivism in Latin America is at once the same and different to the problem identified by Coronil in the dominant Marxist literature of roughly the 1970s to the 1990s. The problem is the same insofar as the predominant dialectic remains dual rather than triadic. It is different insofar as rather than the pivot of the dual dialectic being capital-labor (the problem identified by Coronil), it is instead capital-nature, with labor as the absent category. The study of extractivism in Latin America, while deeply concerned with the destructive impact of capitalism on the natural world, has, with some important exceptions, largely ignored the question of productive labor.

TRENDS IN THE LATIN AMERICAN
LITERATURE ON EXTRACTIVISM

Consider the themes taken up in recent, exemplary edited collections on extractivism and political ecology published by the Latin American Council of Social Sciences. The thematics of Constanza Narancio's edited collection, *Feminismo y ambiente: Un campo emergente en los estudios feministas de América Latina y el Caribe*, for example, include indigenous women's involvement in defensive, anti-extractivist struggles in the Colombian Amazon pivoting on issues of territory and the indigenous concept of *buen vivir* (living well), ecofeminist struggles in defense of the "web of life," public policy alternatives to extractivism, and the centrality of decolonial and communitarian thought and practice to contemporary feminist environmentalism in Latin America (Narancio 2022). The collection, *Defensa del territorio, la cultura y la vida ante el avance extractivista: Una perspectiva desde América Latina*, edited by Hugo Pereira, Eraldo da Silva Ramos Filho, and Angelina Herrera, covers the agrarian question in contemporary Paraguay; capitalist expansion and associated dispossession in the soy and ranching sectors; the growing role of foreign ownership in land tenure in Latin America; conflicts over indigenous territory in areas of extractivist activity; the mining boom and environmental conflicts in Zacatecas, Mexico; the political economy of landholding and palm oil expansion in Colombia; Mapuche indigenous resistance to extractivist expansion in southern Chile; and the role of unpaid, gendered, social-reproductive labor in extractive sectors of Brazil's economy (Pereira, da Silva Ramos Filho, and Herrera 2022). In the one exception that proves the rule, *Defensa del territorio* includes a single chapter on unionism and extractivism, in which the authors lament the dismal state of social scientific work on the topic (López et al. 2022, 95–109).

The absence of productive labor is similarly apparent in Lucas Sablich's edited volume, *Ambiente, cambio climático y buen vivir en América Latina y el Caribe*. This collection features articles on women's role in indigenous territorial defense against extractive expansion in Chiapas, Mexico; the relationship between extractivism, dispossession, and the body/territory in Peru and Brazil; Afro-Colombian community resilience in the face of extractivism in Colombia; indigenous resistance to extractivism in Amazonian Ecuador; the role of glaciers (under threat from mining) in the cosmovision of Mapuche indigenous communities in Chile; feminist, indigenous, and youth organizations responding collectively to extractivism in Paraguay; and visions of *buen vivir* in the face of extractivism throughout Latin America (Sablich 2022). These recent collections repeat many of the concerns taken up by political ecological research over the last decade or so in Latin America by social scientists concerned with extractivism broadly conceived. As a result, pursuing a longer inventory here of the subject areas covered by seminal collections on the political ecology of extraction would quickly prove redundant. Despite insight into multiple areas of the complex assemblage of issues that constitutes contemporary capitalist extractivism in Latin America, what consistently stands out in this research is the total absence, or extreme marginality, of the question of productive labor.

A survey of the recent work of arguably the two most influential scholar-activists working on extractivism in contemporary Latin America—Maristella Svampa and Eduardo Gudynas—is similarly revealing. Significant sections of Svampa's most important and wide-ranging book to date, *Debates Latinoamericanos: Indianismo, desarrollo, dependencia y populismo*, deal directly with theoretical and empirical trends in extractivism in the region. New patterns of economic dependency; indigenous resistance; the "environmentalization of social struggles"; the political, ideological, cultural, and social consequences of the "commodities consensus"; the puzzle of "rights of nature"; the intricacies of different understandings of *buen vinir*; and the "transition problem" (or how societies might shift away from the present developmental model toward "post-extractivism") are among the relevant themes discussed, often with rigor and insight (Svampa 2017a, 151–60). And yet, no comment on workplace struggles in extractivist sectors. Roughly one-third of Svampa's more recent book, *Del cambio de época al fin de ciclo: Gobiernos progresistas, extractivismo y movimientos sociales en América Latina*, is devoted explicitly to issues of extractivism. Here, the "commodities consensus" (an extractivist developmental paradigm shared between progressive and conservative governments alike); the "ecoterritorial" turn taken up by socio-environmental movements in the region; connections between new popular feminisms, extractivism, and patriarchy in Latin America; and the reconfiguration of global North-South power dynamics and associated relations of dependency and extractivism in Latin America are the predominant concerns. As in her earlier work, the issue of extractivist productive labor is absent (Svampa 2017b). The same could be said of Svampa's only book to date available in English, essentially a condensation and reworking of the themes she has developed in her work on extractivism over the last decade (Svampa 2019).

For Eduardo Gudynas, an essay from relatively early in the period of progressive "Pink Tide" governments in the region lays out a number of the themes that would come to animate his research over the next decade (Gudynas 2009, 187–225). In that essay, he begins with the puzzle of the persistence of state support for primary commodity extraction for export over the long durée of Latin American history, despite considerable evidence for the negative long-term effects on national development. In particular, Gudynas is concerned with why progressive governments that started to assume office in several Latin American countries in the mid-2000s continued this trend, rather than embarking on a political-economic strategy of anti-extractivist rupture. In his view, this phenomenon was not simply inertia, that is, a path-dependent holdover from previous regimes. Rather, new progressive governments enthusiastically subsidized and facilitated the acceleration of extractivism. At the same time, Gudynas is careful to note change as well as continuity, notably labeling the patterns of development under progressive governments the "new extractivism." Under the "new extractivism," the state plays a more direct regulatory role, including more transparent rules for concessions, increases in tax and royalty regimes, and the revitalization of state-owned energy companies. The novelty of the "new extractivism" of the mid-2000s also involved a changing dynamic of the world market, in which high commodity prices reigned and capital flowed into Latin American extractive sectors from abroad to take advantage of this fact. The consequent intensification of extractivism across agroindustry, mining, and oil and natural gas, according to Gudynas, was the deterritorialization, and/or territorial fragmentation, of peasant and indigenous communities. This led to growing socio-environmental conflicts, including anti-extractivist movements running up against the policies of progressive governments. Nonetheless, progressive governments were able to legitimate their rule for a time through the distribution of easy rents, while commodity prices remained high (Gudynas 2009).

Elsewhere, Gudynas theoretically developed the legitimacy factor more thoroughly through the concept of the "compensatory state." Skimming from the rent generated during high commodity prices in the early twenty-first century, many progressive governments in Latin America established "compensatory states," in which legitimacy rested on modest redistribution efforts via cash-transfer programs to the extremely poor, while the underlying class structure and property regime of the societies in question remained largely intact (Gudynas 2012, 128–46). The reproduction of these political economies depended upon states continuing to prioritize the maintenance of private property rights and juridical environments in which multinationals could profit. Even before compensatory states ran into economic problems with declining commodity prices, the intensification of extractivism led to socio-environmental conflict, often necessitating state repression for extractivism to continue. The compensatory state, then, was always a mixture of cooptation and coercion (Gudynas 2012). In his most comprehensive and influential book, *Extractivismos: Ecología, economía y política de un modo de entender el desarrollo la naturaleza*, Gudynas synthesizes and elaborates his political-ecological framework for understanding large-scale mining, oil and natural gas extraction, and mono-crop, industrial agriculture, exploring further the negative ecological and health consequences of these various forms of extractivism, the degradation of democracy and justice with which they are often accompanied, and the necessity of cultural and ideological change for a radically different alternative conception of development (Gudynas 2015; 2021). In his most recent book, Gudynas develops an argument on what he sees as the intimate relationship between extractivism and corrupt forms of rule (Gudynas 2018b). Despite the enormous range of Gudynas's work, the problem of productive labor is once again conspicuously neglected.[5]

More surprisingly, perhaps, the absence of productive labor in recent literature on extractivism in Latin America extends to research of an explicitly Marxist orientation. José Seoane, Emilio Taddei, and Clara Algranati's *Extractivismo, despojo y crisis climática: Desafíos para los movimientos sociales y los proyectos emancipatorios de Nuestra América*, is an important example (Seoane, Taddei, and Algranati 2013). One of the best and earliest Marxist interventions on twenty-first-century extractivism, the text is informed theoretically by David Harvey's concept of "accumulation by dispossession," where primitive accumulation is understood as a continuous process necessary for the ongoing reproduction of capitalism. The authors focus on how the extractivist model in twenty-first-century Latin America systematically produces accumulation by dispossession and how this precipitates socio-ecological axes of conflict and the formation of anti-extractivist social movements. With a sophisticated historical sensitivity and political-economic acumen, the book marks an important turning point in social scientific inquiry into extractivist processes. Nonetheless, it is notably silent on the question of the productive labor and workplace struggles at the heart of the extractive sectors it investigates.

Similar themes of dispossession of peasant and indigenous communities as ongoing primitive accumulation, or "enclosure of the commons," constitute the bulk of a special issue of the Marxist journal *Revista Theomai* (no. 26). Another issue of the same journal approaches the question of extractivism through the potentially rich theoretical and praxiological relationship between the traditions of *buen vivir* and ecosocialism (no. 32). But here, too, the question of productive labor is sidelined. Claudio Katz's crucial essay criticizing the "commodities consensus" for failing to distinguish adequately between the extractivist governance orientations of progressive and reactionary governments in the region is another case in point. In many respects a masterful survey on Latin America's subordinate integration into the world market and the implications for the contemporary political economy of extractivism, this essay can nonetheless be added to the list of those ignoring the question of productive labor in extractive sectors (Katz 2015). These examples are broadly representative of the avowedly Marxist literature on extractivism in the region over the last decade.

TRENDS IN THE ANGLOPHONE LITERATURE ON LATIN AMERICAN EXTRACTIVISM

The inattention to productive labor is even starker in the Anglophone literature on Latin American extractivism. Anthony Bebbington and Jeffrey Bury's edited collection, *Subterranean Struggles: New Dynamics of Mining, Oil, and Gas in Latin America*, for example, is a wide-ranging collection of essays from a political-ecological perspective (Bebbington and Bury 2013). The collection covers new geographies of extractive industries, "resource nationalism" in Bolivia under the government of Evo Morales; community, peasant, and indigenous resistance to mining in Peru and Ecuador; the socio-ecological impacts of natural gas and mining extractivism in Bolivia; the political ecology of socio-environmental protest movements in Peru; and social mobilization around extractivist issues region-wide. Labor struggles at the workplace in relevant extractive sectors receive no serious attention in the collection, with the word "union" appearing only once (in reference to the mid-twentieth century) and "strike" (in its labor meaning) not at all.

Despite its critical political-economic perspective, Steve Ellner's edited volume, *Latin American Extractivism: Dependency, Resource Nationalism, and Resistance in Broad Perspective*, is no exception (Ellner 2020). Labor employed in extractive sectors and associated workplace labor struggles receive only fleeting mention in the book, despite sweeping coverage of the political economy of mining in Colombia, foreign direct investment and extractive sector growth in Bolivia, Chinese investment in Venezuelan extractive sectors, resource nationalism and the Pink Tide, public policy with regard to extractive industry in Mexico under Andrés Manuel López Obrador, water conflicts related to mining expansion in Ecuador, the gendered dynamics of soybean extraction in Argentina, mining governance in Honduras and El Salvador, artisanal mining in the Andes, and Black women's anti-extractivism struggles in Colombia.

Ellner's introductory chapter to Latin American extractivism is also, in a sense, a left-wing variation of a more general institutionalist inflection in the mainstream extractivist literature (Ellner 2020). Ellner rejects the "neo-extractivism" perspective[6]: a broad critique of primary commodity dependence, where, in the context of the relative decline of the Pink Tide, scholars argue that extractivism cannot promote meaningful development regardless of the state-specific policy frameworks that govern its characteristics (Ellner 2020, 4–7). While acknowledging that governments across the political spectrum have been responsible for environmental destruction, violating indigenous rights, and failing to diversify economies, Ellner contends that focusing on the "commodity consensus" between governments with different political orientations obscures the real policy differences between Pink Tide and non–Pink Tide governments. By "condemn[ing] progressive and conservative governments more or less equally," Ellner argues that writers committed to the neo-extractivism perspective fail to support the genuinely progressive institutions, policies, and legal reforms of Pink Tide governments (Ellner 2020, 21). When such governments are challenged by neoliberal oppositions with US backing, this position has the unintended consequence of weakening support for the Pink Tide and may help facilitate instability and regime change.

Such an emphasis on governance and institutional variation in extractive sectors across different countries more often assumes a liberal guise, equally inattentive to productive labor. Ann Helwege and Anthony Bebbington are representative of this approach, arguing that good governance, institution-building, and a development-based approach could solve extractive conflicts and facilitate development in Latin America today (Bebbington 2012b; Bebbington et al. 2018; Helwege 2015). Bebbington, for example, argues in favor of institution-building to ameliorate extractive conflicts. In particular, he calls for labor and service markets that create backward and forward linkages to extraction, corporate social responsibility programs, and tax and royalty schemes, all of which will ostensibly impact local economies in positive ways (Bebbington 2012b, 16–18). Relying on political settlements theory, Bebbington et al. argue that political stability is key to institution-building, which includes "pacts and bargains" between different factions of the elite (Bebbington et al. 2018, 16). Recognizing that new actors emerge and decline due to changes in national economic structure, influenced by external markets, and activists, they argue that the political and cultural ideas tied to natural resources, and "the interacting influences of transnational, national, and subnational actors, especially those living in areas where natural resources become rapidly valorized" are key to political stability (Bebbington et al. 2018, 16). This perspective posits that avoiding class conflict and elite pacts are key to building the institutions that will produce stable extractive industries. Axiomatically, a theoretical and empirical focus on the potentiality of extractive labor's capacity to disrupt the accumulation process through its strategic economic positionality, for the benefit of labor and in opposition to the interests of capital, is ideologically ruled out of order from the start.

Reflective of a broader turn in the literature away from political economy and toward theories of decoloniality and critical indigenous studies, Macarena Gómez-Barris's *The Extractive Zone: Social Ecologies and Decolonial Perspectives* assesses the politics, aesthetics, and performative praxis of indigenous movements and in majority indigenous areas of South America (Gómez-Barris 2017). It is perhaps unsurprising that extractivist productive labor receives no attention in the book. Beyond literature that explores dispossession as something that happens to indigenous people and peasants, some literature situates these groups as agents in the process of negotiating the conditions under which their livelihoods and relationships are shaped by the intersection between international extractive industries and changing local economic structures. An edited book by Cecilie Vindal Ødegaard and Juan Javier Rivera Andía explores how indigeneity is represented, performed, and recreated in struggles over extractivism by national and international actors (Ødegaard and Andía 2019). The collection demonstrates that indigenous engagement with extractivism is not limited to opposition or resistance, and rather, explores the ways in which indigenous groups negotiate and adapt to new extractivist industries to "maintain their ability to be part of a localized community in a socially legitimate manner" (Ødegaard and Andía 2019, 29). Adopting a decolonial perspective, Laura Rodríguez Castro explores how extractivism and dispossession associated with foreign tourism and flower export affect rural women (Castro 2021). Castro addresses the question of labor, but specifically through the lens of its gendered potential for empowerment/disempowerment of women. Castro aims both to explore how new flower and tourism industries are exploitative to women, but also to articulate how women navigate and understand their experience participating in these industries. In both cases, Castro finds that the women used work "for their own gains and on their own terms" (Castro 2021, 56). This involved sharing different types of work (cooking, farm work, and care work) with family members, colleagues, and friends, and conceptualizing these forms of work as temporary income supplements, rather than their only option. She argues that the women were neither inherently empowered not disempowered through employment in these industries, and rather "were negotiating within these spaces in conflicting ways" (Castro 2021, 52).

More paradoxical, perhaps, is the absence, or underdeveloped treatment, of productive labor that characterizes recent, high-profile Marxisant ethnographies of extractive sectors in contemporary Bolivia and Ecuador. In *Bolivia in the Age of Gas*, Bret Gustafson provides some plausible opening hypotheses as to why Bolivian oil and gas workers did not form a militant part of the wider labor movement in the twentieth or twenty-first centuries, but the book ultimately never offers a developed explanation, and workers employed directly in the gas sector are excluded from its discussion of labor in the Morales era (Gustafson 2020). In *Resource Radicals: From Petro-Nationalism to Post-Extractivism in Ecuador*, Thea Riofrancos offers an important survey of crucial disputes between the anti-extractivist indigenous social movement left, and the pro-extractivist, progressive government of Rafael Correa. Despite the considerable range of themes broached in the text—particularly vis-à-vis the process of Ecuador's Constituent Assembly and related extra-parliamentary struggles—productive labor in the country's extractive sectors, and how its interests might relate to the disputes between these "two lefts" is unexamined (Riofrancos 2020).

A similar neglect is apparent in most of the explicitly Marxist anglophone literature on extractivism in Latin America. In Todd Gordon and Jeffery R. Webber's *Blood of Extraction: Canadian Imperialism in Latin America*, the theme of anti-extractivist struggles at the point of production is only marginally addressed, despite a region-wide survey of prominent socio-ecological movements confronting extractivist projects in Latin America undertaken by Canadian capital (Gordon and Webber 2016). One further example of the surprising neglect of labor in explicitly Marxist research into extractivism in Latin America is the influential volume edited by James Petras and Henry Veltmeyer, *The New Extractivism: A Post-Neoliberal Development Model or Imperialism of the Twenty-First Century* (Petras and Veltmeyer 2014). Despite wide-ranging discussion of imperial dynamics, capitalist interests in soy and mining in Argentina, extractive governance in Bolivia under Evo Morales, peasant resistance to extractivism in Colombia, government discourse and public policy in extractivist industries in Ecuador, the political ecology of mining in Mexico, socio-ecological conflict in Peru, and extractivism and the "post-neoliberal" state, the question of productive labor struggles in extractivist sectors remains unanswered in the volume.

A partial exception to the trend of productive labor's marginalization is evident in the literature on agroindustrial extractivism, where the labor of direct-producers is generally taken into consideration. For example, Cristóbal Kay demonstrates the connections between changing social relations and agricultural practices in rural areas in Latin America, free market policies under neoliberalism, and the commodity boom that accompanied liberalization (Kay 2015). A shift from traditional crops to more profitable agro-export commodities, and a high concentration of capital as transnational agri-business dominated the sector, led to a process of proletarianization as peasant farmers could not compete and increasingly resorted to off-farm work (Kay 2015, 73). The nature of work changed due to mechanization and a feminization and precarization of labor, all of which led to fewer labor opportunities, and temporary and flexible work that is of greater intensity and subject to greater control by agri-business companies (Kay 2015, 76). However, even here, the bulk of the literature tends to focus on peasants qua peasants (and processes of land dispossession and associated proletarianization) or indigenous communities as collectivities (and processes of territorial dispossession), rather than the theme of agrarian workers, the problem of exploitation, and labor resistance at the point of production (McKay, Alonso-Fradejas, and Ezquerro-Cañete 2021; Vergara-Camus and Kay 2017; Alonso-Fradejas 2015).

A BERGQUISTIAN TURN: WORKERS IN THE EXPORT-PRODUCTION COMPLEX

Why begin with productive labor? Exploitation under capitalism is the foundation of the capital-labor relation, made possible by the fact that capitalists own and control the means of production while laborers must sell their labor power in exchange for a wage in order to survive. On this basis, exploitation consists of the ability of capital to "pay workers a 'fair' wage in the labor market, but then use workers' labor power in the sphere of production to generate greater value (surplus value) than the price of the original wage" (Selwyn

2014, 5). This structurally unequal and antagonistic relationship systematically favors capital, but nonetheless is a relationship in which labor derives a latent, potential power precisely due to its role as value producer. Within the process of accumulation, productive workers enjoy what Erik Olin Wright termed "structural power," simply due to their position within the economic system. Individuals in tight labor markets or a particular group of workers located in a "strategic location" in a "key industrial sector" are instances of structural power (Wright 2000, 962). In her seminal book, *Forces of Labor*, Beverly J. Silver refines Wright's conceptualization of structural power by specifying the two subtypes of structural power implied but underdeveloped in his analysis. She calls the subtype that refers to the consequences of tight labor markets, "marketplace bargaining power," and the subtype that pertains to the strategic location of workers in a key industry, "workplace bargaining power" (Silver 2003, 13). The latter subtype is most crucial for our purposes, and Silver goes on to elaborate that such workplace bargaining power:

> accrues to workers who are enmeshed in tightly integrated production processes, where a localized work stoppage in a key node can cause disruptions on a much wider scale than the stoppage itself. Such bargaining power has been in evidence when entire assembly lines have been shut down by a stoppage in one segment of the line, and when entire corporations relying on just-in-time delivery of parts have been brought to a standstill by railway workers' strikes. (Silver 2003, 13)

Such structural power opens up the possibility of disrupting the process of capitalist accumulation, and in so doing to shift the balance of power toward labor, with improvements in working conditions, among other things, as a potential result of such disruption.

However, structural power is not automatically realizable by workers. Structural power is generally activated only when workers manage to develop a sufficiently robust "associational power," referring to "the various forms of power that result from the formation of collective organization of workers," including "such things as unions and parties," but also potentially extending to "a variety of other forms, such as works councils or forms of institutional representation of workers on boards of directors in schemes of worker codetermination, or even, in certain circumstances, community organizations" (Wright 2000, 962). By adopting a "labor-centered" perspective on Latin American extractivism, our attention is directed toward the myriad forms assumed by labor struggles against exploitation in the sectors of agroindustry, mining, and natural gas and oil, and the various compositions or decompositions, connections or chasms, between these workers' differentiated, potential structural power and their differentiated associational abilities to leverage that power in different countries and sectors. The challenge of a "labor-centered" perspective, in this sense, "is to conceptually connect these struggles and their potential outcomes to a vision of human development free from exploitation" (Selwyn 2014, 208). The analytical perspective advanced in this book is an attempt to add a Latin American perspective to broader, emerging literatures linking themes of ecology and labor, as well as cutting-edge literature on labor regimes and the environment (Malm 2016; Huber 2022; Moore 2015; Campling and Colas 2021; Campling et al. 2016; Baglioni et al. 2022; Taylor 2014; Taylor and Rioux 2017).

The research carried out over several decades by historian Charles Bergquist represents one of the most important, and thus far largely neglected, pool of resources available on the structural and associational power of export workers located in strategic sectors of Latin American economies during the region's modern capitalist era, as well as the consequences of that power in shaping different political and economic development outcomes of distinct national societies (Bergquist 1978; 1986; 1996; Hylton and LeGrand 2021). Bergquist first introduced the analytical centrality of investigating Latin American export workers in order to understand the variegated development patterns of different countries in the region, a region shaped fundamentally by its subordinate integration into the capitalist world market and international division of labor (Bergquist 1984). Bergquist then developed and refined these initial insights in *Labor in Latin America*. In our view, the framework of inquiry developed in that book represents an untapped theoretical resource for correcting the imbalance of contemporary studies of Latin American extractivism insofar as they neglect the question of productive labor (Bergquist 1986). One key purpose of this edited volume, therefore, is to initiate a collective attempt to explore the potentialities (and limits) of critically adapting Bergquist's theoretical axioms—originally formulated almost four decades ago—to the current phenomena of capitalist agroindustrial, mining, and natural gas and oil extraction in Latin America.

In *Labor in Latin America*, Bergquist begins with a disarmingly straightforward thesis:

> Workers, especially those engaged in production for export, have played a determining role in the modern history of Latin American societies. Their struggle for material well-being and control over their own lives has fundamentally altered the direction of national political evolution and the pattern of economic development in the countries of the region. (Bergquist 1986, vii)

Latin American historians attempting to explain the region's modern history should not proceed randomly across all potential explanatory factors (Bergquist 1986, x). In determining the best point of entry, he suggests, there are good analytical and political reasons for beginning with workers in the "export-production complex" (Bergquist 1986, 8).

Analytically, Bergquist draws on classical Latin American structuralist economists to demonstrate that export sectors of Latin American economies have been crucially important to patterns of capitalist development and state formation in the region since the 1880s, when the advanced development of industrial societies in the North Atlantic basin fostered a surplus of capital and technological resources, leading to an enormous boost in the export of European capital to much of the rest of the world, including Latin America. Latin American ruling classes responded to this opportunity to play a vanguard role in the transformation of their societies, with one after another country turning to primary commodity production for export (Bergquist 1986, 1). In the late nineteenth and early twentieth centuries, these export sectors were the main determinant of capital accumulation and the principal source of foreign exchange. They consequently determined a country's capacity to import capital, manufactured goods, and technology. Export sectors, furthermore, underpinned the revenue of governments and were decisive to the expansion and capability of states. Export sectors continued to be important into the mid-twentieth century, even in those countries in which import-substitution industrialization policies led to widescale industrial development. Insofar as exports generated foreign exchange, these sectors substituted for a capital goods sector during the import-substitution industrialization era (Bergquist 1986, 9).

Combining insights from Latin American structuralism with the Marxist premise of class conflict as the integral driver of historical change, and specifically the struggle between capital and labor under capitalism, Bergquist alerts us to "the overwhelming importance of workers in export production within the Latin American working class" (Bergquist 1986, 10). While owners of the means of production in the export sectors of Latin American societies after 1880 were able to exert enormous economic and structural power as the most dynamic section of the capitalist class, so too were export workers structurally possessed "of tremendous inherent economic and political power" (Bergquist 1986, 10). Therefore, when these two leading sections of capital and labor inevitably clashed in the early twentieth century, those conflicts "deeply influenced the pattern of economic and political change, and helped fix the basic direction of twentieth-century developments in the societies of the region" (Bergquist 1986, 9).

Between capital and labor, the historian always chooses a side, implicitly or explicitly. Bergquist is unambiguous on his own position, "hoping that in some small way the vision of the past outlined imperfectly in these pages will help to inform intelligent and effective political activity by the working class in its continuing struggle to forge a more humane world social order" (Bergquist 1986, x). Bergquist adopts a relatively capacious definition of export-production workers in early twentieth-century Latin America. These were, in his view, a motley crew of industrial and urban laborers and agricultural and rural workers, as well as pure wage laborers and more complex class positions. His view of this section of the working class included both direct workers in the export sector in question, together with those employed in transport and processing sectors linked to the entire export-production matrix (Bergquist 1986, 8).

EXPORT VARIATION AND WORKING-CLASS CONSCIOUSNESS/ORGANIZATION

Within the unity of export-oriented Latin America, Bergquist identifies seven key factors that help to explain variation in patterns of economic development and labor-movement formation among different countries in the early twentieth century, via their enabling or inhibiting of working-class consciousness and organization: geographic location and climatic conditions, nationality and concentration of ownership, capital intensiveness and technological sophistication, degree of vulnerability to seasonal cycles and/or world market fluctuation, reservoir of surplus labor, ethnic composition and citizenship status of the workforce, and nationalism.

How were these structural variables decisive? First, geography helped to determine both the strength of the link between export workers and wider society and the degree to which wage workers were dependent on their wage for their social reproduction. Second, nationality and concentration of ownership affected the degree to which workers understood their employers to be members of an antagonistic social class. Third, the level of capital intensiveness and technological sophistication in an export sector had an impact on the way in which the labor process was organized, as well as the size, wages, skill level, and concentration of the workforce. Fourth, an export sector's vulnerability to seasonal and/or world market fluctuation conditioned both the material well-being of workers and their understanding of fairness of the social relations in which they were embedded. Fifth, the ability of export capital to draw on the surplus labor of the unemployed, underemployed, or poorly paid affected its disciplinary power. Sixth, ethnic composition and citizenship status among export workers was a factor in achieving class unity in the sector and enabling or inhibiting the wedding of nationalist sentiment to the material struggles of the working class. Seventh, nationalism played a mediating role in the relationships developed between export workers to other workers, as well as other social layers of society. In polarized export production situations, in which "national labor" was pitted against "foreign capital," patriotic sentiments generally enabled by the dominant culture could have the unintended consequence of bolstering mobilizational capacities of export workers behind their class interests. This dynamic facilitated stronger alliances between labor and other social groups in a manner that strengthened labor, which hindered vigorous growth in the export sector, and thus of the national capitalist economy as a whole. In a virtuous circle, this limiting of capitalist development tended to strengthen potential for encompassing anti-imperialist alliances in the relevant society. Of these seven structural variables, Bergquist singles out the capital requirements of export production as the most important. Where there were high capital necessities, foreign capital tended to be advantaged over national capital to assert control over the means of production. In such scenarios, capitalist relations of production were more likely to prevail over precapitalist ones, as were concentrated rather than dispersed units of production (Bergquist 1986, 11–12).

With this theoretical backdrop, two polar tendencies can be identified and actually existing Latin American societies can be plotted on a continuum between them. On the one hand, foreign ownership and concentrated production tend to privilege culturally autonomous, class-conscious, and anti-capitalist labor organization among export workers while simultaneously weakening prospects for economic development as a whole. On the other hand, national ownership, low capital necessities, and diffuse production units tend to be an obstacle for labor organization in the export sector and anti-capitalist alliances more broadly, and thus improve the potentiality of overall economic development. A country whose export economy closely approximates the structural features of the first scenario (the left pole in Figure 1.1) should consequently witness the development of a stronger more anti-capitalist labor movement. Inversely, a country whose export economy closely approximates the structural features of the second scenario (the right

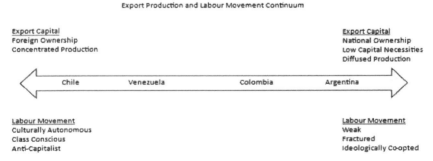

Figure 1.1.   Source: chapter author

pole in figure 1.1) should witness the development of a fractured, weak, and ideologically coopted labor movement. With nothing more than this skeletal set of relationships, one might chart the history of major nations in the region, such that Cuba, Chile, Bolivia, Venezuela, and possibly Mexico would appear on the left of the continuum and Argentina, Uruguay, Brazil, and Colombia, on the right (Bergquist 1986, 12).

In the core comparative chapters of *Labor in Latin America*, Bergquist defends the validity of this framework with detailed, historical case studies of Chile, Argentina, Venezuela, and Colombia. On the left pole, Chile, with its foreign-owned nitrate and copper export sector, developed a strong and anti-capitalist labor movement with the strongest political left in Latin America. Argentina, on the right pole, with its nationally owned livestock and cereal export sector, produced a fractured and weak labor movement, organization-ally incorporated into a corporatist framework, and ideologically aligned with Juan Domingo Perón's "right-wing popular nationalism" (Bergquist 1986, 15). The Venezuelan and Colombian cases, meanwhile, are positioned on different sides of the center. In Venezuela, the foreign-owned petroleum economy privileged the early development of a strong, radical, and autonomous labor movement and political left. Structurally, Venezuela was gravitationally drawn toward the left pole. However, the country's "special feature"—a foreign-owned oil enclave that contributed to growth, but not development of the national economy (Bergquist 1986, 205)—eventually led to the eclipse of the labor movement by consolidated liberal governments in the 1940s that sought to increase state ownership over oil. In Colombia, the nationally owned coffee sector proved an impediment to the formation of a culturally autonomous and anti-capitalist labor movement, with the country's "special feature"—diffuse ownership of the means of export production (Bergquist 1986, 305)—channeling socioeconomic discontent into conservative political channels, and class struggle from below into "intraclass warfare of the period called la violencia in the 1940's and 1950's" (Bergquist 1986, 16).

LIMITS OF ABSTRACTION AND PATHS AHEAD

For Bergquist, this kind of abstract modeling is a useful and necessary point of departure, but on its own, "such modeling is a mechanical exercise, artificially abstracted from life and incapable of touching and moving its human subject matter" (Bergquist 1986, 18). Bergquist is insistent on attending to the "complexity and untidiness of social reality and change," which can be obscured if one's method fails to move from the abstract to the concrete. Against the positivism of mainstream social science that has learned "to cut off a manageable slice of social life and to specify as precisely as possible how various factors combine to influence it in patterned ways," Bergquist's basic sensibility remains with dialectical historicism, and the "conviction that such fragments cannot be adequately understood apart from the whole" (Bergquist 1986, 18). Narrative exposition of complex and untidy historical processes has the dual benefit of (a) capturing "dialectical social processes" that "are best unraveled step by step as they unfold through time," and (b) allowing for an engaging prose style capable of reaching the lay reader.

In an exemplary mode of critical self-reflection, Bergquist sets aside the standard social scientific practice of summarizing the insights of *Labor and Latin America* in the concluding chapter of the book. Instead, he devotes this space to the limits of his study and identifies potential ways forward for future research. He refers especially to three areas requiring more theoretical and empirical refinement. First, he suggests that his extant framework could be bolstered considerably by a more throughgoing integration of the long histori-cal development of political systems (state and party formation, particularly). How did the evolving state forms and party systems of different countries, in many cases initially forged prior to the export booms of the late nineteenth century, dialectically interact with and mediate the social processes unleashed by the onset and consolidation of export economies (Bergquist 1986, 377)? Second, Bergquist suggests that greater attention is necessary to the sheer complexity of "the process of human cognition and the creation of cultural understandings" that has sometimes been simplified under the basic head-ing of "class consciousness." In Bergquist's estimation, he "wrestled more or less unsuccessfully with this issue," in *Labor and Latin America*, "whose full elucidation would require a massive amount of primary investigation by highly trained and unusually perceptive social historians" (Bergquist 1986, 383). Third, Bergquist suggests his approach is ultimately too one-sided with respect to workers in Latin American export sectors, relatively neglecting conflicts and alliances with other social classes in the determination of his-torical processes. Nonetheless, "perhaps these excesses can be excused in the context of a historiography that has for too long left working people out of its central concerns" (Bergquist 1986, 386).

Methodologically, Bergquist conceptualizes his book as an attempt to forge a critical unity between the most promising developments in world historiography (at the time he was writing, world-systems analysis and the new social and labor history coming out of North America and Europe) with the best on offer in Latin American studies (Latin American structuralism and Latin American dependency theory). While world-systems theory and the new social history both constitute "major, albeit partial, breakthroughs in the way we understand the historical evolution of the modern world," one understandable but real shortcoming Bergquist attributes to them is that they "developed largely in isolation from the other" (Bergquist 1986, 381). Any application of the new social history to Latin America must pay attention to the historical particularities of the region, while any engagement with world-systems theory must overcome the tendency of its adherents to "focus so single-mindedly on the global structural 'logic' of the world system that they neglect the concrete dynamics of class struggle within national societies" (Bergquist 1986, 384). The economists of Latin American structuralism, meanwhile, "developed a method of analysis appropriate to the resources of the societies they studied," but their bourgeois ideological commitments and their disregard of the role of labor in export sectors are necessarily to be transcended in any meaningful critical engagement (Bergquist 1986, 385).

What is the promise of Bergquist's paradigm for unlocking core features of modern Latin American development? For Bergquist, the framework he sets out in *Labor in Latin America* is a first step, the promise of which has only been validated in a preliminary and partial way by his initial historical investigations into Argentina, Chile, Colombia, and Venezuela. He hoped much more serious research would be pursued in this vein, with investigations of other countries in light of his interpretive model. He warned against mechanical applications of the model set out in chapter 1, suggesting rather that it be used "heuristically to gain interpretive leverage over a concrete and specific national history, a discrete and complex national historiography," pursued by researchers "willing to immerse themselves fully in the historiography of these separate nations and willing to undertake primary research" (Bergquist 1986, 379). Unfortunately, Bergquist's *Labor in Latin America* has had a muted afterlife, with too little influence on the directionality of Latin American studies since the 1980s. Today, we find ourselves in a period in which Latin American export sectors are once again decidedly determinative of the trajectories of a number of societies in the region, and yet attentiveness to the question of productive export labor is perhaps as neglected as it has ever been. Our volume is intended to help kickstart a revival of attention to this area, in the critical (rather than mechanical) spirit of Bergquist.

LATIN AMERICAN EXTRACTIVE LABOR IN THE NEOLIBERAL ERA

Of course, much has changed in the dynamic evolution of Latin American class structures since Bergquist's book was published in the late 1980s. The uneven roll-out of neoliberal economic restructuring worsened social conditions and transformed labor markets and class structures throughout the region. Traditional working-class organizations and associational forms of power were considerably decomposed as trade union power declined. In the majority of countries in the region, there was a dramatic informalization of the world of work, with deteriorating working conditions, employment security, and the absence of contracts. Women entered the paid labor force on an unprecedented scale (Felder and Patroni 2021; Portes and Hoffman 2003; Hite and Viterna 2005; Braga 2012). The countryside, meanwhile, was characterized by accelerating dispossession of peasant and indigenous communities as agrarian liberalization undercut their ability to sustain livelihoods connected to their land and territories (Robinson 2008; Vergara-Camus and Kay 2017; Vergara-Camus 2014). These new proletarians joined the reserve army of informal laborers—what Jan Breman in a different context called "wage hunters and gatherers" (Breman 1994)—pursuing survival strategies in the gray markets of the region's major cities, while living in the makeshift shantytowns burgeoning on their urban edges (Fischer, McCann, and Auyero 2014; Angotti 2017). Social inequality, poverty, and exploding crime characterized many Latin American societies at the close of the 1990s, two decades after the region first became a laboratory for neoliberal management techniques.

The economic crisis of neoliberalism was transformed into a political crisis for the ruling class in the early twenty-first century, as green shoots of extra-parliamentary social movement sprouted in the countryside and city alike in country after country (Webber 2017; Gaudichaud, Modonesi, and Webber 2022). By the mid-2000s, the social movement left found a muted echo in the institutional terrain of electoral politics, as much of the region—especially in South America—shifted its political colors from conservative to avowedly post-neoliberal rule. This so-called Pink Tide coincided with a boom in commodity prices on the world market, driven above all by China's rapid industrialization. The easy rents to be acquired by progressive governments through opening up primary resource sectors to further foreign investment, combined with modest hikes in taxation and royalties, generated the "commodities consensus" and the associated "compensatory state," discussed earlier (Svampa 2013; Gudynas 2012). As long as commodity prices remained high, many social development indicators improved, and the legitimacy of Pink Tide governments was largely secured, despite the lack of substantive change in the underlying property and class relations of these societies, growing socio-ecological conflicts engendered by the intensification of extractive capitalism, and deepening subordination of the region as a primary commodity producer within the international division of labor and nature. Against this backdrop, what were the structural conditions of work and the forms of resistance/passivity assumed by productive labor in the flourishing zones of agroindustrial, mining, and natural gas and oil extraction?

NEOLIBERAL AND PINK TIDE PRECARITY

Since *Labor in Latin America* was published in 1986, certain tendencies noted by Bergquist—increasing foreign investment, unequal capital flows, and austerity measures—deepened throughout the 1980s and 1990s. The literature on the neoliberal restructuring of Latin American labor markets traces how structural adjustment programs generally resulted in a precarization of labor as markets were further opened up to global capital, and added to a growing reserve army of unemployed laborers (Cypher 2018; Valenzuela et al. 2021). While extractive sectors included varying degrees of foreign investment prior to the 1980s, liberalization and deregulation during this period enhanced international participation in extraction. This included privatizing and increasing foreign investment in extractive operations that had been nationalized in previous eras, both of which reduced profits that accrued to the state and to small scale producers (Smart 2020, 768).

There is a vast literature on the class conflicts that neoliberalism produces around extraction, though productive labor is largely absent from this analysis. Much of the literature focuses on how extractive industries were restructured to benefit international rather than national interests (Alonso-Fradejas 2015). Sebastián Smart argues that with private actors playing a greater role in the international extractive market and its regulation beginning in the neoliberal era, extractive conflicts have mutated from those over distribution to conflicts between the aims of states, the private sector, and communities (Smart 2020, 767–68). Smart characterizes contemporary Latin American extractivism as "predatory," meaning that it is undertaken on a large scale, with a high level of foreign direct investment and without social control of transparency, the result of which is to create enclave economies and to hinder economic diversification (Smart 2020, 770). Conflicts under predatory extractivism have been shaped by the rise of private international law, which protects private investment, while states aim to increase profits and to implement national social, environmental, and economic protections (Smart 2020, 769–70). In countries with low capacity to control extractivism at the local level the "externalities" of extractivism (environmental destruction, displacement, corruption, and killings) are experienced more profoundly and generate local conflicts (Smart 2020, 768).

A marginal but important subset of literature explores the changing nature of work under neoliberalism, including how reforms have altered the structures of extractive industries and the social relations of production (Chiasson-LeBel 2016; Kay 2015). Across extractive sectors, automation and precarization have led to a decline in extractive sector jobs, employment conditions, and traditional labor organizing. This includes subcontracting in mining (Arboleda 2020), short-term contract work for port workers (Fox-Hodess and Rebolledo 2020; Manky 2018), fewer jobs in oil extraction, and a proletarianization of peasant farmers who cannot compete with agri-business (McKay et al. 2021; Vergara-Camus and Kay 2017; Alonso-Fradejas 2015).

For some, the extreme commodification of workers under neoliberal extractivism is representative of modern slavery in a non-institutionalized form (Issa 2017a; 2017b). Modern slavery includes work performed under violence or its threat, economic exploitation, or strenuous low-paid work indirectly coerced because workers have no other means of survival. From this perspective, there is a strong link between extractivism and modern slavery because the former tends to take place in areas with a small labor supply and minimal state presence (Issa 2017a). As a result, workers are recruited to remote areas, and upon their arrival subject to conditions such as debt bondage, and contract slavery where they work for little to no pay. More convincingly, others have argued that the media-driven discourse of "slave labor" is both sociologically incorrect (the workers in question are actually wage laborers, and subjectively do not identify as "slaves") and politically detrimental insofar as it discourages potential conceptual link-ages of shared interests across different sections of the working class and the possibilities of solidaristic, combined collective action (Kabat, Desalvo, and Egan 2017).[7]

Labor markets under Pink Tide governments were, in many ways, charac-terized by continuity with the neoliberal structures they inherited. As James Cypher has shown, for example, the income transfer policies of Pink Tide governments, made possible through reprimarization and export windfalls during the commodities boom, failed to challenge the pervasiveness of infor-mal work, flexibilization, and deunionization enhanced during the neoliberal era (Cypher 2018). Cypher illustrates the linkages between neostructuralist policies that increased labor law protections for formal and informal work-ers; neodevelopmentalism which focused on demand growth, full employ-ment, and income redistribution; and social neoliberalism promoted by the World Bank, which attempted to resolve the tensions between free markets and the survival needs and employment conditions of the majority. These frameworks all failed to reduce neoliberal informalization (Cypher 2018, 34). Instead, there was a focus on anti-poverty programs, which while achieving temporary reductions in poverty lacked sustainable structural change (Cypher 2018, 39).

SPACES OF LABOR

With the intensification of global extractivism in the twenty-first century, an emerging literature in historical materialist geography posits how space is being remade at the international, national, and local levels. New forms of spatialization are influenced by growing global demand for natural resources; increased extraction of oil, minerals, and agriculture; foreign investment and concentration of capital; precarization of work; and displacement from land. These phenomena are altering global commodity networks and social relations at points of extraction and distribution, including the nature of work and worker-organizing.

Hernán Cuevas Valenzuela, Jorge Budrovich Sáez, and Claudia Cerda Becker explore how ports, cities, and hinterland are constituted by global capitalism, which they characterize as a "network of global supply chains that are continually reorganising the international division of labor and the global geography of capitalism" (Valenzuela et al. 2021, 70). They identify five "transformative logics" that are restructuring the port city and its hinterland: neoliberalism, precarization, reterritorialization, extractivism, and logistics (Valenzuela et al. 2021, 71). While ports are modernized, mechanized, automized, and digitalized, it is the cities and related territories that surround them that suffer the environmental and social injustices from this development strategy (Valenzuela et al. 2021, 72). However, the authors find that changes to agriculture in the countryside, namely a reterritorialization of the countryside to produce fruits for large-scale export, are the driving forces behind the logistical modernization of the port (Valenzuela et al. 2021, 86). In this context, port cities function as hubs of global supply chains, and networks of production and circulation in the unequal geography of capitalism (Valenzuela et al. 2021, 71).

Cuevas Valenzuela, Budrovich Sáez, and Cerda Becker analyze the effects of neoliberal spatialization strategies on the social relations of extractive accumulation. Reterritorialization in the countryside favored a new class of local entrepreneurs and transnational agribusiness that can rely on agrichemicals and technology to increase production (Valenzuela et al. 2021, 80–81). Studying the Chilean port city of Valparaíso, the authors note that as both port and hinterland have been constituted by global capitalism, both are characterized by a decline in labor positions and by a rise in precarious work (the port due to mechanization, and the hinterland due to the dominance of agribusiness and capital-intensive agriculture). In the countryside, labor restructuring was initially undertaken via repressive means. Private companies implemented a series of new flexible contracts that segmented the labor force and multiplied labor positions. This created different categories of workers with different income levels and different rights.

Exploring the geography of extraction, Martín Arboleda argues that we are witnessing a shift from a global to a planetary mine due to the "quantum leap in the robotization and computerization of the labor process brought about by the fourth machine age" (Arboleda 2020, 4). Underlying Arboleda's approach is the notion that the planetary mine is irreducible to a singular site of extraction; instead, it ought to be treated as a "dense network of territorial infrastructures and spatial technologies vastly dispersed across space," combining processes of production and exchange across the complex apparatuses and geographies of a circulatory system of extractive capital (Arboleda 2020, 5). The space of extraction in question, then, is never merely a copper mine in northern Chile, say, but also its intricate links to Chile's logistical system of highway grids and nodal ports on the Pacific coast, transoceanic trade routes, geographies of labor on either side of the Pacific, hierarchical supply chains, new forms of state power and imperialism, and the mediation of these ties by novel developments in finance. The increasing spatial separation of extraction and manufacturing due to more capital-intensive mining has led to "a new generalized architecture of social production" and thus a new stage in the struggle of capital against labor (Arboleda 2020, 2). Concerned with "excavating the revolutionary subjectivity of the laboring classes and subaltern groups," Arboleda argues that despite the fragmentation of the productive subjectivity of the international working class under the planetary mine, it produces novel formations of collective consciousness and of collective agency (Arboleda 2020, 16, 20, 27). Building on reinterpretations of the Marxian notion of the collective laborer, Arboleda argues that widespread technological change and industrial expansion have facilitated an unprecedented degree of proletarianization and real subsumption of labor to capital, which has led to a massive increase in the global working class and global reserve army during the neoliberal period (Arboleda 2020, 140–41).

Phillip A. Hough, meanwhile, counters the idea that the movement of capital and production to new geographies marked by cheap labor is leading to a race to the bottom in terms of wages and working conditions, or cumulatively driving the rise of market despotism (Hough 2019, 506–7). Instead, Hough argues that this overlooks two tendencies in twenty-first-century capitalism: the salience of extra-economic forms of labor control (state repression, policing, paramilitarism), and the breakdown of capitalist production and systems of labor control leading to an emerging illegal and informal class, state, and market formations (gangs, warlord economies, illegal and informal markets) (Hough 2019, 507). Drawing on Giovanni Arrighi, Hough explores the social contradictions that arise from peripheral proletarianization and situates local labor regimes in Colombia within the rise and fall of US hegemony (Hough 2019, 508). Comparing labor regimes in three regions, Hough finds that in cases of full proletarianization the struggle over the redistribution of wealth becomes most volatile and potentially destabilizing for both workers and capital (Hough 2019, 522). Full proletarianization does not arise automatically of its own accord, but rather, at least in the case of Colombia, from the convergence of the interests of peripheral capitalists, the developmental state, and US hegemonic initiatives (Hough 2019, 522–23).

UNION ORGANIZING, POWER, AND STRATEGY

The literature broadly notes a decline in worker organizing and trade union activity as a result of changes to labor during the neoliberal era (Trujillo and Spronk 2018; Felder and Patroni 2021). One major trend has been the fragmentation of the workforce, with increasing separation of precarious workers from traditional full-time and permanent workers (Arboleda 2020; Manky 2018). This fragmentation is the result of different work experiences between the two types of workers and the limitations of workplace organizing for precarious workers (Ferre 2020). Limitations include the fact that many precarious workers do no live close to where they work and must commute, the temporary nature of their employment, and the extreme exploitation of precarious work, all of which leave workers with little time, community connections, or incentives to organize. But we should avoid seeing the precarious and permanent, or informal and formal, segments of the working class as separate silos of a "dual" labor market. Juan Cruz Ferre has shown that how we understand the relationship between permanent and precarious work has important implications for worker consciousness and thus collective organizing efforts between precarious and permanent workers. By theorizing the connections between traditional and precarious work and exploitation as part of one complex and stratified labor market, possibilities are opened up for labor organizing between precarious and permanent workers. Considering strategies of resistance to agricultural extractivism in Guatemala, Alberto Alonso-Fradejas argues that how resistance is framed is crucial to creating alliances that resist extractive expansion and proletarianization. He argues framing resistance as "defense of territory" offers the possibility to build alliances between peasant, indigenous and women's movements, while protecting both collective indigenous identities and rights to land, as well as peasant-based farming livelihoods and practices (Alonso-Fradejas 2015, 26–27).

A subset of literature on extractive labor focuses on worker and union organizing, power, and strategy (Manky 2020a; 2018; Fox-Hodess and Rebolledo 2020; Fox-Hodess 2019; Chomsky and Striffler 2014). This literature explores the challenges and changing nature of labor organizing given the precarization and flexibilization of extractive labor in the twenty-first century. Omar Manky, for example, argues that rather than the disappearance of labor conflicts in the mining industry, we are witnessing a transformation in the dynamic of workers' collective action (Manky 2018; 2020a). Mine workers are increasingly employed through subcontracting, including workers employed by mining companies for nonessential services (catering and cleaning), and for specialized tasks (explosives setting or equipment maintenance), which means they organize in novel ways (Manky 2020a, 1122). For example, in Los Bronces, Chile, commuting created a mobile and disbursed workforce; however, workers coordinated while riding the bus together commuting to the mine (Manky 2020a, 1126). In this way, worker agency does not necessarily decline, rather, it "evolves, adapts and reformulates" at different political scales (Manky 2020a, 1122). Given the changing nature of extractive labor, as well as decline in the number of workers employed in extractive sectors due to automation, much of the literature focuses on the ability of extractive workers to network and cooperate with other groups and organizations in order to increase their bargaining power. Relying on an application of resource mobilization theory to labor studies in the Global South, Manky argues that political activists have aided precarious worker organizations in post-authoritarian societies by providing moral, material, informational, and human resources (Manky 2018, 584). These include safe meeting spaces, sustaining union leaders' livelihoods, informational resources and strategies on how to organize work stoppages, and party networks to build national organization and overcome organizational fragmentation.

Via a case study of Chilean dock workers, Katy Fox-Hodess and Camilo Santibáñez Rebolledo argue that associational power and social power—which enable dock workers to form alliances with external actors—are crucial factors in explaining the revitalization of the trade union movement. The structural power of strategic positionality of dock workers is derived from their centrality to key global commodity export chains. Innovatively, however, Fox-Hodess and Santibáñez Rebolledo argue that strategic economic bargaining power had the potential to undermine the hegemonic position of dock workers in society due to the wide-ranging economic impacts of port strikes on both capital and labor (Fox-Hodess and Rebolledo 2020, 234). Instead, the associational and social power of dock workers, manifested via alliances with other workers from "productive" national sectors and with dockworkers internationally, as well as with students and university professionals, enabled dock workers to increase pressure on the state to achieve their demands.

Elsewhere, Fox-Hodess argues that the types of alliances formed by unions, and their resultant organizing strategies, are also influenced by the role of state action (Fox-Hodess 2019, 33–34). Relying on, but also critiquing, the varieties of capitalism approach, Fox-Hodess argues that the presumption of institutional stability of this perspective does not adequately explain labor relations in the Global South. Rather, "sociopolitical factors," such as the state's willingness to intervene on behalf of capital or labor, explain the differences between trade union strategy in cases like Chile and Colombia. In Colombia, pervasive state-sanctioned violence and the absence of labor law prevented workers from striking, and instead Colombian dock workers pursued a limited strategy of "human rights unionism" that relied on international pressure and lawsuits outside of the workplace for union recognition and a workers' contract. In the absence of these limitations, Chilean dock workers developed a largely successful "class struggle unionism" based on port strikes and local and international allies.

Such alliances between trade unions and other groups and organizations can be situated within a longer, little-known history of extractive sector unions in Latin America aligned with an integrated commitment to the left, anti-imperialism, and critique of the negative environmental impacts of extractivism (Chomsky 2019, 293). Based on an interview with Jairo Quiroz, the president of Colombia's largest coal mining union, Aviva Chomsky and Steve Striffler demonstrate that contemporary labor movements maintain this multifaceted critique of extractivism (Chomsky and Striffler 2014). Colombian unionists draw on a critique of capitalism and imperialism and demand for resources in the Global North, while also supporting the interests of peasant and indigenous movements focused on environmentalism, traditional land and lifestyles, and access to jobs and basic consumer needs (Chomsky and Striffler 2014, 195–97). Chomsky and Striffler point out that Colombian unions demanded that the mines operate to the benefit of local populations, possibly through nationalization, and committed themselves to participating in the elaboration of a broader, alternative model of development. The linkages pursued by Colombian extractive unions included prioritizing the local reproductive needs of the surrounding communities, resisting environmental destruction, opposing imperialism, fighting for better distribution of the material benefits derived from extractive activities, and supporting indigenous rights (Chomsky and Striffler 2014, 198–99).

THE ARCHITECTURE OF THE BOOK

Part II of the book explores and critically engages with cases first analyzed by Bergquist, considering the relevance of Bergquist's theoretical framework for labor in a key contemporary sector of extraction in the same country. In chapter 2, Ruth Felder and Viviana Patroni address the Argentinian case, assessing both the historical validity of Bergquist's treatment of the classical Peronist era, as well as the potential and limits of extending elements of his framework to the contemporary era of Argentine extractivism, especially with regard to its implications for workers situated in the country's informal economy. In chapter 3, Kristin Ciupa analyzes the Venezuelan case, drawing on elements of Bergquist's framework to assess labor-corporate-state relations within the country's rentier oil economy across three periods: neoliberalism (1980–1999), the Pink Tide (2000–2014), and the post–Pink Tide (2014–present). In chapter 4, Phillip A. Hough assesses the validity of Bergquist's interpretation of the coffee growers of mid-twentieth-century Colombia, as well as extending Bergquist's framework into the contemporary era of coca growers and accelerating extractive sectors of the economy. In chapter 5, Omar Manky compares the classic case of Chile with Peru, examining the strengths and limits of Bergquist's framework for understanding both countries during the late nineteenth and early to mid-twentieth centuries, as well as the possibilities for extending the framework forward in time to understand the contemporary extractive sectors of both countries. In chapter 6, Guido Starosta and Fernando Cazón develop a fundamental theoretical critique of the general analytical framework found in Bergquist's *Labor in Latin America*, as well as a grounded critique of his empirical findings in the Argentine and Chilean cases.

Part III of the book includes chapters assessing the viability of extending Bergquist's analytical framework to countries he did not cover in his seminal book, as well as to subject areas beyond his original remit. In chapter 7, Anna Zalik and Aleida Hernández-Cervantes analyze the case of Mexico, investigating the trajectory of the oil and energy sectors, as well as the more recent emergence of the maquila sector. In chapter 8, Andrea Marston engages with Bergquist by tracing the transformations of the labor movement in the Bolivian mining sector, from the mid-twentieth-century heyday of tin miners in the state-owned sector to the cooperativism dominant in the mining sector since neoliberal restructuring was introduced in the mid-1980s. In chapter 9, Christopher Little extends Bergquist's method by inverting its focus, from labor concentrated in Latin American export sectors to the export of labor-power itself by specific Latin American countries through migration.

Part IV consists of Jeffery R. Webber's concluding chapter. It seeks to place the different contributions to the volume in conversation with each other, to flesh out recurring themes as well as recurring tensions and unresolved subject matter. It assesses the basic aim of the project as a whole and measures the extent to which it lived up to that aim. It concludes by linking the intellectual puzzles explored in the volume with the most pressing issues of political strategy facing Latin America today.

NOTES

1. Over the past several years there has been a revival of Latin American Marxist dependency theory, which engages with parallel debates to this chapter on extractive capitalism, value, and labor. Initially formulated between 1967 and 1982 in response to crises of national developmentalism in Latin America (Martins 2022, 18), Marxist dependency theories explore the tendency of capitalism to create regions from which value is extracted, and other regions to which that value is appropriated (Treacy 2022, 226). According to much of this literature, capitalist expansion in pursuit of cheaper raw materials and a labor force under more precarious working and living conditions (Raposo, Filho, and Amaral 2022, 175) is the source of the historical-structural dependent capitalist form—characterized in particular by Latin American countries—which exists alongside developed capitalism in the global system (Osorio 2022, 163). The revival of dependency theory occurred in the context of the rise and decline of progressive and neodevelopmentalist regimes at the turn of the century (Chilcote and Salém 2022, 7). Neodevelopmentalism is a political project that sought to overcome economic underdevelopment via state aid, low interest rates, and competitive exchange rates (Katz 2022, 12), by projecting a new relationship among the bourgeoisie, state, and workers (Clemente 2022, 87–88). Contemporary Marxist dependency theories critique the neodevelopmentalist project for reproducing the conditions that facilitate dependency, albeit with some unique features under contemporary capitalism. The neodevelopmental model of export extractivism, characterized by increasing technification and capitalization, was facilitated by state alliances with key sectoral players and with transnational corporations (Katz 2022, 11–12). It was adopted in the context of a decline in manufacturing and a new cycle of financial capitalism, characterized by inflation, structural adjustment, and indebtedness magnified by price fluctuations in the region (Raposo et al. 2022, 175–76; Katz 2022, 11). While neodevelopmentalism appeared to broadly serve national interests, Antunes de Oliveira (2022, 50–51) argues that it subordinated the priorities of the working classes and is "just an updated strategy of the historically privileged ruling classes to mobilize the state in defense of their interests in a context of increasing international competition." Discussions on value of the workforce are central to debates on ongoing dependency, with position in the international division of labor—in this case, as extractive exporter—as well as degree of foreign investment, being closely connected to the value of labor (Katz 2022, 19–20). The recent publication of Ruy Mauro Marini's classic *The Dialectics of Dependency* in English for the first time (2022) will undoubtedly spawn renewed debate in the anglophone world on "super-exploitation" under dependent capitalism: the reduction of the cost of labor power below its value in order to re-establish surplus value and profit in competition with sectors and firms with higher technical and organic capital (Martins 2022, 20). While treatment of this complex theoretical puzzle is beyond the scope of the present volume, see Katz (2022), Osorio (2022), and Martins (2022) for contemporary applications of super-exploitation; Acosta and Cajas-Guijarro (2022) on subimperialism; Felix (2022) on the reserve army of labor; and Machado (2022) on dependent fascism.

2. While most contributors to this volume focus exclusively on productive labor as we define it here, not all the contributors concur with the specific distinctions we draw between productive and social reproductive labor, nor with our insistence on the analytical utility of an exclusive focus on productive labor for the purposes of our collective analysis. In allowing space for these tensions and disagreements in the collection, there is therefore a certain intentional inconsistency across the volume on this question (and some others) for the purpose of clarifying what is at stake theoretically and empirically, as well as advancing the debate on labor generally vis-à-vis extractivism in the region.

3. Social reproductive labor carried out in capitalist enterprises, such as private education or childcare, on the other hand, *is* labor set in motion to directly produce a commodity for sale on the market for a profit, and is therefore value-productive labor even as it is also labor which reproduces labor power (Ferguson 2019, 165).

4. Our definition is intentionally restrictive and designed to contrast with more expansive definitions that are at risk, in our view, of subsuming all processes in contemporary capitalism under the extractivist banner, and therefore become less and less able to say anything specific about the parts that make up capitalist totality, and the dialectical relationships that exist between them. See, for example, Gago (2015). Again, not all contributors to this volume accept such a restrictive definition.

5. One could easily repeat the exercise just carried out in relation to Svampa and Gudynas with, say, the prominent work of Ecuadorian political-ecologist Alberto Acosta or the influential Mexican political ecologist Enrique Leff.

6. For a review of the literature on the concept of "neo-extractivism," see Burchardt and Dietz (2014).

7. While we disagree with those who would categorize extractive labor in Latin America as "modern slavery," we do take seriously the need for further investigation into the continuum of unfree labor (including "free" wage labor) in extractive capitalist sectors in the region today. For clearer conceptual guidance on free and unfree labor, see Banaji (2003) and Gordon (2019).

Part II

REVISITING THE CLASSICAL CASES

Chapter Two

The Political Economy of the Labor Movement in Contemporary Argentina

Ruth Felder and Viviana Patroni

Studies about the economic and political transformation of Latin America during the twentieth century have often overlooked the roles workers and their organizations have played as a force shaping these trajectories of change. Charles Bergquist's (1986) insights into Latin American labor history were intended as a way to overcome this deficit. While this oversight might describe less the case of Argentina—where most observers would be hard pressed not to recognize the power organized labor has exercised on politics, particularly over the second half of the twentieth century—it is nonetheless pertinent insofar as it opens the possibility of thinking anew labor and its role in shaping the tortuous patterns of capital accumulation followed by the country in its contemporary history.

Our objective in this chapter is to revisit Bergquist's journey into the history of the labor movement in Argentina to explore the factors that account for its current strengths and weaknesses. Doing so allows us to appraise the complex relationship between the structural conditions that inform patterns of growth and job creation, and influence, but do not determine, forms of workers' agency. Organized labor, which through their unions and union federations—in particular the General Confederation of Labor (Confederación General del Trabajo [CGT])—in general terms has not directly challenged capitalist social relations, but has nonetheless hindered attempts to reset the patterns of capital accumulation in the country on the basis of a drastic cheapening of labor costs. This is both a testament to the power of labor organizations and the complexities of labor politics.

We pay attention to the experience of workers in Argentina after the economic collapse and political crisis resulting from the neoliberal reforms of the 1990s. We address the implications of the centrality of the export of natural resources to the pattern of capitalist accumulation that followed this crisis by looking at its underbelly: the poor performance of job creation. This is critical to understand the persistence of labor precarity and informality even in periods of robust gross domestic product growth and, equally important, to interpret the contemporary dynamics of labor organizing in the country.[1] With a focus on the capacity of precarious workers who are "surplus to the needs of capital" (Li 2017, 1249) to organize and mobilize to secure their livelihoods, we problematize some of the assumptions about the forces, tensions, and boundaries that condition the transformative potential of working-class politics. Our argument is that while precarious workers lack structural power linked to their position in the current pattern of capital accumulation, a fuller understanding of their transformative potential requires a consideration of their ability to organize under adverse conditions in an attempt to deal with the contingency of their reproduction, and potentially build bridges to overcome the political fragmentation of an increasingly heterogeneous working class.

To foreground our own understanding of the promise, contributions, and also shortcomings of Bergquist's approach, we start with a brief discussion of the theoretical approach that informs our chapter. Because of the centrality of Peronism in Bergquist's analysis of both working-class organizing in Argentina and workers' role during and after Perón's government (1946–1955), our discussion continues in the third section by appraising the significance of Peronism as the political expression of a large majority of workers in Argentina. Through this we seek to frame the discussion in the fourth section where we address the effects of neoliberalism on the collective power of workers since the 1990. With this as the backdrop, we tackle what for us is one of the important implications of Bergquist's analysis: the need to widen the lenses through which the working class is defined. Thus, in the subsequent three sections we address the power that against all historical odds have acquired precarious workers in Argentina. While their struggles cannot readily be understood as politically radical, they have been central in exploring new terrains for organizing around both what constitutes work and the insecurity of reproduction for workers in contemporary capitalist societies. We conclude in the final section by renewing the call to place workers understood in this encompassing way at the core of the political economy of development in Argentina and, equally important, the political conflicts the country confronts.

WORKERS, THEIR POWER, AND DEVELOPMENT TRAJECTORIES

Published in the mid-1980s, Bergquist's comparative study came at the time of the closing of the "development age" in Latin America and the early stages of the neoliberal structural transformations in the region. In creating a more hospitable environment for business, and thus also altering the balances of forces between capital and labor, these transformations failed to deliver on the promises of sustained growth and job creation. More recent changes in the twenty-first century have to some extent addressed some of the most pressing problems created by neoliberal reforms but have again fallen short of fulfilling the long-held aspirations to make sustainable development alternatives a reality. The limitations of the policy experimentations associated with the Latin American left turn of the 2000s to establish the structural conditions for the creation of good-quality jobs even in the context the commodity boom are especially telling.

Our reading of Bergquist's study of Argentina's labor movement is informed by a political economy of development approach that allows us to integrate the interplay between three dimensions. The first dimension corresponds to the scope and limitations for job creation associated with successive patterns of capital accumulation in the country. The second dimension relates to the varying forms of collective action of different sections of the labor movement and their interaction with the initiatives and practices of other relevant actors. The third dimension refers to the institutional arrangements and policies that help to shape, and to some extent are shaped by, patterns of job creation, labor relations, and forms of workers' organizing and mobilization, including the capacity of the state to extend social protection and regulate economic activity and labor markets to affect the creation and the quality of jobs created. The interconnections among these three dimensions provide a way of understanding the structural and associational power of the working class (see the introduction to this volume). In our study of precarious workers' organizing, we suggest that associational power can be developed even in the absence of significant structural power. Thus, we consider the potential that those workers excluded from direct participation in capital accumulation have to contest, and to some extent, influence development options in the country.

Finally, we pay attention to the centrality of social reproduction in precarious workers' organizing strategies. This is one way in which our chapter extends its focus beyond the productive labor framework of other contributions to the volume. Our discussion also falls outside of both a conceptualization of social reproduction understood as unpaid labor performed by women within the confines of the household, and struggles about social reproduction as separate from working-class struggles. Instead, we suggest that central in understanding the full meaning of precarity is the collapse of the limited responsibility both employers and the state used to share in ensuring the social reproduction of workers, especially of those deemed "unnecessary" for capital accumulation (Katz 2001, 711). Even though these workers are seen as "disposable" and definitively lack structural power, their refusal to be "disposed of" constitutes a political challenge to the existing pattern of capital accumulation. More generally, we find particularly compelling the role of precarious workers in reminding us that what is central to capitalism is not the wage relation but rather "the imperative to earn a living" (Denning 2010, 80), which is just another way of referring to the uncertainties workers confront about their reproduction.

THE WORKING CLASSES AND PERONISM

One of Bergquist's pivotal contributions to debates about labor in Latin America is his proposal to situate workers' political action, and thus the specific forms of conflict between capital and labor, as critical in understanding development trajectories. Likewise, he calls attention to how patterns of capital accumulation affect the power of labor in various ways, for example in determining levels of employment and the degree to which the national economy is sheltered or exposed to global forces. It is in this context that Bergquist accounts for the impact of Peronism on organized labor in Argentina, and its eventual inability to either advance an agenda of radical change or to be part of a settlement buttressing the power of capital to ensure a sustained path of growth and labor discipline. While the discussion lends itself to a critical re-examination of the dilemmas of mid-twentieth-century populism to overcome existing structural limitations to more dynamic forms of capitalist accumulation, the text suffers from a partial analysis of the complex and contradictory outcomes of organized labor's alignment with Peronism. Even though, as Bergquist argues, Perón and some factions within Peronism have aimed at containing social struggles, other sectors also identified with Peronism have disputed the limits of what has been seen as possible, placing themselves at the forefront of working-class struggles in different historical moments. It is our understanding of this shortcoming in his work that prompts us to focus on the nature of the labor movement in Argentina at the time of Perón's ascent to power and during his first two presidencies (1946–1955).[2] Following Bergquist's call to engage with different levels of analysis, we situate labor struggles in the context of patterns of capital accumulation and the institutional arrangements that accompany them.

   As in the rest of Latin America, the 1930s were very trying times for Argentina. The 1929 crisis put an end to the illusions of prosperity based on the agricultural exports and the manufacturing associated with them, due to the combination of falling international demand and the declining competitiveness of local agriculture (Schvarzer 1998, 25). The economic downturn was accompanied by the advent of highly repressive and conservative governments. However, the crisis was also the context in which some sectors of the local bourgeoisie saw the substitution of imported manufacturing goods as a temporary relief, while others perceived that Argentina would not recover its previous position as an exporter of food and successfully pushed for sustaining import substitution (Murmis and Portantiero 1971, 11–12). Economic growth resumed by the second half of the decade on the basis of this incipient industrialization. With the growth of employment in manufacturing, unions pushed once again for improvements in wages and working conditions. While labor organizing was significant, just as critical a factor was the rather meager victories unions could claim for themselves.

In this line, we understand the moment leading to the emergence of Peronism as being the outcome of two critical political processes. First, the political and economic exclusion of the working classes in the country was central in consolidating a unifying identity within the working class, notwithstanding the various objective conditions dividing them and complicating their capacity to organize (Murmis and Portantiero 1971, 76; Bergquist 1986, 102–3). This is the experience that Perón promised to transform as he became gradually more prominent within the government that had come to power in a military coup in 1943. The appeal of Peronism, as James (1988, 36) suggests, was precisely the promise of gains for the working class without the costs unions had paid so far for their struggles. While there were reasons for the government and Perón to fear the power of the organized working class of Argentina, they also saw in it an untapped political ally of critical importance. The challenge for Perón was how to ensure that opening the doors to working-class organizations did not weaken the capacity of the state to effectively manage social conflict. He would soon succeed in keeping the labor forces he had activated effectively under control, away from the dreaded influence of communism and socialism (Altamirano 2001, 29).

Second, the common identity workers had forged during this critical period also implied that there was a large diversity of working-class organizations that found Perón's leadership appealing. Yet organized workers responded with caution regarding the potential risks involved in the political opportunities Perón offered (Patroni 2018a, 20). As Perón consolidated his own bases of power, he was careful to frame his political project in the context of organized labor's long-held demands, for example the establishment of an explicitly working-class party, the Labor Party (Partido Laborista) (Murmis and Portantiero 1971, 96). His power with workers increased rapidly and substantially in the critical period between 1943 and 1945 when he was the Labor and Social Security Secretary, and consolidated further during his first two presidential terms. This was, not by chance, the period of most rapid growth of unionization from approximately half a million organized workers in 1945 to 2.5 million in 1954, that is a five-fold increase in just one decade (Collier and Collier 1991, 341–42). Unions gained institutional recognition as relevant political actors and as mediators between workers and employers, while the opposition to Peronism within the labor movement became increasingly marginalized. All in all, Perón's first presidency (1946–1952) was a period of distribution of wealth toward workers through new labor and social legislation and other forms of income distribution. Over time, however, distributive policies affected investments and profits, and hindered Perón's efforts to reconcile capital and labor.

The process summarized here seems to us critical to understand not only the power that Perón gained over the labor movement but also the way in which unions imprinted on populism in Argentina its labor ethos. Perón introduced critical new labor and social policy in the country that, despite changing economic circumstances, implied important long-term material gains for workers. The consolidation of industrialization via import substitution (ISI) bears the mark of this political dynamic. In particular, the centrality of redistribution and the strengthening of the domestic market as central components of the industrial policy were evidence of the weight of the working class in the political alliance supporting Perón in power (Rougier and Schorr 2012, 18). Nonetheless, as many countries following ISI, Argentina experienced cyclical balance of payment crises. Expansionary policies that boosted import substitution but affected the balance of payments were followed by stabilization plans that produced recession and a massive transfer of wealth to agricultural exporters (Smith 1989, 37).

Peronism gave the working class a new political identity that would stand the test of time, allowing it to become a central political actor over the critical twenty years after the downfall of Perón in 1955 as the country confronted an increasingly violent deadlock. Clearly, the incorporation of labor unions into the coalition that brought Perón to power, and the discipline imposed through the legal framework regulating unions' activity, set in unambiguous ways the limits to what most labor leaders came to understand as politically feasible (Patroni 2000, 244). However, both also were represented the channels through which labor gained access to the state and came to occupy institutional and political spaces that altered the relationship among labor, capital, and the state in critical ways. Labor legislation granted CGT enormous power as it secured the organization's monopoly of representation as the only confederation recognized by the state. Moreover, by ensuring that only one industry-wide union per sector was legally entitled to negotiate collective agreements, labor legislation accorded extraordinary clout to these unions and their leaderships. The outcome was, no doubt, the consolidation of a labor leadership that became increasingly bureaucratic and undemocratic.

Yet this pattern of labor control—what came to be known as state corporatism—was never completely effective. In particular, it could not suffocate the persistent and ongoing challenges to labor leaderships emerging from the rank and file (Patroni 2018a, 23). Furthermore, while Peronism gave the labor movement ideological unity, Peronism itself became increasingly an arena of contention especially after the coup d'etat that ousted Perón in 1955. Peronism's malleable contours as a political movement led to its growing ideological and political heterogeneity, ensuring room for a full spectrum of political forces, including left-wing factions that became increasingly influential over the 1960s and 1970s. These changes affected the labor movement, creating not only new perspectives about radical change in Argentina, but also an increasingly violent confrontation with more orthodox groups within CGT. The scope of labor mobilization, the nature of its demands, and the segments within organized labor that understood Peronism as encompassing the prospect of revolutionary change, provide an illustration of the complexity of labor struggles in Argentina during this period. In our view, Bergquist's (1986, 187) assertion that "after 1955 labor remained solidly anti-Marxist" does not capture the complexity of labor politics during this period. Granting centrality and agency to workers and their organizations requires some reconsideration of the understanding of Peronism as the obstacle for more radical ideals among the working class. Moreover, it requires us to abandon the premise of Peronism as an immutable political force (Horowicz 2007, 317–25).

Proof of this was the difficulties facing the state's attempts to discipline workers after the 1955 coup d'etat that ousted Perón. Not only did distributive conflicts continue but also the proscription of Peronism following the coup became a main factor promoting political instability (Felder 2013, 57). "Stop-and-go" cycles of recession and growth were accompanied by the exacerbation of struggles between the groups benefited and affected in each stage of the cycle, and by an alternation between elected governments and military dictatorships (Patroni 2018b, 106).

Despite these conflicts and repeated economic crises, between the 1950s and 1970s the country experienced substantial levels of economic growth. Indeed, over the last decade of ISI in Argentina, the country underwent a process of both sustained economic growth and rising real income. Nonetheless, if political conflict did not immobilize the country's economy, by the mid-1970s it resulted in a major crisis in which Peronism itself became the main arena of increasingly violent confrontations. The process culminated with the military coup of 1976 and the installation of a regime of terror. Labor organizations and workers suffered the heaviest losses, as the military not only pursued the physical elimination of any dissent but also the dismantling of ISI, and the power of the working class associated with it (Flichman 1985). In other words, the dictatorship was a moment of inflection which signaled in an unambiguous way the diminishing capacity of labor to contest the country's development trajectory. The subsequent transition to democracy failed to address the economic legacy of the dictatorship, which led to macroeconomic, fiscal, and external crises during Raúl Alfonsín's government (1983–1989) and eventually paved the way for the neoliberal reforms that would be initiated soon after Carlos Menem (1989–1999) won the presidential election and took power.

WORKERS AND THE CONSOLIDATION OF NEOLIBERALISM

Even though structural reforms had gradually changed the country since the mid-1970s, it was not until the 1990s that a full package of neoliberal policies was put into place in Argentina. Central to this package was the effective control of inflation—following the hyperinflationary episodes of 1989 and 1990—through the implementation of a currency board (the Convertibility Plan) in 1991. Over the decade, this approach would result in currency overvaluation, the declining competitiveness of domestic manufacturing, growing external deficits, recession, rising levels of unemployment, precarity and poverty, and financial crisis, all leading to a major political crisis and the collapse of the economy in 2001, and eventually to the abandonment of convertibility in 2002.

The Menem administration (1989–1999) proposed critical legal changes to the labor legislation that, as we suggested earlier, had provided a certain level of protection and rights to workers. Equally important, the restructuring of the economy and the destruction of jobs it generated imposed a discipline of its own, intensifying flexibilization and precarization, and undermining workers' rights.

During this period, CGT and unions faced the challenges of crumbling labor rights amidst rising unemployment and precarization. Critical outcomes of this process were the division of the labor movement leadership between those who unreservedly supported the government and its reformist agenda and those who raised warnings about it, which ultimately led to the emergence of alternative labor organizations and, equally important, the growth of organizations of the unemployed. Workers, their organizations and actions, and the responses they elicited from the state are central to understand the collapse of neoliberal reforms in 2001 and the nature of the government that succeeded this collapse.

As mentioned before, labor market indicators worsened over the 1990s. By 1995 unemployment had increased threefold when compared to 1991, from 6.9 percent to over 18.4 percent (Novick, Lengyel, and Sarabia 2009, 239). By the turn of the century as recession set in, all indicators in the labor market deteriorated further. By 2002 unemployment reached 21.5 percent and involuntary underemployment 24.3 percent. In 2003 unregistered employment affected almost 44 percent of workers.

This was also the context of innovation and experimentation in workers' collective action. Unemployed workers, unable to rely on the most conventional forms of labor action, used roadblocks (piquetes) instead (Bascuas et al. 2021, 250). The piquetero movements, as they came to be known, were diverse in political leanings and goals, ranging from autonomist groups that explored forms of self-sufficiency to others that affiliated with several political parties and groups. Starting in the mid-1990s, their demands for state assistance and jobs transformed the political dynamics of the labor movement in Argentina. It was within these experiments that many in the organizations of precarious workers of the following decade trace their political roots.

Some unions and groups within them came to see the growing number of unemployed and precarious workers as a major source of strength in the struggles against neoliberalism. This understanding, along with the failure of most unions within CGT to position themselves as a strong voice of opposition to neoliberal reforms and austerity, opened the doors to big divisions within the labor movement. Most relevant among those divisions was the splinter in 1992 of major unions within the public sector and their confluence into an alternative labor organization, the Argentine Workers' Central (Central de Trabajadores de la Argentina [CTA]). By the turn of the decade, the confluence of some dissident unions within CGT, CTA, the piquetero movements, and other political forces created a powerful opposition movement that became critical in the final downfall of the austerity measures with which governments until 2001 responded to the crisis in Argentina.

Between the end of 2001 and the beginning of 2002, as the crisis deepened, many of the legal and institutional arrangements that had made the implementation of neoliberal restructuring possible were modified. In particular, the government abandoned the decade-long currency board and allowed the peso to depreciate. Initially, this pushed the country deeper into depression combined with very high levels of inflation. By mid-2002, the economic decline that had begun in 1998 and led to total social and political turmoil in December 2001 and early 2002 reached its worst moment. By May of that year, unemployment had risen to 21.5 percent and underemployment to 18.6 percent. Poverty and extreme poverty also reached their all-time historic highs in modern Argentina. In May 2002, 53 percent of the population was living below the poverty line and 24.8 percent was living below the extreme poverty line. Moreover, while poverty levels were related to the growth of unemployment, work itself was not necessarily a safeguard against poverty, as many wages were not sufficient to satisfy basic needs (Felder and Patroni, 2018a, 6–11).

ECONOMIC RECOVERY AND THE UNEVEN PERFORMANCE OF LABOR MARKETS

After the long recession, the economy resumed growth in late 2002. Central to explaining the country's changing economic outlook was the approach taken by the incoming administration of Néstor Kirchner (2003–2007), who won the 2003 presidential election. In many respects, this administration, along with the subsequent terms of Cristina Fernández de Kirchner (2007–2011 and 2011–2015), marked a departure from the neoliberal policy blueprint of the 1990s. Recognizing that the uprising of 2001 had set political limits to neoliberal policies, Kirchner moved away from strict austerity and introduced several policy reorientations that would eventually lead both to a period of growth and to improvements in labor market and other social indicators.

Equally important was the agricultural export bonanza of the mid-2000s that allowed the country to sustain robust economic expansion with external and fiscal surpluses between 2003 and 2008. This was central in expanding the room within which the state could maneuver to carry out expansionary and distributive policies amid more favorable conditions for extractive activities (Gudynas 2012, 131–32). The reduction in the rate of unemployment from 24.4 percent to around 8.5 percent between 2002 and 2008 was without question one of the most significant features of this period. However, the economy slowed down with the 2008–2009 crisis, with negative consequences for unemployment, which grew to 8.80 percent of the active economic population in 2009. The economy recovered quickly from the crisis, and by the end of that year, unemployment had fallen to 7.3 percent.

The increase in the number of new formal salaried jobs, that is jobs registered for social security purposes, was also remarkable: while during the 1990s only 6 percent of new jobs satisfied this legal requirement, between 2003 and 2008, 85 percent of new jobs were registered (Panigo and Neffa 2009, 14). Yet this transformation was not sufficient to alter the structural trend toward precarity: approximately 34 percent of salaried workers were still unable to join formal labor markets, and by 2011—that is, once the period of most rapid economic growth had ended—almost 45 percent of all workers in Argentina, both salaried and self-employed, were still working informally (Bertranou, Casanova and Sarabia 2013, 6).

This changing economic and political landscape of Argentina opened up a new stage in the organization of working-class struggles, both for the traditional CGT and other sectors within alternative unionism like CTA, as well as for organizations of the unemployed. Beginning in 2004, with the consolidation of growth, wage bargaining between unions and employers with the mediation of the state resumed after more than a decade of inactivity. This development gave CGT and unions, especially those in strategic sectors that were leading the economic recovery and in sectors that were highly subsidized by the state, a new role. Understandably, in a highly fragmented labor market, workers' gains were very unevenly distributed (Felder and Patroni 2018a).

As economic growth slowed down and fiscal and external balances became less favorable after 2010, tensions between sectors of CGT and the government mounted, resulting in the split of CGT into three fractions, with two of them strongly opposed to the Fernández de Kirchner administration. Likewise, CTA split between those who considered it essential to retain the organization's autonomy from the government and those who were closely aligned with it. These splits occurred when the government was making efforts to decelerate the pace of wage rises with the expectation that this would help control inflation.

The economic and political changes the country experienced after 2003 also brought fundamental changes to the organizations of the unemployed. At a most basic level, the growth of employment that accompanied the economic recovery implied the reduction in the membership of piquetero organizations and their political influence. Nonetheless, as the decade went by, as we will discuss in the following section, the high unemployment of 2001–2002 mutated into a growing concern over informality, other forms of precarity, and poverty more generally.

The political scenario under which the organizations of the unemployed had mobilized their grassroots and framed their demands also changed substantially after 2003. This was connected in part to Kirchner's acknowledgment of the scope and nature of the social crisis and, equally important, the legitimacy the piquetero movement had achieved as a political force. With the goal of reducing social conflict, Kirchner announced that his government would neither resort to repression of protests, nor would it increase the number of social assistance plans, as the expectation was that acute social conflict would gradually decline along with employment creation. The government also extended new opportunities for some of the piquetero organizations to participate in policy making and included some of their leaders within the government. Not surprisingly, participation in the government also deep-ened some of the divisions that had characterized this sector from its very beginning.

Lacking a legal minimum wage, union representation, social security, and other benefits, informal and precarious workers remained excluded from many of the benefits that economic growth brought for formal workers. Criti-cal for the tensions that mounted in the late 2000s, the government perception of the significance of this segment of workers was marked by its initial under-standing that unemployment and underemployment and, equally important, high levels of labor informality, were temporary problems that economic growth would solve. However, labor precarity and informality among waged and self-employed workers remained high even as the economy continued to grow (Felder and Patroni 2018a). In our view, this tendency reflects new accumulation strategies cemented through the profound economic restructur-ing operating in the country since the 1970s that limit formal employment creation. This key structural change in labor markets stands at the core of the struggles unemployed workers had initiated in the 1990s and is central in understanding the growing universe of movements organizing precarious workers since the last decade.

One key implication of this transformation has been the centrality of the state as the key arena of struggle. This has been the case with social assis-tance policy. While a comprehensive discussion of policy in this area is beyond the scope of this chapter, it is important to mention the relevance of programs for the unemployed both in addressing some of their most urgent demands and in defining their relationship with the state. These programs have undergone important changes since their mass-scale implementation during the 2001–2002 crisis, the two most significant being based on the understanding of employability of recipients and on the nature of condi-tionality imposed on beneficiaries (Logiudice 2022, 118–26). Regarding the former, the government recognized in the mid-2000s that a portion of the population affected would remain "unemployable" regardless of the eco-nomic performance of the country. Following this criterion, it implemented programs aimed at ensuring some very minimum income for them. For the rest of the unemployed but potentially "employable" population, social pol-icy provided workfare programs. Workfare has implied the active engage-ment of the organizations of unemployed and precarious workers in the management of assistance. Strengthened by the administration of programs and funding, these organizations have also become central in providing basic social services and public infrastructure in some extremely poor urban areas (Bascuas et al. 2021, 252).

PRECARIOUS WORKERS' ORGANIZING AGAINST ALL THE ODDS

The transformation and sustained political presence of unemployed and precarious workers' organizations constitute a critical facet of politics in Argentina, one that has imprinted new dynamics to labor politics in the country still not sufficiently understood. As we argue in this chapter, while organizations of precarious workers might lack structural power, at least in the traditional sense, their capacity to mobilize members and articulate some demands associated with the reproduction of workers who are unable to sell their labor power speaks to new practices of building associational power. To elucidate the relevance of these changes, we will turn now to the example of the Confederation of Popular Economy Workers (Confederación de Trabajadores de la Economía Popular [CTEP]), an organization founded in 2011 and transformed in 2019 into the Union of Popular Economy Workers.[3] We focus on this organization because its struggles are emblematic of the demands of a very broad and diverse group of precarious workers, in particular, workers from cooperatives formed under the umbrella of social assistance programs, street and popular market vendors, worker-controlled companies, recycling cooperatives (cartoneros), garment cooperatives, and small agricultural producers.

Central to the articulation of their demands is the conception of "popular economy."[4] The notion is used to delimit the space where wageless workers "invent their own work" (Pérsico and Grabois 2014, cited in Felder and Patroni 2018b, 13). These are workers without steady access to waged jobs—although they might enter into wage relations sporadically and under the most precarious circumstances, as is the case with unregistered work—who manage to secure some cash by collecting refuse, selling cheap commodities in public spaces, working in small cooperatives, making repairs, or toiling in small family farms. Many, in particular women, work in the construction and maintenance of basic community infrastructure, or run daycares, soup kitchens, or other basic services that make everyday life possible in neighborhoods in which the state had abandoned the provision of these infrastructure and services long ago. Some of these community initiatives are made possible through workfare programs and other subsidies some of these workers receive as social assistance from the state. Insofar as they ensure the very basic conditions for social reproduction, it is possible to think of these activities as embodying the little power these sectors exercise. Moreover, as Li (2017, 1255) suggests, wageless workers "do not die, or not immediately, hence they may exert some leverage simply through their presence." In our view, the power precarious workers have managed to gain derives in no small part from their ability to reassert their presence in the ways available to them. This is most tellingly the fact in their capacity to mobilize around their demands and in so doing disrupt the public space, reminding everyone of their right to at least have a presence.

Arguably, the existence of the popular economy and its workers expresses the structural segmentation of labor markets and, with it, the fragmentation of the working class (Felder and Patroni 2018b). But the true innovation associated with the use of the term comes from its political conceptualization as the social space where workers, who have lost the connection to a workplace and to the rights other workers enjoy, can find common grounds for their struggles and unity, notwithstanding the wider range of paths leading them to precarity (Felder and Patroni 2018b, 9–10; Fernández-Álvarez 2019, 62–65). Furthermore, the emphasis on the popular economy has been central in challenging the notion of wageless workers as unemployed. On the contrary, CTEP has insisted through its practices on buttressing the identification of the activities of its members as workers. Such an understanding carries with it the insight that under the current pattern of capital accumulation, there will not be sufficient waged jobs to absorb all those seeking them. It is also a tacit recognition that under the existing balance of forces it is just as difficult to imagine more radical solutions in the allocation of work. CTEP's analysis of the structural conditions underlying unemployment contrasts sharply with the emphasis the government and also many conventional unions have continued to place on economic growth as the most effective means to create good quality formal employment (Palomino 2010). Furthermore, CTEP has stressed that workers in the popular economy often perform activities that are critical for the capitalist economy, not to mention society more generally (Grabois 2014, cited in Felder and Patroni 2018b, 10). This principle of identifying workers in the popular economy as workers accounts also for CTEP's strategy to demand recognition as a union with all the rights of other unions, and to demand a social salary in lieu of social assistance programs. Arguably, this strategy highlights the limitations of the current pattern of capital accumulation to guarantee the reproduction of all workers. Yet the transformational prospects of such strategy depend on organized popular economy workers' capacity and willingness to situate their struggles and demands within a broader political project. Otherwise, rather than radicalize workers, working in the popular economy may constitute a form of managing and containing the potentially disruptive effects of widespread precarity and poverty.

Since its creation, CTEP has demanded its certification as a union with the ability to negotiate collective agreements to protect the working conditions of its members. Although some of its leaders were politically close to the government of Cristina Fernández de Kirchner, the demand remained unfulfilled. It was only in December 2015 and on the eve of the assumption to power of conservative president Mauricio Macri (2015–2019) that the outgoing Fernández de Kirchner government agreed to some concessions, in particular the granting of partial legal recognition as a labor organization with the capacity to institute its own health-care plan. Furthermore, CTEP, along with some other organizations representing precarious workers, had to wait until the change of government that took Peronist Alberto Fernández (2019–2023) to power to gain legal recognition as a union. The recognition of the state, however, has not been accompanied by the recognition of CGT despite CTEP's numerous attempts to join it. CGT's disinclination to welcome popular economy workers to its rank and file can be explained in several ways. Two points seem to us fundamental. First, CGT has historically proven quite reticent to experiment with new organizational forms, and incorporating such a large union with a very diverse membership implies a risk that it is simply not willing to take (Patroni 2018b, 133–34). The second relates to a consideration fundamental for CGT as a labor organization: the prospect of addressing precarity and informality in any way other than demanding the creation of standard employment runs against all its instincts. After all, the expansion of standard employment has been the pillar upon which the structural power of unions has been sustained, in Argentina as elsewhere.

Nonetheless, while CTEP's initiative to be incorporated into CGT might not have found satisfaction, it proved to be more effective in creating the conditions for common action under the new administration of President Mauricio Macri (2015–2019).

WORKERS AND THEIR ORGANIZATIONS FROM THE "RIGHT TURN" TO THE COVID-19 PANDEMIC

Mauricio Macri won the presidential election attacking assistance and workfare programs that allegedly damaged the "culture of work" and perpetuated poverty. In the following years, social and labor market indicators deteriorated amid a long economic slowdown and several periods of acute macroeconomic instability. Between the second trimester of 2015 and the second trimester of 2019, unemployment rose from 6.6 percent to 10.6 percent. Unregistered employment grew from 33.1 percent in the second trimester of 2015 to 35.9 percent during the third trimester of 2019, and 369,000 formal jobs were eliminated in the four years between September 2015 and September 2019 (CETyD 2019). The purchasing power of salaries also deteriorated as inflation accelerated. Overall, by mid-2019, wages in the private sector had lost approximately 12 percent of their purchasing power when compared to

2015, and public sector wages more than 30 percent (Basualdo et al. 2019, 17).

In this context of losses for workers, especially for popular economy workers, CGT opened a space for agreements and joint actions with CTEP. Both organizations agreed on the need to defend workers' rights regardless of whether they are formal or informal (Rodríguez 2016). Growing impoverishment and, of more concern for the government, the demonstrated ability of CTEP along with CGT, CTA, and other workers' organizations to mobilize with a unified agenda against deteriorating living conditions left no option to the government but to keep some channels of communication with CTEP open and to back down on the downsizing of social assistance it had promised in its electoral campaign.

By the end of 2016, after CTEP's effective mobilization, the Congress sanctioned a Social Emergency Law that mandated the creation of one million workfare subsidies and the creation of a Council for Popular Economy and Social Salary in charge of establishing a Complementary Social Salary with the participation of members of the government and of popular economy workers (*La Nación* 2016). The social salary would allow popular economy workers to receive an income established as a proportion of the legal minimum wage in exchange for the economic activities they were already performing. For CTEP, the concept of social salary—rather than social assistance for the unemployed—was key as it entailed a recognition that popular economy workers' activities constitute work and, as such, deserves compensation.

With the worsening of economic, labor market and social indicators, mobilization intensified in 2018 despite the government's attempts to curtail the power of precarious workers' organizations. By 2019, social mobilization became increasingly influenced by the upcoming presidential election in which a broad number of sectoral demands were combined with calls to defeat Macri's bid for reelection on the part of several union leaders. The change of government in December 2019 created expectations of recovery from the losses suffered during the previous years among the various sections of the labor movement.

The incoming government led by Alberto Fernández acknowledged the relevance of the popular economy by appointing several of CTEP's leaders to key positions in the presidential cabinet and announcing the implementation of some of the clauses of the Social Emergency Law approved in 2016, in particular a Registry of Popular Economy Workers (Registro de Trabajadores de la Economía Popular) that would allow popular economy workers a certain degree of formalization. These political decisions no doubt reflected the power these organizations have accumulated through active mobilization. Nonetheless, for some organizations, participating in the government meant undermining the very basis of their power as organizations, that is, their ability to mobilize and remain politically visible.

Against the backdrop of a serious economic crisis inherited from the Macri government and the multiplication of demands, the irruption of the COVID-19 pandemic entailed momentous transformations in the social and political landscapes of the country. It made the relevance of the work of popular economy workers, especially of their care work, evident while at the same time greatly restricted their livelihood and, equally important, the forms of mobilization that had been previously effective in securing some forms of support from the state.

As it happened elsewhere, the pandemic appeared to be a more propitious moment to invite reflection about the value of the essential work of those who for many appeared marginal in their contribution to society. While that recognition has not materialized, it has been workers in the popular economy, notwithstanding their weak structural power, who have remained central in organizing around issues essential to all workers, especially the contingencies of workers' reproduction in a pattern of capital accumulation in which a growing number of workers are seen as "disposable."

FINAL REFLECTIONS: WHICH WAY FORWARD? WORKERS AND THEIR STRUGGLES IN TODAY'S ARGENTINA

In the context of increasingly heterogeneous labor markets, organizations like CTEP have found innovative ways of overcoming the obstacles to organizing precarious workers. Likewise, their efforts have also been critical in giving new impetus to debates about what constitutes work and who is a worker in a capitalist society and, equally important, about the precarity of reproduction for workers as wage employment continues to decline.

A key dilemma—and a very evident limitation—for organizations within the popular economy is that the viability of their initiatives entails some form of access to state funding in the form of assistance programs. While reliance on the state might be inescapable, it has created two fundamental problems. One is its contingency. Popular economy organizations have very little leverage in ensuring the availability of these resources, and this creates political vulnerabilities the state can manipulate in its favor. The other problem relates to the political risks that the subordination to state assistance generates as it brings to the surface assumptions about the poor under capitalism, in particular their being unproductive and superfluous to society. In struggles by popular economy workers, we thus see an ideological battle to vindicate the worth of these workers' contributions to society in terms of the value of their productive and reproductive activities and, therefore, their rightful claim to a share of the wealth generated.

Equally important, popular economy workers' organizing is—as other historical forms of workers' collective action—an open-ended process. These collective forms have been portrayed in some cases as the starting point of radical moves away from surplus value producing labor to forms of work that are mostly aimed at satisfying needs and freeing workers from the subordination to capital (Mazzeo and Stratta 2021, 21–24). In our understanding, emerging forms of organizing precarious workers have the potential of transforming working-class struggles more broadly in positive ways as these workers push the boundaries of what is politically relevant and desirable. But there are dangers that cannot be underestimated as the recognition and institutionalization of the popular economy could also legitimize the expansion of very precarious forms of survival.

The case of CTEP allows us to reflect on the structural position and the political prospects of the growing surplus population whose survival seems increasingly disassociated from the reproduction of the labor force required by capital accumulation. In all its limitations and contradictions, we are certain these workers' actions bring along a new opportunity to confront the irrationality of our capitalist societies for their inability to ensure the survival, well-being, and dignity of a very large segment of the population. Equally important, it reminds us that workers' search for forms of collective action to deal with this irrationality has the potential to overcome the "fate" of the precarization of life.

NOTES

1. Precarious labor is a broad and heterogeneous range of working conditions including nonregistered labor, self-employment, family work, etc. Informal labor is often used to refer to nonstandard employment or unregistered employment. Our study focuses on various combinations of these categories which in general expose workers to forms of vulnerability and uncertainty.

2. Space does not permit us to develop a systematic analysis of the historical evolution of the Argentinean labor movement. We focus on Perón's first two presidential periods because of their relevance in the identities and dynamics of the labor movement in the country. We refer to key moments the historical evolution of the labor movement in the following decades with an emphasis on the momentous transformations occurred amidst neoliberal reforms and their aftermath.

3. In this chapter, we use CTEP to refer to the organization.

4. The popular economy demarcates a reality different from common understandings of the "social economy," a concept used to identify economic activities undertaken on the basis of solidarity of voluntary participation.

Chapter Three

Oil and the Dualization of Venezuela's Labor Movement

Kristin Ciupa

Since the mid-1940s, Venezuela's labor movement has been characterized by a dualization between large bureaucratic unions aligned with the state content to advocate for material gains within the confines of extractive capitalism, and smaller Marxist unions intent on achieving socialism via a critique of oil extraction. First forming at the same time as the country's political parties, the major unions aligned with parties in an historical process of state consolidation. This process was driven by national demands to achieve liberal democracy in order to capture growing oil revenues from foreign oil companies for the benefit of the nation. Venezuela's oil export economy, and the performance of oil as a commodity in the international market, have thus shaped workers' movements that struggle both within, and against, the extractivist model.

This chapter analyzes the dualization of Venezuela's labor movement focusing on national oil dependency and on the relationship between the state, oil companies, and union organizing. It does so through an engagement with Bergquist's original case study of Venezuela. Seemingly foreshadowing what was to come, Bergquist ends his study with the following:

> As long as the petroleum character retains the historical characteristics that have made it unique among Latin American export economies, and as long as liberal democrats remain in power . . . the Marxist left will have to content itself with making trenchant critiques of the pattern of Venezuela's oil-based development, and resign itself to a long, uphill struggle to regain its influence in Venezuela's labor movement and politics. (Bergquist 1986, 273)

Shortly after *Labor in Latin America* was published, conditions in the global oil market, Venezuela's oil sector, and the nature of class conflict in

Venezuela changed substantially. Volatile oil prices and neoliberal reforms in Venezuela undermined political and economic stability (the unique character-istics to which Bergquist refers), and national oil operations were privatized. This led to an increase in informal labor, and class conflicts were institu-tionalized via the Confederation of Workers of Venezuela (CTV): the main workers' union aligned with the social democratic Acción Democrática (AD) party. In response, there was renewal of the Marxist left and other radical elements of class struggle in the political arena during the Pink Tide period, represented by class coalitions between formal and informal labor, the urban poor, peasants, and indigenous people. Yet, while new government-endorsed workers' unions were created, the division between large party-aligned bureaucratic unions and small radical unions at odds with the government remained. In the post–Pink Tide period, low oil prices and a decline in pro-ductive capacity, and US sanctions, led to a decline in the standard of living for workers, an increase in informal labor, and mass migration out of the country. Privatization policies and government assaults on workers' rights increasingly fragmented labor unions and the political left in general, with the right being equally fragmented in its response. This chapter analyzes these developments by adopting Bergquist's claim that class struggle, shaped by the Venezuelan oil export economy, best explains the country's social and political trajectory (Bergquist 1986, 204).

Beginning where Bergquist's study ends, this chapter explores contem-porary developments in the labor movement since 1980. It situates these developments in the context of oil price volatility where Venezuela no longer appears unique among Latin American export economies, and where, after forty years of pacted democracy, the liberal democrats are no longer in power. The chapter adopts three units of analysis outlined by Bergquist: variation in economic development and labor formation, nationality and concentration of ownership, and the mediating role played by nationalism (Bergquist 1986, 10–12). It adds to this analysis three themes: the relationship between the state, oil companies, and the labor movement; the cyclicality of oil prices and rentier social relations; and worker-organizing beyond oil. It argues that the nature of oil dependency, situated in the rentier social relation between the Venezuelan state and oil companies, is crucial to understanding the country's economic and social organization, as well as the possibilities for worker-organizing. First, it theorizes the nature of Venezuelan oil dependency and the rentier social relation. This section focuses on how rents affect state form; the relationship between state, unions, and oil companies; and the potential for worker-organizing. Second, it traces changes to labor, worker-organizing, and oil export over three time periods, situating them within changes in the global oil market and Venezuelan political economy since the 1980s.

LABOR UNIONS, THE RENTIER STATE, AND FOREIGN OIL COMPANIES

Venezuela's labor movement has been shaped by a tripartite relationship between foreign oil companies, the state, and workers' organizations. In *Labor in Latin America*, Bergquist notes several limitations of his analysis, one of which was a relative inattention to processes of state consolidation and the emergence of modern political systems (Bergquist 1986, 376–77). Focusing on explicating processes of state consolidation and political party formation, this section outlines a theoretical framework, focusing on oil export and the rentier state, the relationship between parties and unions, and class struggle and worker-organizing in the rentier economy.

Oil Export and the Consolidation of the Rentier State

After gradually decreasing in the early 1980s, the price of oil declined sharply by mid-decade. This marked the end of what Bergquist noted to be the particularly stable performance of oil as a global commodity. While Venezuela had experienced less severe cycles of boom and bust in the past, the combination of record-high prices in the late 1970s and extensive state spending followed by rapid price decline created an unparalleled crisis under the oil export model. Theories of resource dependency emerged in the late 1970s, explaining this general phenomenon as the "resource curse" (Auty 2001) or "paradox of plenty" (Karl 1997). The basic principle of these theories is that resource-rich countries tend to underperform economically, despite having an abundance of a valuable commodity, due to growing dependency on one profitable export sector and deindustrialization in other areas.

The Marxian theory of rent explains that these economic processes are actually the result of a particular social relationship between capitalist and landlord: in this case, between foreign oil companies and the Venezuelan state. With the state acting as the sovereign owner of land, and thus of oil reserves, it collects rents from international oil companies operating in Venezuela. Land does not produce value, but rather appropriates it through rents, which is the economic form of the social relationship between capitalist oil companies and the landlord state (Coronil 1997, 59). It is this social relationship that has fundamentally shaped the Venezuelan economy, providing the impetus to expand oil production and thus increase state revenues.

The Venezuelan state expanded and was consolidated around oil as the government negotiated contracts with foreign oil companies, enacted oil legislation, and sought to capture a portion of oil rents from companies exploring and extracting oil on Venezuelan soil (Coronil 1997, 76). Acting as a mediator between the nation and foreign oil companies, the state became responsible not only for regulating oil production, but also for managing natural resource extraction, transforming productive structures, and collecting and distributing rents to the population (Coronil 1997, 32). Nationalist discourses frame the struggle to increase state oil revenues to be for the benefit of the Venezuelan nation, with the state representing the interests of Venezuelans both within the country and in the international sphere. The simultaneous process of state consolidation, and the rise of Venezuelan oil extraction and export, inextricably connected state legitimacy and power to oil, thereby making the state, acting on behalf of national capital, a key player in the oil sector.

Political Parties and Labor Unions

The process of state consolidation began under the dictatorship of Juan Vicente Gómez from 1908 to 1935 (Tinker Salas 2009, 2). Upon Gómez's death in 1935, labor unions and political parties that had been prohibited from openly organizing emerged simultaneously. They initially collaborated to challenge the traditional oligarchy and gain control of the state, with oil workers playing a vital role given their strategic ability to stop oil production. This was first achieved via collaboration between Marxist and social democratic factions of workers and unions (Bergquist 1986, 231). Over time however, the power of Marxist unions and the Communist Party (PCV) were undermined by a growing liberal reformist movement among the AD and other middle-class parties that sought a compromise between capital and labor. Collective struggle won oil workers more and more benefits, while mistakes made by the PCV, and the AD's attempts to dominate the union landscape, served to undermine the influence of Marxist unions in the oil fields (Bergquist 1986, 248, 259).

After 1958, unions were remade to be corporatist, centralized, and bureaucratic. They were sanctioned by the state, which negotiated with oil companies to win benefits for workers without resorting to strikes (Bergquist 1986, 272). This affiliation between corporatist unions and political parties continued throughout the twentieth and into the twenty-first century. Interviewing union leaders and workers affiliated with either the AD or COPEI (The Social Christian Party) in the city of Barguisimeto, Davis found that they tended to "accept a social democratic bargain of peace between labor and management and to play down the ideological rhetoric" (Davis 2014, 21). The unions engaged in minimal strike activity, and referring to "class conflict" one leader said: "We simply don't use this phrase; it is a hollow expression."

Instead of in the workplace, struggles over access to economic resources tend to take place in the political sphere where oil rents are maintained, which explains in part the ongoing alliance between labor unions and political parties. Aligning with parties and the state, however, presents certain limitations for unions. When oil prices are high, the interests of the state (national capital) more closely align with those of the working class and there are sufficient resources to materially provide for various class sectors. Increased national ownership over oil and ample rent transfers mitigate conflicts between capital and labor. When oil prices decline, however, the government is more likely to align with the interests of international capital in order to attract investment. This results in privatization, lower state revenues, and a deterioration of conditions for workers. This chapter demonstrates that the compromises between unions and the state, and the nature of class struggle, shifted with the 1980s decline in oil prices, which shattered the illusion of Venezuelan exceptionalism (Ellner and Tinker Salas 2005, 5), faith in pacted democracy, and the idea of the state as protector of national interests. I argue that struggles among factions and classes over state power, as well as confrontations between capital and workers (Nore and Turner 1980, 1–2), characterize the nature of class struggle in an unstable oil economy. Drawing on Bergquist, I argue that these struggles, shaped by oil export, explain Venezuela's social and political trajectory since the 1980s.

Rent and the Possibilities for Worker-Organizing

Bergquist posits oil workers as a key sector in the struggle against foreign oil companies, the capitalist state, and Venezuela's export-oriented economy (Bergquist 1986, 230–31). This idea has been echoed in contemporary literature on the strategic role of workers at key junctures in processes of resource extraction and circulation that have the potential to disrupt major sectors via work stoppages (for example, Fox-Hodess and Santibáñez Rebolledo 2020). Others have questioned the revolutionary potential of Venezuelan oil workers, referring to them as the country's "labor aristocracy" (Lebowitz 2008; Ciccariello-Maher 2013). Given the relatively high pay, social benefits, and material comfort of oil workers compared to other workers, this latter position argues that oil workers are not interested in fundamentally disrupting the production process, their relationship with oil companies, and Venezuela's export-oriented economy.

Rather than understand the strategic potential of workers as static, this chapter argues that worker-organizing and power is constantly in flux. Relying on the work of Erik Olin Wright,[1] it argues that the structural power enjoyed by oil workers due to their position in production is only activated when workers develop sufficient "associational power" as the result of collective organizing (Wright 2000, 962). The associational power of oil workers is influenced by perceived collective interests among workers and attempts by capital to divide workers, affecting worker-consciousness. The structural power of oil workers and the labor movement in general is influenced by the expansion and contraction of public sector employment, congruous with cycles of boom and bust in the economy, which influences the importance of particular industries in a given period.

Contrary to Bergquist, who focuses on oil workers as the main protagonists affecting the export sector, this chapter adopts a broad conceptualization of extractive labor. In Venezuela's oil-dependent economy, the majority of national revenues accrue to the state, and it is the government that becomes responsible for investing in and upgrading productive structures across different sectors of the economy. State subsidies to other sectors—made possible by oil rents—mean that the availability and nature of work, and the experience of the working class across formal and informal sectors, is tied to extractive accumulation.

In this context, the "associational power" of extractive workers can be conceptualized to include the organizing capacity of formal and informal workers outside of the oil sector that sometimes organize with oil workers. Connected by the rentier economy, these sectors are recipients of oil rents via distribution networks coordinated by the state, which is sometimes also the employer. This conceptualization of associational power not only quantitatively and qualitatively expands the organizing capacity of Venezuelan workers; it also demonstrates the tendency for collective organizing to take place outside of the workplace and instead in the political arena. In Venezuela, the associational power of the working class is often realized in the political arena as a result of the historical relationship between unions and parties, and the consolidation of the rentier state as a center of economic distribution. The collective interests of the working class are formed by conditions of global oil export, as well as by the political projects and distribution networks of particular governments. Given the small number of laborers working at key points of oil production, and that the majority of Venezuelan workers are informal, structural power manifests as the ability to stop oil production not only via work stoppages, but also to affect production via political channels. Conceptualizing extractive labor beyond the confines of oil workers is thus crucial to understanding the possibilities for worker-organizing and consciousness in Venezuela.

The next section explores these theoretical considerations over three eras: the neoliberal period, the Pink Tide period, and the post–Pink Tide period.

THE NEOLIBERAL PERIOD

During the neoliberal period (1980–1999), labor distribution changed substantially with a decline in formal employment, particularly in the public sector, and a massive rise in informal labor. This occurred in the context of a sharp oil price decline in the mid-1980s, and a neoliberal adjustment package adopted by the government in 1989. Neoliberal reforms included mass firing of workers, creating workplace hierarchies and cutting social benefits. The success of neoliberal assaults on labor was aided by the weakened bargaining power of unions that had adopted a corporatist model of collaborating with the state to advocate for material benefits for workers. In the context of severe economic crisis, the government privatized oil operations, thereby supporting the interests of international capital over labor, in order to resolve declining state capacity and protect the interests of national capital.

Oil Price Decline and Neoliberal Reforms

As oil prices declined, the value of Venezuelan exports fell from $19.3 billion[2] to $13.5 billion between 1981 and 1983 (Santiago 2008). On February 18, 1983, in what became known as "Black Friday," President Luis Herrera Campíns devalued the currency and imposed foreign exchange controls (*The Economist* 2010), in response to massive capital flight that threatened to leave the country without reserves (Lander and Fierro 1996, 50).

Despite the contraction of the oil sector, government spending continued throughout the 1980s to support the national development program put in place under President Carlos Andres Pérez of the AD (Naím 1993, 28). Low oil prices throughout the decade, paired with high spending, meant that debt was high, foreign currency reserves were depleted, and the government could not access more credit from international banks (Naím 1993, 28). In this context, the government turned to international capital at the expense of Venezuelan workers. In order to access a $4.5 billion loan, the Pérez government agreed to a structural adjustment program with the International Monetary Fund (Mommer 2003, 137). The main requirements of the program were restricting public expenditures, restricting wage levels, unifying the exchange rate, flexible interest rates, reducing price controls, reducing subsidies, and trade liberalization (Lander and Fierro 1996, 52).

These economic changes were met with responses from workers. A rise in gas prices as part of the adjustment package sparked the Caracazo: a week-long series of protests and violent clashes with government, beginning on February 27, 1989. Informal workers commuting into the city responded to doubled public transportation fares, refusing to pay fares and rioting on the first day of the price hikes (Ciccariello-Maher 2013, 92). To control the protests, the government declared a state of emergency and martial law was imposed on February 28, 1989. A number of constitutional rights were suspended and throughout the protests, the military took aggressive action against the public. Deaths are officially listed at 276, but many estimates put the number at up to three thousand (TeleSUR 2016).

Initially, CTV leaders ascribed the riots to "nihilistic tendencies of lumpen elements" and denied that organized workers were involved (Ellner 1993, 102). This explanation was quickly discarded, and the CTV attempted to serve as spokesperson for formulating demands, attributing the event to the deterioration in living conditions of workers throughout the decade. In the context of these developments, there was a change in labor organization within the CTV in two ways. First, while the CTV remained absent from subsequent street protests, Steve Ellner argues that a general strike on May 18, 1989, was an attempt by the CTV to extend its leadership role in organized labor beyond its immediate constituency by incorporating protesting workers into the organization (1993, 102). Second, speaking out in favor of workers, and organizing a general strike against the AD government, served to weaken alliances between the CTV and the AD during this period when the state pursued capitalist interests over labor (Coker 2001, 191). Trudie Coker, however, explains the changing alliances between the CTV and AD government of the time as being "more of a reaction to economic realities, rather than being politically motivated" (2001, 188). In this sense, the protests, strike, and actions of the CTV were characterized by perceived collective economic interests against structural adjustment and the decline in working-class standards of living, indicative of strong associational power between various sectors of the working class. They failed, however, to challenge the oil export model itself, instead seeking an improvement of material conditions within it.

Changes to Production and Labor

Trade liberalization was met with mixed reactions by entrepreneurial sectors, whose interests are also shaped by the rentier economy. Liberalization increased low-cost imports, which was beneficial for importers who, due to limited productive capacity in Venezuela, are responsible for importing food, medicine, and consumer goods, supported by state subsidies. The influx of cheap goods, however, led to the contraction of national productive sectors (Jongkind 1993), as many small and medium-sized enterprises in textile, apparel, and footwear experienced increased pressure due to international competition (Lander and Fierro 1996, 60). There were confrontations between industrialists and importers, the former who have been limited by the rentier economy, while the interests of the latter are tied to oil extraction.

Most industries attempted to survive this period of economic bust by shifting the costs of adjustment to the workers (Lander and Fierro 1996, 61). This was achieved by reducing employees, labor flexibilization, cutbacks in social benefits, dualization between permanent and contract workers, intensification of work, and the decline of real wages (Lander and Fierro 1996, 61–62). With job losses in productive sectors (Green 2003, 60–61), the share of the manufacturing sector in total employment fell from 18 percent in 1988 to 16 percent in 1992. In textiles, apparel, leather products, and food, beverages, and tobacco industries there were absolute decreases in the labor force between 1988 and 1992 (Lander and Fierro 1996, 61). Following the privatisation of the state-owned telephone, ports, airlines, and steel industries, job security rules were eliminated or made "flexible" (Jonakin 2009, 1290). Public sector employment declined significantly as a result of privatization initiatives during the 1990s and was not compensated by growth in formal private employment (Portes and Hoffman 2003, 48).

There was a change in class structure as labor shifted from agriculture and industry to the service sector, including a shift from formal to informal employment, with lower wages and more precarious work (Roberts 2003, 60). At the end of the 1970s, more than twice as many workers were employed in the formal sector than in the informal sector. By 1997, the formal and informal sectors were roughly equal (Smilde 2008, 39). The number of people living in official poverty nearly doubled between 1984 and 1995 from 36 to 66 percent, and those living in extreme poverty more than tripled during the same period from 11 to 36 percent (Roberts 2003, 59). Ultimately, the cyclicality of Venezuela's oil economy, and low oil prices in this period, negatively affected the rentier state and national capital, with the effects being disproportionately borne by labor via structural adjustment.

Prejudices against informal workers (Ciccariello-Maher 2013, 231) meant that they were not incorporated into labor organizing, and after 1980, the workers' movement was divided due to an increase in contract workers (Ellner 1993, 144). The CTV made unsuccessful attempts to incorporate new professional sectors like doctors and lawyers; however, it remained exclusionary in a number of other ways. Non-AD trade unionists continued to have limited power in the CTV, and the AD retained three of the four positions on the CTV's executive committee (Ellner 1993, 97). Women remained in largely token positions outside of union leadership even in female-dominated industries, like the garment industry (Ellner 1993, 104–5). The failure of CTV organizers to recognize common interests, and the associational potential of organizing with informal workers, limited the power of the union to counter neoliberal assaults on labor.

Oil Reforms and Workers

During the neoliberal period, the oil industry went through an *Apertura*, or opening to foreign investment, where international oil companies were given more control over operations via new contract models with the state for exploration and extraction. Changes to the ownership structure of oil operations negatively affected the material conditions of oil laborers. The state-owned oil company (PDVSA) sought to undermine many of the benefits it had promised workers during the 1976 nationalization relying on tactics that divided workers and facilitated dualization of the workforce. The oil union, Fedepetrol, which was part of the CTV, supported these practices during contract negotiations (Ellner 1993, 140). For example, PDVSA attempted to justify the eradication of commissaries—company stores that sold food and goods to oil workers at subsidized rates—by claiming that remote communities where most commissaries were located enjoyed elite privileges not shared by other workers (Ellner 1993, 141). PDVSA pledged to provide aid to establish workers' cooperatives if the commissaries were eliminated. This pitted workers in central and remote communities against each other, and it was particularly young workers who had not received a commissary card that wanted to see the cooperative scheme implemented. It had the effect of limiting the associational power of oil workers, all of whom were negatively affected by cutbacks to benefits. By the end of the decade, many oil workers that had entered the industry in the 1980s were not recipients of either company houses or the commissary card (Ellner 1993, 145).

PDVSA was able to reduce the workforce via rationalization, where branch organizations were relocated, and decentralization, where headquarters were moved outside of the capital. These changes meant that workers either had to transfer to other parts of the country or quit. PDVSA also began to increase contract work, a practice which it had promised to avoid during nationalization. This was justified on the basis that certain tasks necessitated specialized equipment that PDVSA did not possess, or that services such as transportation were not in PDVSA's line of business and better carried out by specialized firms (Ellner 1993, 138).

During the neoliberal period, faith in Venezuela's liberal democratic two-party system was weakened by Pérez's AD government that immediately after being elected in 1989 agreed to a package of neoliberal reforms. This was seen as a betrayal by many who voted for Pérez, and the mediating role played by oil nationalism was undermined when the state could no longer maintain a relative level of material comfort across different class sectors via distribution. With the flow of material benefits to workers cut off, and the nature of work changing, the compromise between labor and capital outlined by Bergquist was violated. The relationship between the state, oil companies, and labor was altered in the context of low oil prices, wherein the state turned to foreign capital and oil companies at the expense of labor in order to maintain the oil sector. Unions were ineffective at protecting workers' rights against state-led neoliberal assaults on labor, as they had become extensions of state bureaucracy. Further, union numbers declined significantly as workers lost their jobs, making the formal workplace a less significant site of struggle, and negatively affecting the structural power of workers. While workers' response to structural adjustment was an example of strong associational power between workers across various sectors, this was undermined due to employer practices that divided workers, and due to prejudices against informal workers that limited organizing. Instead, mass numbers of newly unemployed and informal workers, members of the working class, and members of the middle class who had seen their class position decline during the neoliberal era responded in the political arena, electing a leader outside of the two-party system that promised an alternative to business as usual.

THE PINK TIDE

The Pink Tide period (2000–2014) was characterized by popular mobilizations that engaged in class struggle predominantly in the political arena over access to state power. Dissatisfaction with the political elitism of pacted democracy between the AD and COPEI, and socioeconomic decline in the wake of neoliberal reform, precipitated the election of an "outsider" and member of the Movimiento V República party, Hugo Chávez, in 1999. This shaped a new political terrain and relationship between the state and social movements. There was a revival of Marxist thinking and organizing, alongside feminist, peasant, indigenous, and anti-extractivist movements. People living in the barrios surrounding Caracas—informal workers of all kinds— were crucial in supporting the Chávez government, which in turn engaged in massive redistributive programs, productive experiments, and extended new rights and powers to decentralized community organizations. Worker-organizing around the goal of increasing political and economic inclusion led to the realization of these interests in state policy, demonstrating the structural and associational power across working-class sectors. New unions were created that broke with the old AD/CTV relationship. Unions remained largely aligned with the state, however, with the associational power of workers undermined by ideological divisions between those connected to government and those that wanted to be autonomous.

The Attempted Coup and Oil Lock-Out

During the first five years of Chávez's presidency, the government attempted to enact a number of reforms that would break with neoliberalism and position more closely with the national developmentalist model of the 1970s. This included re-establishing government majority ownership in public/private oil operations, and land redistribution (Webber 2011, 186). In response to initiatives that would increase oil rents accruing to the state and would redistribute wealth, a number of attempts were made to remove Chávez from power. These attempts were instigated by not only the country's most important business association, Fedecámaras, but also by CTV union leaders who remained loyal to the AD.

Several general strikes were called by CTV union leaders and Fedecámaras, which culminated in a violent confrontation in the center of Caracas on April 11, 2002, and a coup orchestrated by the military, the CTV, Fedecámaras, and media outlets that supported opposition parties. The popular response to the coup was immediate with millions of poor Venezuelans streaming down from the hills surrounding Caracas (Ciccariello-Maher 2013, 169). Widespread mobilizations emboldened supporters in the military, which made possible the overthrow of the interim government, the return of Chávez's cabinet to power, and subsequently, Chávez's return to power on April 13, 2002. The failed coup and actions of the interim Pedro Carmona government significantly divided those opposing Chávez between sectors that supported neoliberalism (the Fedecámaras), and those that were ambivalent toward it yet sought a return to the two-party system (the CTV and AD).

A subsequent oil lock-out in late 2002, initiated by PDVSA directors and management, was a second attempt to undermine the government's agenda to bring PDVSA under state control. While CTV leaders had been relatively unchallenged by union members during the attempted coup, this changed by late 2002. The strike began on December 2 and was largely supported by white-collar workers (aligned with the AD). Blue-collar unions supported Chávez (Kellogg 2015, 158), and the strike was defeated by skilled and unskilled oil workers restarting production with the assistance of technical personnel and people from surrounding communities. Divisions in the workplace, along party lines, reflected the differing class interests between white-collar and blue-collar oil workers that predated the 1976 oil sector nationalization and continued throughout the neoliberal period.

Ultimately, while the associational power of the working class in the streets influenced the government's political project, the lack of associational power between white- and blue-collar oil workers obstructed changes to oil production and rentier social relations. The division between workers allowed the government to reassert control over the oil sector, limiting workers' control in the industry. The government regained control of oil operations after the lock-out with the assistance of retired workers, foreign contractors, and the military, citing the oil sector as a national "strategic industry" (Webber 2011, 188). Around eighteen thousand upper- and middle-level managers who opposed the government, and who exercised control of the company, were dismissed for their involvement in the lock-out and were replaced with government supporters.

The Bolivarian Process and Changes to Labor

While the coup and oil lock-out did not alter oil workplace relations, they did serve to solidify support for the Chávez government and radicalize the government's political agenda. Oil prices rose throughout the 2000s, and in the context of widespread support and strong associational power of popular classes, the Chávez government made sweeping changes to the oil sector, as well as to rent distribution, with a focus on those excluded from mainstream politics and the formal labor market. Workers' interests and power were thus more substantively realized in the political arena due to political coordination across working-class sectors.

In 2001, the government implemented an Organic Hydrocarbons Law, which increased royalties accruing to the state to 30 percent per barrel of oil extracted (Article 44) from the previous 16.1 percent, with excess profit taxes when the price of oil rose to over seventy US dollars, and over one hundred US dollars, per barrel. Privatization was reversed, with PDVSA holding a majority share in all oil operations. With increased oil rents and widespread support, the Chávez government undertook a massive rent distribution program to achieve Twenty-First Century Socialism (Proyecto Nacional 2007–2013). However, while some policies benefited workers via social spending, participatory politics, and new forms of cooperative work, others served to maintain rentier capitalism by supporting productive monopolies and capitalist importers.

National labor statistics demonstrate that productive spending and public sector hiring led to a decline in informal labor from the end of 2004. Between 2004 and 2013, informal labor as a percentage of the labor market declined from approximately 50 percent to approximately 40 percent. While there was an improvement through the reduction of informal work in this period

(Smilde 2008, 40; Weisbrot, Ray and Sandoval 2009, 12), informal work continued to constitute a large percentage of all work, with the majority of informal workers being women (Leary 2007). For some, the large percentage of informal employment during this period is evidence of the failure of the Chávez government to break from the neoliberal model (Leary 2007), with informal work increasing again once oil prices declined.

Other forms of rent distribution followed suit: while temporarily improving social and economic conditions for the working class, they remained dependent on continual state transfers, which became impossible to sustain when oil prices declined in the mid-2010s. For example, co-managed enterprises remained dependent on the state for rent transfers because bureaucratic factions within the state remained unconcerned with technical upgrading of production, and companies did not operate at a scale necessary to recover the costs of production independently (Purcell 2013, 156). From 2012, a wave of labor conflicts in state companies centered on rank-and-file workers' dissatisfaction with the failure of government managers and institutions to efficiently manage state enterprises (Azzellini 2018, 82). Eventually, many state enterprises closed.

Thus, despite the material benefits to the working class from rent distribution, there was no substantive redistribution between capital and labor. Workers lacked the associational power to collectively challenge the extractive model, as well as the structural power to do so once oil prices declined. Rather, high oil prices made it possible for the state to provide materially for different class sectors, and thereby to mitigate antagonistic conflicts between classes during this period, without altering the oil export-oriented model of accumulation and the relations of power that sustain it.

New Union Formation

The attempted coup and oil lock-out also affected labor union formation, which shaped worker-consciousness and -organizing. After the CTV leaders' participation in these events, it became clear that CTV leadership would remain opposed to the government. In response to lock-outs in various sectors, a new labor federation was formed: the National Union of Workers (UNT). The UNT supported government initiatives such as co-management (Gindin 2005, 74) and a government-imposed prohibition on layoffs for the lowest paid workers. The UNT held its founding meeting in Caracas on April 5, 2003, and its first congress five months later, which included fifteen hundred delegates, 120 unions, and twenty-five regional federations. While the group was heterogeneous, they agreed to a program that included nationalization of banks, workers' occupation of abandoned factories, nonpayment of "fraudulent" foreign debt, and a reduced work week of thirty-six hours (Rodríguez

Porras and Sorans 2018, 40). A total of 76.5 percent of collective agreements signed in the public sector in 2003 and 2004 were with unions affiliated with the UNT, while 20.2 percent were with the CTV (Gindin 2005, 76). These numbers demonstrate that a new alliance was being formed between the Movimiento V República and the UNT, which despite the increasingly radical political project of the Chávez government, maintained the historical model of union/party associations. Even in the private sector, the UNT represented 50.3 percent of all collective agreements signed in 2003 and 2004, compared to 45.2 percent with the CTV (Gindin 2005, 76).

Debates over how to balance support for, with autonomy from, the Chávez government characterized the first two years of UNT's formation (Gindin 2005, 83), which limited the associational power of its members. The Bolivarian Workers Force (FBT), a group of pro-Chávez unions that preceded the UNT, was part of the "Chavista unionism" current that called for a new federation to be established to replace the CTV, even if this slightly curtailed the federation's democratic nature. The "autonomous unionism" current argued that the new federation should make a comprehensive break with the old party-aligned unionism, and should be built on autonomous democratic foundations (Gindin 2005, 84). As a result of these differences, by 2006 there were five major currents that acted independently of each other.[3] At the second congress in 2006, the different factions fought over defining the terms of the UNT, and the congress ended in physical fights between C-CURA and pro-government sectors (Rodríguez Porras and Sorans 2018, 43). Conflicts over union autonomy, democracy, and uneven experiences with co-management led to the further fracturing of the UNT in subsequent years.

The Chávez government, for its part, sought to institutionalize the relationship between government, party, and civil society organizations via formalized coalitions. These efforts further entrenched divisions between pro-government and autonomous union factions, and impeded the associational power of workers. The UNT was divided in 2007 when, shortly after Chávez's re-election, the government announced the launching of the United Socialist Party of Venezuela (PSUV): a coalition including grassroots parties and organizations. Those that refused to join argued that regressive government policies were not an anomaly attributable to the actions of certain officials, and instead that bureaucratism and corruption were structural features of the capitalist state (Rodríguez Porras and Sorans 2018, 42). Growing pressure to align with the government manifested in increasing repression of autonomous unions and support for government-aligned unions. At the launch of PSUV, Chávez described supporters of autonomous unions as "counter-revolutionaries," and some government employees that supported autonomous factions were fired from PDVSA, despite having supported the government during the attempted coup and lock-out (Rodríguez Porras and Sorans 2018, 46).

At the same time, the Chávez government intervened in union activities in a number of other capacities. In January 2007, FBT leader José Ramón Rivero was appointed minister of labor,[4] a move that was unpopular with other unions that argued he was using the post to promote the interests of the government-aligned FBT, as the CTV had similarly done in the past. In April 2007, a new oil workers' union—the United Federation of Venezuelan Oil Workers—was formed in collaboration with PDVSA management and the labor ministry as an attempt to unite the four main union federations in the oil industry. By 2009, it represented more than half of oil workers. Elections for the United Federation of Venezuelan Oil Workers never took place, and rather a provisional national leadership committee was appointed by the Ministry of Labor under Rivero. Rodríguez Porras and Sorans (2018, 52) argue that by the time of Chávez's death in 2013, the government had consolidated a union bureaucracy that had weakened unions, atomized workers, and that was heavily dependent on the state. In this way, the Chávez government developed its own union alliances that paralleled those of earlier governments with the CTV. This reproduced the union-party model that had limited associational power and the potential for worker-organizing in the past.

POST–PINK TIDE ERA

In the post–Pink Tide era (2015–2023), a decline in oil prices beginning in 2014 and oil production, as well as US sanctions, reduced state revenues. This led to a decline in formal employment, product shortages, increased poverty, and mass migration out of Venezuela. State-imposed currency controls and a multitiered exchange rate contributed to inflation and attempts to profiteer from the discrepancy between the official and black-market rates, while growing contradictions within the Bolivarian process led to a decline in support for the government. In the context of these worsening economic conditions, President Nicolás Maduro sought foreign investment, flexibilizing labor and undermining collective bargaining rights. Labor unions aligned with the PSUV have been unsuccessful in challenging neoliberal assaults on labor implemented by the Maduro government since 2018.

Declining Oil Production and US Sanctions

Alongside low prices, oil production in Venezuela declined due to lack of technical upgrades to production, owing in part to low government revenues, and worsened by US sanctions in 2017 and 2019 (Rodríguez 2023). Sanctions prohibited the government from borrowing in US financial markets (Weisbrot and Sachs 2019, 1), leading to foreign debt default (Buxton 2020, 1372), and cut Venezuela off from the United States, its largest oil market (Weisbrot and Sachs 2019, 2). Oil output began dropping in 2016 from close to twenty-five hundred barrels per day to a low of around four hundred barrels per day in 2020 (Weisbrot 2023). Between 2020 and 2022, operational oil rigs in Venezuela declined from fifteen, to six, then three (Organization of the Petroleum Exporting Countries 2023, 80). This led to a contraction of the economy with a real gross domestic product growth rate of –22 percent in 2019 and –25 percent in 2020 (Organization of the Petroleum Exporting Countries 2020, 9). Alongside the decline in oil production, the multitiered exchange rate led to increasing inflation rates, which negatively affected the purchasing power of Venezuelans. At the start of 2019, hyperinflation reached an historic high of 2,688,670 percent (Buxton 2020, 1372). In 2023, Venezuela continued to suffer from high inflation although it was no longer experiencing hyperinflation as a result of currency revaluation and use of the US dollar (Organization of the Petroleum Exporting Countries 2023, 35). During this economic downturn, the Maduro government limited imports of medicine, food, and medical equipment, as well as equipment for electricity generation, water systems and transportation (Weisbrot and Sachs 2019, 2). Lack of access to medicines and food had a severe impact on human life and health, resulting in increased poverty rates, reports of weight loss, and an increase in malnutrition among children (United Nations 2019).

Class Relations and Labor Reforms under the Bolivarian Process

In the midst of economic crisis, certain sectors were enriched based on their relationship with the government—including importers, bureaucrats, bankers, and the military—all of whom had access to preferential exchange rates under the Chávez and Maduro governments. These channels of rent distribution served to reproduce rentier social relations despite government discourse to the contrary. Importers and bureaucrats who were granted import licenses, benefited from fraudulent activities like over-invoicing, and by 2018, Manuel Sutherland found that for every ten dollars transferred by the Maduro government, 9.5 dollars was transferred to importers (2018, 146). Under the Maduro government, the role of the military was substantially increased, first through the exchange rate system, and later via the creation of companies run by the military (Webber 2019). Between 2013 and 2017, fourteen military companies were established, including The Bank of the Bolivarian National Armed Forces in 2013 and a mining company CAMIMPEG in 2016. As of 2019, at least 785 active and retired military officers managed private companies that won contracts with government in imports, medicine, food, health, and construction (Guillaudat 2019). By 2019, military figures controlled key national corporations including PDVSA, the Caracas Metro, steel and aluminium enterprises, and the National Electric Corporation (Webber 2019).

At the same time, sectors that supported the Bolivarian process, but challenged national and international capital, were undermined by the government as it sought to align with foreign capital in order to maintain the rentier economy. In 2018, the Maduro government implemented the "Plan for Economic Recovery, Growth and Prosperity" in an attempt to attract foreign investment—in part by cheapening labor costs. This plan included Memorandum 2792, which overturned many of the labor rights outlined in the 2012 Organic Law of Labor and Workers. Memorandum 2792 decrees worker salaries that used to be established through discussion between workers and employer with the labor ministry as an arbiter, freezes or modifies collective bargaining agreements, eliminates the right to strike, freezes social benefits, and results in the loss of medical coverage for the majority of workers. The Office of the United Nations High Commissioner for Human Rights found that Memorandum 2792 did not involve consultations with affected parties on labor issues, "which raises concerns related to trade unions' independence and full enjoyment of their members' rights" (Office of the United Nations High Commissioner for Human Rights 2021).

In addition to changes in labor laws instigated by the government, private companies sought to undermine workers' rights. Relying on a misinterpretation of the 2012 Labor Law,[5] private companies justified mass layoffs of full-time workers, with temporary workers hired in their place (Marquina 2021). A number of companies began paying workers primarily in bonuses.[6] Unlike salaries, employers are under no future obligation to continue to provide bonuses to workers, and bonuses do not count toward retirement income or social security benefits. Further, by paying bonuses to some workers and not others, employers can divide workers within a workplace, thereby limiting their associational power to challenge workplace assaults on labor.

Under these conditions, the government stopped releasing labor statistics at the end of 2018. In 2018, 58.6 percent of the total workforce had formal jobs, while 41.4 percent worked in the informal sector. This means that 6,144,125 were employed in the informal sector. Further, 1,089,331 were unemployed (Abreu 2020). Given Venezuela's negative gross domestic product growth and decline in oil production, it is likely that the proportion of informal employment is rising. A household survey directed by the Universidad Católica Andrés Bello found that in 2021, 71 percent of workers were informal (Caruso et al. 2021, 13). In particular, COVID-19 lockdowns disproportionately affected informal employees and self-employed workers, who were more likely than formal employees, employers, cooperative workers, and domestic workers to experience unemployment during severe lockdown (Caruso et al. 2021, 12).

Union Activity and Strikes

Despite the decline in working and living conditions, mass mobilization has been limited. Eduardo Sánchez, president of the University Workers' National Union and the University Workers' Federation, argues that the decline in worker-organizing can be understood within the broader context of political polarization, which has led to the fragmentation of the labor movement (Sánchez 2021). This fragmentation is defined along party lines, which reproduces the historical union/party model, where the Bolivarian Socialist Workers Central (formerly FBT) is aligned with PSUV, and the CTV with the AD. Sánchez argues that the Bolivarian Socialist Workers Central has become an arm of the government, with unlimited access to state media, opposing strikes and rubberstamping decisions to repeal workers' rights and collective agreements. Given that both unions lack political autonomy, Sánchez argues that most workers do not identify with either organization. Arguing that the trade union movement has lost credibility, he states that the main reason workers are not mobilizing is due to the unlivable salaries they now make. The need to find work, along with state repression of street mobilizations and arrests of long-time union advocates (Marquina 2020), has led to a decline in associational power between workers of different sectors. Rather, high inflation and a decline in purchasing power and real wages (Marquina 2021), lack of access to essential imports, and few employment opportunities have led to a mass migration out of the country. In March 2023, the United Nations estimated that over 7.1 million Venezuelans had left their homes, with more than six million relocating to other countries in the Americas (United Nations High Commissioner for Refugees 2023).

Still, there have been some protests against Memorandum 2792, though they have been fragmented and lacked coordination between different sectors of the working class. Protests led by oil workers in PDVSA whose collective agreement became null with Memorandum 2792, and workers of other state-owned industries such as SIDOR (a steel mill) where around 80 percent were declared "non-active"[7] due to the pandemic, have had limited success. State companies have sought to divide workers and thereby limit their associational power by bargaining with management, while some workers have faced dismissal or arrest for protesting, or military repression of strikes. Any wage increases achieved have been minimal and insufficient to counter inflation (Dobson 2021).

Aligning With and Fracturing From the PSUV

In the political arena, in response to assaults on labor and the declining purchasing power of workers, the PCV and National Front of Struggle of the Working Class union called for a minimum wage increase, transforming workers' income into salary, a sliding scale of salaries that reference prices constituting Venezuela's basic goods basket, and mandating the Central Bank to regularly publish consumer price indexes (Eusse, cited in Gilbert and Marquina 2020, 201). In February 2018, a Unitary Agreement was signed by the PCV and PSUV wherein the PSUV committed to protecting workers' rights, and which in turn solidified PCV support for Maduro in an upcoming presidential election (Tribuna Popular 2018). The agreement represents a new alignment between union and party, with workers' rights being advocated for in the political sphere. It outlines recovering state enterprises, as well as a number of workers' rights, including protecting autonomous unions, new job creation, increasing formal employment, and implementing a new management model incorporating workers (Tribuna Popular 2018). These worker protections have not been achieved, however. With strong parallels to the late 1950s wherein the PCV and interests of labor were excluded from the 1958 democratic pact, the PCV and workers were excluded after the Maduro government was re-elected. At the same time, middle-class opposition parties and organizations formed their own coalition, which has engaged in several successful negotiations with the government. The opposition-based "Unitary Platform" signed a memorandum of understanding with the government in 2021 and a social agreement in 2022, wherein the United States would release assets into Venezuela that would be used toward reducing poverty and improving other social conditions (Lowenthal 2023). These agreements are indicative of state realignment with private national and international capital, and away from labor in the context of economic decline.

As the Maduro government engaged in the privatization and flexibilization of labor, a new bloc of left-wing groups was formed in 2020 separate from the PSUV, called the Popular Revolutionary Alternative (APR). The APR includes the PCV that had aligned with PSUV for many years, as well as majority currents of Homeland for All Party, Tupamaro Party, United Left Party, and a host of grassroots activists and trade unions. The APR critiques the government's failure to develop infrastructure in local oil, gas, and electrical generation, arguing that these could have helped to alleviate the impact of sanctions, government corruption, landlord-led attacks against small farmers, and the dwindling power of communal organizations (Lunn and Dobson 2020; Molina 2021). It also critiques alliances between the Maduro government and the national business sector, as well as economic policy that promotes privatization, dollarization, concessions to capital, destruction of collective labor rights, persecution of workers and unionists, and the decline in wages. Since its formation, a number of APR leaders have been fired from public sector jobs, and have had homes searched by police without warrants (Lunn and Dobson 2020). The formation of the APR draws some parallels to the creation of earlier parties and coalitions, like the Movimiento V República and PSUV, in that it is an attempt to collectively organize working-class interests in the political arena against the government in order to gain control of the rentier state. The goal of gaining state power is, like its predecessors, to use oil distribution to more egalitarian ends, rather than to alter the oil export model itself.

CONCLUSION

Given the nature of rentier social relations and the rentier state in Venezuela, there is a tendency for class struggle to revolve around capturing state power, and thus access to oil rents. For the labor movement, this has manifested with unions aligning with political parties both due to the concentration of national wealth managed by the state, as well as to the historical process through which unions and parties emerged in support of democracy. With the cyclicality of oil market prices since the mid-1980s, relationships between large unions like the CTV and the government have become less predictable. Instead, governments have sought to attract foreign investment and to support private capital in moments of economic downturn, like the neoliberal and post–Pink tide periods. The bureaucratic model of union organizing, supported by institutionalized processes and relationships with government and employer, has limited the associational and structural power of Venezuela's major trade unions as they have either supported, or been too weak to challenge, neoliberal reforms to labor.

In the Pink tide and post–Pink tide periods, debates about the limitations of aligning with the state permeated union-organizing. Policy reforms that increased social inequality, and attempts in the workplace to divide and disorganize workers led to a massive rise in informal labor and revealed the restrictions of collective organizing under a bureaucratic model. New unions were formed, yet the dualization of unions continued, as some chose to support the Chávez government, while autonomous unions were undermined and marginalized over time. This reproduced the dualization seen in earlier eras between large bureaucratic unions aligned with the state content to advocate for material gains within the confines of extractive capitalism, and smaller radical unions intent on achieving socialism via a critique of extractivism.

Throughout the three periods explored in this chapter, a major limitation of union organizing was the exclusion of Venezuela's large informal working class. George Ciccariello-Maher (2013) demonstrates the associational power of informal workers, arguing that they assert their class interests in the political arena through both electoral participation and street mobilizations, and by their interests being represented and recognized via state policy. Given their diverse participation in the Venezuelan economy, Ciccariello-Maher (2013) argues that the class interests of this group are reflected in common culture and geographical proximity afforded by barrio life, with communal councils being the preferred form of association to reflect these class interests.

On their own, however, informal workers appear to lack structural power because they are not tied to a formal workplace. This chapter argues that the informal sector may not participate in collective organizing through a formal workplace, but because it is integrated into the rentier economy as recipient of oil rents via state coordinated distribution networks, it has the potential to affect production in the political arena via intersectoral working class alliances. Beyond the associational power of informal workers, this group shares collective interests with the formal working class and oil workers, formed by conditions of oil export and the global oil market, as well as by the political projects and distribution networks of particular governments. Given the small number of laborers working at key points of oil production, and that the majority of Venezuelan workers are in the informal sector, structural power manifests as the ability to stop oil production not only via work stoppages, but also to affect oil production via political channels.

There are challenges to achieving these forms of organizing, however, not only in terms of coordinating informal workers across diverse work experiences, but also given ongoing discrimination against informal workers by those on the left who "failed to recognize either the structural origins of the lumpen or its explosive potential" (Ciccariello-Maher 2013, 231). The associational possibilities and structural power of the working class thus depend on identifying forms of oppression collectively tied to the rentier economy, and on organizing both within and outside of the workplace against private capital and the rentier state.

NOTES

1. See chapter 1 to this volume.
2. All dollar figures are in US dollars.
3. The Bolivarian Workers' Force; Alfredo Maneiro Current; Collective of Workers in Revolution; United Revolutionary Autonomous Class Current; Union Autonomy.
4. Under pressure from the workers' movement, Chávez removed Rivero from the position in April 2008 after Rivero called striking Sidor workers "counterrevolutionaries," but the FBT remained an arm of the government.
5. Article 148 states that when a company faces technological or economic difficulties, a protection committee can be established to agree upon conditions to keep its doors open. While the intention was to avoid job loss, it has been used to justify layoffs.
6. For example, in April 2021, all university employees earned less than five US dollars a month, while receiving a bonus of about ten US dollars a month.
7. Active and nonactive workers receive the same salary, but active workers receive bonuses.

Chapter Four

A Labor History of Extractivism in Colombia

From Coffee to Coca and Beyond

Phillip A. Hough

Charles Bergquist's groundbreaking *Labor in Latin America* (Bergquist 1986) introduced a comparative and world-historical perspective that offered a novel understanding of the region's political and economic development over the longue durée of historical capitalism. At the center of Bergquist's analysis were Latin American export workers, whose lived experiences shaped national processes of economic insertion and laid the institutional foundation for the region's divergent national political trajectories into the twentieth century. His comparative case study of Chilean nitrate workers, Argentine meat workers, Venezuelan oil workers, and Colombian cafetero farmers drew attention to the structural leverage they deployed in their struggles against exploitative capitalist labor processes and elitist institutional politics. Their formation into powerful labor movements by the early decades of the twentieth century, he argued, was shaped by the particular structures of production and ownership associated with each export commodity, which in turn facilitated the rise of distinct types of national working-class politics: Marxist in Chile, Peronist in Argentina, Nationalist in Venezuela, and Conservative in Colombia. By shifting scholarly attention to the lived experiences of workers positioned within developmentally consequential national export industries, Bergquist developed what might be described as a labor-centered world historical approach that retained the insights of world-systems and dependency theories about the structural experiences of peripheralization while averting their economic determinism. In this sense, Bergquist's *Labor in Latin America*, in addition to his *Labor in the Capitalist World Economy* (Bergquist 1984) and *Labor and the Course of American Democracy* (Bergquist 1996), carved space for future analyses of labor and labor movements in an era that was becoming increasingly critical of labor's capacity to challenge the power of global capital.

Nowhere was Bergquist's influence greater than in Colombia. Indeed, Bergquist's *Coffee and Conflict in Colombia* (Bergquist 1978) and his two co-edited volumes, *Violence in Colombia I and II* (Bergquist 2001; Bergquist, Peñaranda, and Sánchez 1992), did not only provide invaluable historical context to the country's devolution into widespread violence and instability in the closing decades of the twentieth century. His dogged commitment to analyzing the social history of Colombia's coffee regions, rather than those regions directly affected by the country's political violence, provided scholars with a powerful set of insights into the social origins of the crisis. Echoing his work in *Labor in Latin America*, and much to the chagrin of Colombia's political left during that time, Bergquist (2001) argued Colombia's history of violence stemmed from the hegemony, rather than despotism, of the country's Liberal and Conservative political parties that retained electoral support from significant groups of working-class voters:

> Throughout the twentieth century, Colombians experienced, under liberal economic and political institutions, a degree of economic growth and social mobility unmatched in most of Latin America. In this history, the role of small producers—part reality and part myth—has been of central importance. The experience and influence of small coffee farmers, in particular, helps to explain both the economic dynamics and political conservatism of twentieth-century Colombian history. (Bergquist 2001, 203–04)

He then went on to develop an interesting counterfactual argument:

> The revolutionary insurgents of the 1960s in Colombia, like their middle-class intellectual supporters, tended to equate Colombian history with that of countries such as Cuba, whose economies revolved around industries owned by foreign capitalists and worked by proletarianized labor. If the Colombian economy had come to depend on banana or oil exports, the twentieth-century history of the nation in general, and the fate of leftist third parties in particular, might have been different. . . . But it was coffee, much of it produced by small owner-operators, that became the axis of the modern Colombian economy. And it is the economic, social, political, and cultural ramifications of coffee production, I believe, that largely explain the historical weakness of the Colombian left in the Latin American context. (Bergquist 2001, 204)

This thesis that twentieth-century Colombian history has been shaped by the lived experiences of the country's most economically and culturally significant segment of the working class—cafetero farmers—inspired a generation of Colombianista scholars to analyze the political and developmental repercussions of working-class formations that have arisen across other national industries (Farmsworth-Alvear 2000; Gill 2016; Hough 2022).

As we propel deeper into the turbulence of the twenty-first century, however, the social and political imprint of Colombian cafeteros has receded as coffee exports have been eclipsed by other export commodities and as the extractivist sector has become the top developmental priority of elites.[1] If we are to take Bergquist's insights seriously, as I believe we should, we will need to understand how these shifts have shaped and been shaped by emergent working-class formations. In this chapter, I turn our attention to the experiences of another group of smallholding farmers: cocaleros. Like their cafetero predecessors, Colombian cocaleros have ridden a wave of land colonization and generated a highly lucrative commodity-export sector that has absorbed surplus labor, stimulated domestic processes of economic growth, and ultimately facilitated Colombia's re-insertion into the global economy of the twenty-first century. While the coffee sector undergirded the institutions that shaped the country's developmental trajectory into the twentieth century, it is the rise of the cocaine sector that has shaped the country's developmental trajectory today.

This chapter takes off from Bergquist's analysis by highlighting four important historical conjunctures that help us connect the dots from coffee to cocaine and ultimately to the contemporary extractivist economy. First, I highlight how the conservativism of Colombia's cafetero regions helped buttress a set of rural developmental initiatives that laid the groundwork for the emergence of coca farming. Second, I highlight how the consolidation of the coca economy rested upon a set of market interventions instituted by the self-avowedly Marxist-Leninist guerrilla group, Revolutionary Armed Forces of Colombia (FARC). Here, I point out the surprising similarities in the market politics of the FARC in the coca economy and the National Federation of Coffee Growers (Fedecafé) in the mid-twentieth-century coffee sector. Third, I describe how Colombian rural developmental agencies were rolled back in the 1990s in an effort to institute a neoliberal model of development that would open the countryside to flows of capital. However, these flows remained obstructed by the entrenched territorial presence of the FARC. Finally, I demonstrate how control of the countryside finally tilted in favor of elites following a series of war-making and peace-making actions that culminated in the 2016 Santos-FARC peace agreement. It is this history—the removal of leftist control of the countryside—that forms the historical context underpinning the rise of Colombia's extractivist economy.

While my analysis of the historical connections linking Colombian coffee to coca to extractivism stands heavily on the shoulders of Bergquist, it also extends Bergquist's labor-centered perspective in key ways. First, it builds upon insights developed in the field of Marxist ecology on the need to view "nature" along with labor and capital as an active social force in the reproduction of historical capitalism.[2] As Fernando Coronil (1997, 61) notes, viewing capitalism through a "triadic dialectic" that includes nature, labor, and capital allows us to see more clearly how processes of commodity production are shaped by struggles over control of land and territory. In rural Colombia, land and labor conflicts have been enveloped in broader political struggles over the territorial legitimacy of state and parastatal agencies with distinct claims on uses of local land and labor and distinct logics of violence. What commodities are produced and how much control workers leverage over the production process are therefore determined in part by which armed political actor controls the territory—state, paramilitary, or revolutionary insurgent.

Second, by including the reproduction of nature alongside that of labor and capital as an essential feature of capitalist production, this chapter draws attention to the hidden labor histories that shaped Colombia's extractivism today. In its prototypical capital-intensive and foreign-controlled structure of production, labor struggles in the extractivist sectors of mining and natural resource extraction are not merely conflicts between proletarianized workers and capitalists. Nor are they simply struggles between an ecologically destructive mode of production and rural communities seeking sustainable forms of development. As this chapter highlights, the labor struggles that arise in extractivist industries refract prior histories of class conflict, state and class formation, and land struggles. By drawing upon a triadic dialectic perspective that brings together labor, capital, and land, I show how the victories of landless campesinos and rural farmers of the twentieth century facilitated political formations that undermined rural labor over time and thus paved the way for the adoption of neoliberal practices today. Through their advocacy of capital-intensive and foreign-owned extractivism as the new engine of rural economic growth, contemporary Colombian elites have attempted to politically erase rural labor from their economic blueprint while propelling a dystopian neoliberal vision that prioritizes capital accumulation above all else.

COFFEE AND THE RISE AND DEMISE OF RURAL DEVELOPMENTALISM

Unique to Bergquist's historical analysis was his attention to the role played by cafetero farmers in propping up Colombia's traditional Liberal and Conservative political parties from their early origins in the nineteenth century into the developmentalist era of the twentieth century. As Bergquist notes, the Hobbesian individualism that arose across Colombia's coffee regions redirected emergent class conflicts inward, taking the forms of partisan political struggles and internecine localized conflict rather than social revolution. This pressure cooker of a situation, marked by rapid socioeconomic change arising within the confines of elitist party politics, ultimately erupted in 1948 with a decade of bloody partisan wars known as La Violencia. The political violence was eventually quelled following the military coup of Gustavo Rojas Pinilla in 1957 and the return of the political establishment under the guise of the National Front regime the following year.

Politically, the National Front (1958–1974) was essentially a power-sharing agreement in which Liberal and Conservative party leaders agreed to rotate presidential power every four years, appoint local and departmental executives by national party bosses, and restrict third parties from running for office. It was through the National Front that Colombian elites obtained the political stability needed to institute a range of state-directed capitalist development policies meant to expand export production and domestic industrialization. Coffee's role in the National Front system was twofold. First, as Bergquist notes, the conservatism of cafetero farmers provided national party leaders with a ready bastion of electoral support. The abatement of partisan violence in the central coffee-axis regions in the 1960s converged with a similarly fortuitous boost in coffee prices that climaxed into the boom years of the mid- to late 1970s. Not surprisingly, Colombia's coffee parastatal organization, the National Federation of Coffee Growers (Fedecafé), remained a powerful ally and advocate of National Front policies. Second, and less evident, was how the successful growth of coffee exports acted as an economic blueprint for the development of other domestic agro-export sectors. During the first administration of the National Front, for example, President Alberto Lleras Camargo (1958–1962) introduced "Plan Vallejo" to boost domestic exports through a system of tariff exemptions, import restrictions, and direct subsidies via tax credit certificates allocated to domestic capitalist producers (Villar and Esguerra 2007). Over the next two decades, Liberal and Conservative party leaders used the sustained growth of the coffee sector to justify their support for rapid industrialization, domestic market expansion, and export production elsewhere even though such policies habitually dispossessed rural inhabitants from their lands and—in the absence of social reforms—exacerbated urban and rural social divisions.

In my own work, I have highlighted two rural regions that typified the ways that National Front developmental policies generated deep social conflicts that would ultimately come to undermine the political legitimacy of the traditional party establishment (Hough 2022). In the northern coastal region of Urabá, National Front leaders took advantage of favorable world market opportunities that opened to domestic capitalists following the vertical disintegration of United Fruit Company and other monopolistic banana transnational corporations in the 1960s. With the help of government subsidies, tax breaks, and development aid, the region quickly transformed from a rural backwater into Colombia's principal site of banana export production. Along the southern frontier regions of Caquetá, Meta, and Guaviare, National Front leaders developed a series of land colonization initiatives meant to provide land to rural inhabitants who had been displaced during La Violencia in order to facilitate their transformation into domestic farmers who would produce cheap agricultural staples, meats, and hides for a rapidly urbanizing national populace. At least on paper, the country's key rural development agencies—INCORA, IDEMA, and Caja Agraria—were meant to work in tandem to distribute land titles and provide extensions services, market outlets, and credit to landless campesinos and frontier settlers in order to integrate rural land and labor into the national developmentalist model. As it turned out, both regions quickly transformed into highly exploitative regimes of commodity production marked by heightened class conflict, intractable political corruption, and labor repression. In Urabá, banana production arose on large-scale plantations using fully proletarianized labor systems. Acquiring new lands and managing labor costs fell into the hands of the newly established Association of Cattle Ranchers and Banana Producers of Urabá (Augura, established in 1963), a parastatal group with strong political connections to the local "Guerrista" wing of the Liberal Party. By the early 1970s, banana workers began to organize collectively via labor unions on the plantations, revolutionary worker parties in local elections, and civic organizations in their neighborhoods. A similar pattern of radicalization arose in the frontier regions of Caquetá. Rather than transform into a site of stable agricultural production from farmer families, regional development agencies became corrupted by affiliates of the local "Turbayista" wing of the Liberal Party, who used their political influence to legally (and often illegally) obtain large tracts of frontier lands that were subsequently converted into cattle grazing zones. These efforts to expand cattle lands at the expense of frontier settlers gained impetus through the establishment of the parastatal Colombian Cattle Ranchers Federation (Fedegán, established in 1963). Under the aegis of Fedegán, the region's cattle ranchers expanded their production of meats and hides through cycles of land dispossession and colonization in which landless settlers carved new tracts of land out of the frontier, only to be forced off these lands due to ownership claims by cattle ranchers.

By the early 1970s, both systems of commodity production—bananas in Urabá and meats and hides in Caquetá—had developed into despotic labor regimes driven by local elites and parastatal agencies that came to rely heavily on the authoritarian practices of the National Front system to maintain local control. In Urabá, local class struggles centered on the lived experiences of an exploited class of banana workers who were denied access to local political office and basic workers' rights on the plantations. In Caquetá, local class struggles centered on the lived experiences of frontier migrants who were denied access to local political offices and therefore lacked the capacity to maintain their hold on the land. With their access to social and political avenues blocked, it is not too surprising that regions like Urabá and Caquetá transformed into sites of radicalization and eventually to sites of guerrilla insurgency. In Urabá, for example, the region's labor unions gained support from the FARC and from the Maoist Popular Revolutionary Army, both of which also created local political organizations that began organizing working-class communities in the region's urban shantytowns. In Caquetá, the FARC established a territorial presence along the external frontier zones, where they protected settler land and livelihoods from the dispossessing practices of the domestic cattle industry.

The formal termination of the National Front regime at the close of the Misael Pastrana Borrero administration in 1974 did little to ameliorate these types of local class conflicts. The practice of rotating power and appointing local executives, for example, continued informally into the administrations of Alfonso López Michelson (1974–1978) and Julio César Turbay Ayala (1978–1982). And by then, the radicalized land and labor struggles of the nascent agro-export zones and frontier regions were conjoined by mass protests in the country's urban centers organized by student, labor, and civic groups that demanded a democratization of the political system and social reforms.[3] A national civic strike that shut down the national economy in 1977 signaled the growing strength of Colombian labor and leftist organizations. Yet President Turbay responded by instituting a state of siege that further exposed the authoritarianism of the political establishment inherited from the National Front. It was not until the election of Belisario Betancur (1982–1986), who ran on a campaign of social reform and political dialogue, that the institutional edifices of the National Front system began to unravel. Betancur's peace negotiations with the FARC and April 19 Movement, while tumultuous and ultimately unsuccessful, opened new spaces for social and political organizing. The Barco administration carried these reforms further by formally dismantling the National Front's system of political appointees and paving the way for a constitutional assembly that would include social organizations and demobilized guerrilla groups. By 1991, a new constitution was ratified, and a number of guerrilla groups had demobilized in order to participate in formal political conventions.[4]

It is important to note that this historical swing from radicalization and repression in the 1970s to processes of political democratization in the 1980s had relatively little direct impact on the livelihoods of Colombia's cafetero farmers or the developmentalist institutions of the National Federation of Coffee Growers. As the livelihoods of workers, farmers, and urban inhabitants living outside of the country's coffee regions were jolted back and forth by national political machinations, the country's cafeteros retained a relatively privileged position as "junior partners" in a protective social compact (Pacto Cafetero) that exchanged Fedecafé provisions of price floors and guaranteed purchases, extensions services, flows of credit, and other investments for cafetero commitment to coffee production as a nationalist vocation. Outside of the coffee-producing regions, however, the formal opening of new political spaces to working-class organizations pulled the rug out from under domestic capitalists and parastatal organizations that had become reliant upon the repressive tools afforded by the National Front system.

Beginning in the 1980s, Colombian economic elites began to rely increasingly upon the coercive terror of private militias and paramilitary violence to stem the tide of working-class mobilization. Paramilitarism, it turns out, became a particularly useful modality of labor control for domestic capitalists and local elites who could no longer rely directly upon the use of state repression as calls for peace negotiations with guerrilla groups and demands for political democratization ensued. Establishment political officials, in turn, could evade responsibility for the spread of paramilitary violence, which they described as "autonomous self-defense groups."[5] Nowhere was this more apparent than in Urabá, where paramilitary forces engaged in a brutal practice of attacking civilian allies of guerrilla groups in a strategy described as "draining the water to catch the fish." By the mid-1990s, this strategy of paramilitary terror was expanding through the country's most lucrative agro-export zones (excluding coffee) as regional paramilitary groups grew into a national paramilitary organization under the aegis of the United Self-Defense Forces of Colombia (AUC, established in 1997). By facilitating elite control of key export sectors, the AUC helped domestic capitalist organizations like Augura adapt to what was becoming an increasingly competitive global market in agro-exports.

FROM FEDECAFÉ'S PACTO CAFETERO TO THE FARC'S PACTO COCALERO

Charles Bergquist himself never elaborated on the historical linkages connecting Colombia's coffee sector to the rise of the cocaine sector and the growing power of the FARC guerrillas in the closing decades of the twentieth century. As highlighted earlier, throughout the postwar developmental decades, Colombian elites were unwilling to address the social problems generated by the National Front's developmentalist agrarian policies. In emergent agro-export sectors like banana production in Urabá, the Colombian state sided with planters and exporters whose competitive edge in the world market rested upon a highly exploitative system of production. That is, capitalist expansion rested heavily upon the National Front's authoritarian practices that repressed labor unions and excluded working-class parties from accessing political power. In frontier regions like southern Caquetá, where class struggles over rural land rather than labor predominated, National Front policies similarly propped the interests of traditional landed elite groups and cattle ranchers at the expense of frontier settlers. And while guerrilla insurgency groups came to play a critical protective role for agro-export workers as well as subsistence farmers and landless peasants in the 1970s, it was in the latter type—struggles over access to land—that ultimately paved the way for a radical transformation of Colombia's rural economy.

In the early 1970s, struggles for land still tipped in favor of landed elites and agro-capitalists. This is evident in the geography of rural Caquetá, for example, where Fedegán and their Turbayista allies retained effective control over the regions surrounding the departmental capital of Florencia and the more settled regions of the Caguán River. In the more remote areas of the Lower and Middle Caguán regions, the Revolutionary Armed Forces of Colombia were able to forge a tentative form of territorial hegemony vis-à-vis frontier settlers. In these regions, the FARC acted as a de facto state that engaged in war-making and proto-state-making activities. As insurgent combatants, they protected settler land and livelihoods from encroachment by cattle ranchers and state forces. As revolutionary proto state makers, they used their territorial monopoly of violence to extract resources from local residents (via revolutionary taxes on production and agricultural sales) while enforcing systems of justice and authority to preserve local order. To be sure, the FARC's territorial presence during this period was sparse and generally ineffective in full-scale clashes with the Colombian military because their war chest was limited by their reliance on the local agricultural economy. This said, given the frontier settlers' historical distrust of the state and landed elites, the FARC's presence was generally welcomed by locals who gained access to land, cultivated subsistence goods, and secured a degree of social and economic security that was unattainable in most other agricultural regions of the country.

The FARC's ability to engage in war making and proto state making, however, changed significantly in the closing years of the 1970s when frontier settlers began to supplant their subsistence produce with the cultivation of coca plants. Increasingly, the region's coca-producing farmers (cocaleros) would plant coca and harvest leaves using family systems of labor. Once harvested, they would process their coca leaves into coca paste using basic inputs and readily available technologies (water, sulfuric acid, gasoline, buckets, tarps, weed wackers, heat stoves, etc.), which they would then sell to intermediaries working with urban drug trafficking organizations that would further process it into powdered cocaine for export. While FARC leaders were initially reticent to permit the production of coca in the regions under its territorial control, they changed their stance to avert the intrusion of drug trafficking groups into their strongholds and to benefit from the increased revenues generated by the lucrative export commodity. This decision, as it turned out, did not undermine their hegemonic relations with frontier settlers or transform them from revolutionaries to self-interested drug traffickers. Instead, as I argue elsewhere, the FARC's involvement in the coca market actually bolstered their territorial hegemony and strengthened their war making over the next two decades (Hough 2011).

This influx of coca revenues into the coffers of the FARC certainly facilitated the group's geographic and organizational expansion in the 1980s and 1990s. Less evident, however, was how the FARC's territorial power was also affected by the particularities of coca production itself. Like coffee and unlike cattle ranching, coca cultivation is a labor-intensive process that requires few expensive capital inputs, can be harvested throughout the year, and can be planted alongside subsistence agricultural produce. It is therefore an agricultural commodity that can readily absorb rural surplus labor. Not surprisingly, this promise of protection and stability pulled new migrants to the FARC's coca-producing regions as they were being pushed out of the legal economy by paramilitarism and economic instability.

But it was not merely that migration to FARC-controlled territories provided cocaleros with access to land. The FARC also politically regulated the local coca market in ways that mirrored the developmentalist interventions of Fedecafé in the coffee sector. Like Fedecafé, they established a system of price floors and guaranteed purchases of farmer yields, thus protecting cocaleros from both the potential vitriol of drug trafficking organizations as well as from the volatility of cocaine prices in the international market. Cocaleros, like cafeteros, were therefore incentivized to specialize in the production of cash crops as market outlets were ensured for the short and medium term. They also coordinated and financed local infrastructural projects, provided credit to farmers, and developed stable wage payment systems for coca harvesters (raspachines). Like Fedecafé's Pacto Cafetero, which was intended to create a lucrative smallholder structure of coffee production by imbuing coffee production with nationalist importance, the FARC consolidated its own Pacto Cocalero that actively invested in the growth and consolidation of a stable smallholder structure of production and that imbued coca production with revolutionary social significance. Thus, despite their vast differences—the FARC being a revolutionary insurgency group and Fedecafé a parastatal entity—both organizations developed systems of commodity production that absorbed rural surplus labor through hegemonic social pacts that provided a degree of dignity and stability to rural communities that was unattainable elsewhere (Hough 2010).[6]

During the heyday of FARC's hegemony, Caquetá's population more than doubled from roughly 218,000 in 1985 to 446,000 by 2003, with over 70 percent migrating to the coca-producing municipalities under their territorial control (Departamento Administrativo Nacional de Estadística 2004). Moreover, the FARC readily integrated this influx of human labor into their war- and state-making apparatus. Revenues generated from the taxation of local coca sales helped them finance a major expansion of their military armaments, organizational strength, and logistical technologies. The number of FARC "guerrilla fronts" (i.e., battalions consisting of forty to two hundred armed soldiers), for example, jumped from seven in the late 1970s to roughly seventy by the close of the 1990s (Richani 2002, 70, 76). At their peak, the FARC was estimated to have a force of over eighteen thousand soldiers and a total income of over three hundred million US dollars per year (Hough 2011).

The 1990s was therefore a critical decade in Colombian history. On the one hand, guerrilla insurgency groups like the FARC were expanding their territorial control into new regions of the countryside while deepening their roots in existing rural strongholds.[7] On the other hand, the expansion of the power of drug trafficking organizations like the Medellín and Cali Cartels deteriorated the institutional legitimacy of the state at the same time that Colombian economic elites turned to paramilitarism as a key mechanism of labor control. Importantly, it was also during this time that Colombian political leaders began to supplant the state-led developmental policies instituted under the National Front with neoliberal policies meant to "shake the economy out of its slow-growth pattern [by taking] advantage of the new opportunities offered by world trade" (Jaramillo 1998, 38). During the presidential administrations of César Gaviria (1990–1994), Ernesto Samper (1994–1998), and Andes Pastrana Arango (1998–2002), Colombia liquidated or privatized its core agrarian development agencies (IDEMA, Caja Agraria, INCORA), phased out tariffs and other trade restrictions, eliminated exchange rate controls, loosened labor and environmental safety laws, entered bilateral and regional free trade talks, signed onto the Uruguay Round of the General Agreement on Tariffs and Trade (1994), and became a member of the World Trade Organization.

To be sure, while Colombia's neoliberal turn constituted a major ideological shift in elite politics, its actual impact on the lives of rural Colombians was quite uneven across the country's social geography. Expectedly, its impact has been largest on those producing staple goods for the domestic market (including potatoes, wheat, cotton, barley, among others), who found it increasingly difficult to compete in a market flooded with cheap food imports.[8] It had little impact, however, on the economic livelihoods of Colombia's cafeteros, whose own experiences with market liberalization came following the abrogation of the geopolitically regulated coffee quota system established under the International Coffee Agreements (1961–1989) rather than from changes to the country's national agricultural development policies.[9]

Even for large-scale agro-exporters, the impact of neoliberalism has not been straightforward. In Urabá, for example, banana plantation owners had found ways to adapt to what has been an unregulated international market since the 1960s, well before the adoption of neoliberal reforms in the 1990s and early 2000s. Moreover, it was not necessarily neoliberalism, but paramilitarism, that undermined the growing strength of the region's banana workers. A similar reliance upon paramilitarism to keep labor costs competitive has arisen across other major agro-export sectors, including sugar cane and African palm production. All three of these agro-export sectors actually experienced increasing yields during the 1990s and early 2000s.

Perhaps the most unintended consequence of the neoliberal turn in Colombia was its impact on the FARC. By undermining rural livelihoods in some regions of the country, neoliberalism provided the "push factors" driving rural surplus migrants to FARC-controlled regions where they ascertained new livelihoods as coca growers and insurgent militants. Overall, Colombia's neoliberal agricultural turn was more than simply uneven across the country's rural geography. It was effectively stalled by the growing power of the FARC, which became the major obstacle to the neoliberalization of the countryside. The major question facing Colombian advocates of neoliberalism was therefore how to best uproot the guerrillas without further deteriorating the legitimacy of the state.

REMOVING RURAL OBSTACLES TO CAPITAL ACCUMULATION IN THE COUNTRYSIDE

Colombian presidential administrations since the 1990s have deployed both carrots and sticks in their efforts to uproot the FARC from their territorial strongholds in the countryside. Under the Gaviria and Samper governments, this strategy took the form of a low-intensity conflict led by the Colombian military. During the Pastrana years, the FARC's stronghold in the Caguán was deemed a "demilitarized zone" to lure the insurgents into peace talks and under the banner of Plan Colombia. As it turned out, when negotiations broke down and the fighting resumed, the Plan shapeshifted into a predominantly militarized strategy. During his remaining months in office, Pastrana's Plan Colombia was slated to receive unprecedented amounts of military aid from the United States under the guise of the US War on Drugs. However, the onset of the US War on Terror that followed al-Qaeda's attack on the World Trade Center granted Colombia's incoming hardliner, Álvaro Uribe Vélez (2002–2010), the rationale and means to transform the government's erstwhile "containment strategy" into a full-scale "elimination strategy." Under the rubric of the War on Terror, the FARC were described as purely self-interested "narco-terrorists." This label was then used to justify the Colombian military's focused attacks on the FARC's main territorial strongholds along the southern frontier zones of Caquetá, Meta, and Guaviare (Tate 2015).

This militarization strategy was complemented by President Uribe's so-called Democratic Security policies that established legal networks of civilian informants, criminalized protests, and otherwise blurred the boundaries between civilian and military life. In doing so, Uribe sought to undermine the FARC's social bases of support by giving nods of implicit (and sometimes not so implicit) support for paramilitary violence used against social activists and community members living in FARC-controlled areas (Human Rights Watch 2010). In the Caguán, for example, FARC territorial hegemony vis-à-vis cocalero residents deteriorated steadily under the combined weight of an escalating military campaign under Plan Colombia and the expansion of paramilitarism to the region in the early 2000s. As I demonstrate elsewhere, the FARC's incapacity to protect locals against military and paramilitary encroachments occurred precisely when the FARC needed to extract greater revenues from locals in order to finance their own military operations. By the early 2010s, the FARC had lost the trust of large portions of its social base and was essentially forced to retreat into the most remote regions of the country (Hough 2011).

Meanwhile, Uribe began laying the ground for "peace talks" with the AUC paramilitary federation in order to facilitate their eventual reincorporation into civilian life. In 2004, Uribe granted the AUC a "demilitarized zone" in their own territorial stronghold of Santa Fe de Ralito in the country's northern coast. By the close of 2006 some thirty thousand AUC fighters had formally demobilized with immunity. Two years later, AUC leaders officially turned in their weapons and accepted their extradition to the United States for drug trafficking crimes. Critics of the AUC's demobilization during the Uribe administration, of course, point out how the process did little to either address the wide-scale theft of rural lands and property forcibly grabbed by Colombian paramilitaries or to provide justice to the tens of thousands of rural inhabitants whose lives were terrorized by paramilitary violence (Human Rights Watch 2020). Nevertheless, the demobilization of the AUC appears to have signaled a significant victory of Colombian elites in their efforts to weed most regions of the country from guerrilla influence.

By the time that Uribe's handpicked successor, Juan Manuel Santos (2010–2018), took office, FARC rural hegemony was in shambles and its forces on the run. With their backs to the wall, FARC leaders agreed to engage in formal peace negotiations with Santos. By November 2016, following some road bumps, the agreement was ratified, and the FARC began a process of demobilization. Hopes were high in the country that the agreement would become a model for the still-active National Liberation Army and that a new era of peace was close at hand.

On paper, the Santos-FARC peace agreement set out an ambitious agenda that included government commitment to (a) comprehensive rural development; (b) promotion of political participation and democratic pluralism; (c) reincorporation of FARC militants back into civilian life; (d) development of legal alternatives to the problem of illegal drug cultivation, use, and commercialization; (e) promotion of victims' rights; and (f) establishment of rules to implement and verify the process. Overall, these measures were meant to formally recognize the social origins of the FARC and the coca economy and to address their underlying causes by providing an economic blueprint meant to absorb rural surplus labor and generate a stable class of campesino farmers. The problem with this plan, of course, was that Colombian economic elites were even less willing to invest in the needs of rural campesinos than they were during the developmentalist years, when at least the idea of putting rural labor to work seemed like a viable strategy of economic development. By the 2010s, not only did the country's predominantly export-oriented agricultural sector require fewer laboring bodies. Facilitating rural access to land would also undermine what was becoming one of Colombia's most valued assets in the global economy—the land itself, or rather, what lay below the surface of the land, precious minerals, hydrocarbons, and petroleum.

It is perhaps not surprising then that the promise for a "new era of peace, justice and economic development" following the 2016 peace agreement gave way to a less sanguine reality. Like the agricultural practices of the 1960s and 1970s, the rural development programs established through the peace negotiations lacked teeth and elite support. Almost as soon as the coca crop substitution programs were implemented, many cocalero farmers who uprooted their coca plants expecting cash payments and food assistance to subsidize their transition to legal crops complained that the payments were delivered late, far less than the amount promised, or not at all (Fundación Ideas para la Paz 2018). Moreover, families that were displaced by paramilitary violence also complained that they were not able to obtain land titles under the government's new Land Fund system, which appeared to be doling out titles to existing landowners in ways that contributed to, rather than redressing, the country's endemic problem of land concentration (Fundación Ideas para la Paz 2020). In an effort to pressure the state to comply with the promises of the 2016 agreement, Colombian cocaleros and other rural producers formed a social movement organization—Coordinadora Nacional de Cultivadores de Coca, Amapola y Marijuana (established in 2017) that took to the streets demanding cash payments and government protection of cocalero livelihoods. However, these efforts fell on deaf ears under the presidency of Iván Duque Márquez (2018–2022), a long-time critic of the peace process who threw various monkey wrenches into the alternative crop production programs and other political reforms created by the accords.[10]

It was not only that the agrarian reform measures created by the 2016 accords floundered in the absence of meaningful state support. Coca production has actually increased since then. According to the UN High Office of Drug Control (2019), Colombia's coca cultivation jumped from a decade-long low of ninety-six thousand hectares in 2015 to a record high of 169,000 hectares by 2018. Caquetá, which had always ranked high among coca-cultivating departments, increased its production from roughly 7,700 hectares to 11,800 over this time. Moreover, the removal of FARC control from the lower rungs of the cocaine market created a power vacuum that was quickly filled by new armed groups, including criminal gangs (bandas criminales), emergent paramilitary groups, and dissident FARC guerrillas that refused to demobilize, whose efforts to monopolize local market activities have resulted in an upswing in drug-related violence and anomic terror. Not surprisingly, those regions most affected by this criminal violence have been former FARC-controlled communities whose populations have been most willing to undergo the government's coca substitution practices (Diamond 2018; UN Verification Mission in Colombia 2019). Moreover, the drug trafficking groups that have moved into the lower rungs of the market appear to have little vested interest in developing a protective social compact akin to the FARC's Pacto Cocalero or in preserving the stability and dignity of cocalero smallholding farmers or local residents. Consequently, it is cocalero community leaders and Coordinadora Nacional de Cultivadores de Coca, Amapola y Marijuana activists who have borne the brunt of the deregulation and criminalization of the market (Fiscalía General 2019; UN Verification Mission in Colombia 2019).

EXTRACTIVISM AS SOCIAL AND
ECOLOGICAL DISPOSSESSION

When viewed from the historical perspective presented here, it becomes clear that Colombian elite efforts to transform the countryside into a site of capitalist development have a long and troubled history of dispossession and violence. During the developmental years, efforts to stabilize conditions in the countryside through state-directed measures were undermined by the authoritarian and corrupting influence of the National Front. As the developmentalist economy was rolled back by neoliberal policies, the state redirected its attention to the promotion of agro-export sectors that came to rely heavily on paramilitarism as its predominant mechanism of labor control. Over the past three decades, Colombian political leaders have systematically engaged in a series of strategies meant to break down any social or political obstacles standing in the way of the capitalization of the countryside. Early on, these obstacles arose from farmers and agricultural workers who organized against the exploitative and dispossessing practices of the National Front regime. By the 1970s and 1980s, the predominant modality of rural working-class mobilization arose through armed insurgency groups. Since then, Colombian elites have engaged in efforts to uproot these groups through militarism, paramilitarism, peace negotiations, and promises of social reform. Under Uribe, the military and paramilitary strategy gained new impetus through aid from the United States under the guise of the War on Terror. Under Santos, these efforts shifted to a process of rural dispossession via peace making and the promise of social reforms and alternative development. Under Duque, these measures were largely upended. What is clear, however, is that the removal of the FARC as de facto protector of rural land and livelihoods has now exposed rural surplus labor, including cocalero families and communities, to the full weight of Colombian neoliberalism.

As the social stability of the coca sector has diminished, the industries that have expanded since the demobilization of the FARC have been overwhelmingly labor expulsive. Cattle ranching, for example, has flourished with the removal of the FARC from frontier lands. Between 2014 and 2019, Colombian herds of bovine cattle nearly doubled in rural regions of Caquetá (Torrijos Rivera 2019). Moreover, this expansion of the cattle grazing lands has brought with it historically high rates of deforestation of virgin timber forest hinterlands, with the former FARC strongholds in the Caguán region ranking among the worst in terms of rates of deforestation (Mendez Garzón and Valánszki 2019).[11]

The most important sector to emerge in nascent rural areas of capitalist expansion, however, has been the extractivist economy. To be sure, neoliberal advocates since the Gaviria years in the early 1990s have sought to liberalize Colombia's mining and energy sectors to lure foreign corporations and take advantage of world market booms in oil, coal, and gold and nickel mining. In 2000, President Pastrana signed off on measures to liquidate Colombia's state mining company (Minercol) and sell the public coal corporation (Carbocol) to a private foreign consortium with connections to ExxonMobil and other energy companies. In an effort to break the monopoly of Colombia's state oil company (Ecopetrol), he also signed Law 685 of 2001, which opened up the titling process to a "first come, first served" basis that offered transnational mining companies equal access to the country's oil reserves. These hopes for a vibrant extractivist sector only deepened under President Uribe, who set a goal of making Colombia's mining sector the third-largest recipient of foreign investment by assuring liberal concessions and extending the military's presence in regions where foreign companies like BP, Repsol, and Harken were operating (Unidad de Planeación Minero Energética 2006). Consequently, Colombia's mining sector grew from US$466 million in 2002 to US$4.5 billion by 2010, with mining's share of total foreign investment growing from 42 to 67 percent (Sankey 2018, 64).

These policies of luring extractivist capital to Colombia have continued under the Santos and Duque governments, with the major difference being that new lands and contracts were opened to mining companies that were unavailable prior to the demobilization of the FARC. For example, land values increased by over 300 percent in regions like rural Caquetá in the years following the peace accords, as wealthy investors and companies grabbed large swaths of virgin hinterland and untapped sites of energy and oil production. Seven hydroelectric plants cropped up along the Caguán River ways while concessions were granted to corporate investors to tap forty-four new sites of petroleum extraction. Additionally, the Santos government approved the provision of new licenses to extract gold in the alluvial waterways of the southern external frontier regions that had previously been FARC strongholds. Consequently, the region has experienced a veritable gold rush of desperate landless families who currently dredge the streams and dynamite mountaintops in search of gold and other precious metals, while leaving the region's water sources polluted with cyanide, mercury, and other noxious chemicals used to separate alluvial minerals from ore and sediment (Hough 2022).

Overall, as this chapter points out, these efforts to replace the FARC's coca political economy with an emergent extractivist economy have not merely undermined one of the few remaining stable livelihoods available to Colombian surplus rural labor. In the absence of real efforts to integrate rural land and labor into a developmental economy that preserves rural livelihoods and social ecologies, the prioritization of natural resource extraction appears to reflect a larger history of elite unwillingness to recognize the social value of rural stability and proclivity to use violence when confronted with rural opposition. Seen through the labor-centered perspective advocated by Charles Bergquist, we see how these major shifts in Colombian development policies—from developmentalism to neoliberalism to extractivism—were indeed shaped by the everyday realities of working-class opposition in the countryside.

The rise of the extractivist economy, as I point out here, is the latest attempt to open rural Colombia to flows of capital. However, the particular form of capital accumulation that has taken root under the extractivist model differs starkly from previous processes of capitalist development because it is capital-intensive and labor expulsive. Or put differently, it is not merely extractive in terms of the way that it exploits the region's natural resources and destroys the fabric of the local ecology. Perhaps more insidiously, it is socially extractive in that it requires the removal of rural populations, including both their access to the land and the use of their labor, without generating an alternative modality of social inclusion into the country's developmental goals. The consequences of this emergent form of development without rural labor has been the extreme precaritization of the country's rural population.

It is not exactly clear just how far this process of social extractivism can go. While the current historical conjuncture appears to reflect the growing power of Colombian elites, we might draw some optimism from Charles Bergquist's historical analysis of what has happened to Latin American working-class formations that have arisen in leading economic sectors that are capital-intensive and foreign-owned. Indeed, since this chapter was first submitted, the Colombian electorate seems to have shifted sharply away from the Uribismo of the Duque administration by electing the country's first left-ist president, Gustavo Petro, in June 2022. Petro promises to uphold the 2016 Peace Agreement's commitments to socially and ecologically sustainable forms of rural development and seems willing to critique the neoliberalism of Colombian elites. Perhaps this election is the first indication of an emergent political imaginary and working-class politics that seeks to preserve rather than destroy the dignity of rural life.

NOTES

1. See Toro Pérez et al. (2012) and Fajardo (2014) for research on the rise of extractivism in Colombia.

2. I conceptualize each of these concepts broadly. Like Bergquist (1986), I conceptualize "labor" to include both fully proletarianized agricultural workers such as those working in Urabá's banana plantation as well as commodity-producing farmers like Colombian cafeteros and cocaleros who, while retaining control of the land, have lost control over the labor process (what they produce, how they produce, etc.). Following Coronil (1997), I conceptualize "nature" as the materiality of commodities that emanates from the transformation of land, natural resources, and human labor through the production process.

3. The Popular Revolutionary Army, for example, had established territorial strongholds in some of the agricultural export zones and other marginalized rural regions of the country's north. The FARC had established a presence alongside the Popular Revolutionary Army, but also developed a strategic presence in the external frontier zones of the south. The National Liberation Army, another avowedly Marxist-Leninist insurgency group with origins in the 1960s and that was influenced by liberation theology, had established a presence in the oil-producing regions. The student-led, radical nationalist April 19 Movement established a presence in some of the country's major urban centers. Finally, the indigenous Quintín Lame also developed a presence in some rural regions to protect indigenous groups.

4. The groups to demobilize included the April 19 Movement, Quintín Lame, the Maoist Revolutionary Workers Party, and most of the Popular Revolutionary Army.

5. See Hristov (2009) for an analysis of Colombian paramilitarism and its connection to drug traffickers and local elites. For an analysis connecting Colombian democratization to paramilitarization, see Hough (2022).

6. As I point out in *At the Margins of the Global Market* (2022), the distinct legal status of these political economies, however, has had a significantly distinct impact on the livelihoods of coffee- and coca-producing farmers. Producing coffee has been viewed as a nationalist endeavor that merits continued state support and protection. Coca farming, in contrast, has been stigmatized by its association with illegal armed groups and sociopolitical violence.

7. The National Liberation Army guerrillas also expanded their territorial control during this period, predominantly in oil-producing regions where they obtained revenues through the extortion of oil company executives and other wealthy residents.

8. Between 1990 and 2010, agricultural imports grew from 1.2 million tons (worth roughly US$404 million) to nearly nine million (US$4.2 billion) by 2010, agriculture's overall contribution to Colombian gross domestic product shrank from 17 percent to 7 percent, and agricultural employment dropped from 31 percent to 19 percent (Fajardo 2014, 72, 129, 101).

9. As I point out elsewhere, the liberalization of the world coffee market weakened, but did not fundamentally undermine, Fedecafé's domestic regulatory institutions. Since the 1990s, recurrent waves of cafetero protests have succeeded in pressuring Fedecafé to delivery on its promises that were historically established under the Pacto Cafetero (Bair and Hough 2012; Hough 2022).

10. Duque's unwillingness to recognize the social dimensions of the coca economy, made most emblematic by his support for the reinstatement of the controversial

practice of aerial spraying of glyphosate over coca fields, is merely the latest iteration of a longer history of elite aversion to the adoption of measures that might threaten their continued access to rural resources.

11. Deforestation nearly doubled from roughly 120,000 hectares in 2015 to over 220,000 hectares by the close of 2017 (Mendez Garzón and Valánszki 2019).

Chapter Five

Reading Peru from Chile

*Examining Mining Unionism in the
Twentieth and Twenty-First Centuries*

Omar Manky

Though Peru is not examined by Charles Bergquist in *Labor in Latin America*, this is one case that may fit into his analytical framework. Like other countries covered in his book, it is a society whose economy is based mainly on raw material exports. As in Chile's case, mining has been a central element in obtaining foreign currencies from the beginning of the twentieth century to the present, while some of the most salient social conflicts in Peruvian history occurred in this sector. Furthermore, as in Chile, foreign investments played a crucial role in Peru.

Notwithstanding the conditions noted, the country failed to produce a radical labor movement that could significantly alter the political system throughout the twentieth century. The Peruvian case is paradoxical if we read it from the standpoint of *Labor in Latin America* and the hypotheses underlying the book. This chapter ponders this paradox based on two comparisons. The first compares the Chilean and Peruvian experiences. As in Chile, the export of minerals has been vital in Peru, and this sector witnessed the emergence of a powerful labor movement in relation to the rest of the working class (Sulmont 1985). This can be partially grasped from Bergquist's arguments: For him, an export economy that impedes economic diversification should "feature a historically strong, anticapitalist labor movement . . . the political left should be strong and the historical possibility for socialist transformation greatest" (Bergquist 1986, 13). However, the Peruvian case shows the limits of this reasoning, given the limited organizational capacity of its trade unionism compared with Chile or Bolivia. The second contrast through which I am interested in analyzing the Peruvian experience is a temporal one, dealing with the changes experienced in mining unionism in both Chile and Peru since the end of the twentieth century. Specifically, I will draw attention to how key dynamics identified by Bergquist have radically transformed after three decades of neoliberalism and shifts in labor organization. As noted by Kristin Ciupa and Jeffery R. Webber in the introduction to this volume, most studies on the mining sector ignore the contemporary relevance of labor struggles. One purpose of this chapter, therefore, is to illustrate that they have not disappeared, and in fact, continue to play a crucial role in the dynamics of the Chilean and Peruvian worlds of labor, albeit in a context of dramatically transformed structures of production following decades of neoliberalism.

The second aim of these comparisons is to critically dialogue with *Labor in Latin America* to highlight three aspects concerning the relevance of export economies for Latin American trade unionism. The first refers to an element scarcely analyzed in the book, namely the role of elites in the formation of states able to meet workers' demands. The second delves into an implicit aspect in the book: the effects of space on the constitution of labor dynamics. Finally, I stress that, in a context of a crisis in the politics of representation, it is necessary to update the discussion on the relationship between export workers and political activists.

Labor in Latin America does not have a unified theory of workers' movements; I do not aspire to amend any particular aspect of the book, nor am I interested in proposing an alternative to its central themes. But I do consider it necessary to develop, in light of recent discussions in the sociology of labor, core issues not sufficiently explored in this valuable work. By attending to the role of elites, geography, and political activists in structuring export unionism, I hope to better explain the particularities of the Peruvian case. But I also hope to throw light on lines of research that may inspire new debates on other countries of the Global South.

ELITES AND STATE BUILDING

Labor in Latin America posits that in countries where dependence on natural resource export is greater, stronger and more radical labor movements are likely to emerge, eventually institutionalizing their demands through leftist regimes. The standard example is that of Chilean nitrate workers, who became radicalized in the context of living together with foreign capital. Faced with the impossibility of achieving sustainable development at the local level, they demanded major transformations. These claims would soon spread to other economic sectors, such as the public sector and the copper miners (Bergquist 1986; Klubock 1998). More specifically, Bergquist notes that:

> The location of nitrate production, the structure of ownership in the industry, the demography of the labor force, the nature of the work process, and the conditions of life in nitrate oficinas and northern port towns all had important effects

on workers and created among them special needs and opportunities. Their considerable success in defining an autonomous working-class culture and in building progressive social and political institutions for their class reflects not only their determination and creativity but also the unique environment in which they worked. (1986, 37–38)

This organizational strength became a crucial component of a popular movement in favor of a stronger and more democratic state. For Bergquist, this occurred in Chile during the 1920s and 1930s, when workers pushed the political system to the left (1986, 60–61). In fact, Bergquist points out that labor radicalism led the Chilean elite to initiate a process of incorporating labor into political life both by electoral participation in leftist parties and the creation of institutional channels for conflict resolution. As the Chilean sociologist Francisco Zapata (2002, 97) has noted, from this labor institutionality, "mining unionism began a trajectory that lasted several decades in which collective contracts regulating working life in the mines took shape. In this process, the decision of the Communist Party in 1935 to insert itself into political-institutional life . . . contributed to the stabilization of negotiation processes throughout the period 1935-1955."

Despite several crucial transformations, it should be possible to extend this argument to the present day, as the social unrest of 2019 in Chile demonstrates the continued capacity of popular sectors to effectively exert pressure on political elites. In fact, between 2003 and 2012 Chilean society experienced mobilizations that were led by export workers (Aravena and Núñez 2009) and miners in particular (Donoso 2013). Though these protests have not always ended in thoroughgoing successes for workers, it is worth noting that workers were able to change the institutional rules for labor negotiations for subcontracted workers, which is unthinkable in countries such as Peru or Colombia, where mining subcontracting is also common. It would be difficult to imagine these changes without the ability of Socialist and Communist Party militants to exert pressure in different areas of state action (Manky 2018).

The Peruvian economy is also dependent on mining as a core economic activity, and miners worked in isolated areas of the Andes under poor working conditions offered by multinational companies (Sulmont 1980). However, the Peruvian case has differed from that of its southern neighbor since the early twentieth century. Without nitrate, the first serious experiences of mining unionization occurred later, in the 1920s, in the camps of the Cerro de Pasco Corporation, an American copper company. This unionization process was prolonged and restricted to small groups of workers, as most of them came from the rural economy and maintained strong ties with the peasant world. These circumstances made it almost impossible for a large part of the labor force to consider the economic demands of the unions as decisive (Flores Galindo 1974).

But beyond this limitation—which I explore in greater depth in the next section—even when workers succeeded in forming a trade union that threatened the production of the mining companies, their organizations were quickly crushed by the state. Over thirty workers lost their lives in confrontations with the army, which supported the employers in the face of the US embassy's requests in 1930 (Renique 1989). After the government's repression, the labor movement would not regain its strength until two decades later. It is important to note that this was not only repression organized by one government. Instead, it was a general state policy, which we must understand in the context of the "oligarchic state," defined as "excluding the popular masses, particularly the peasantry, from basic democratic rights, through the institutional violence of the state, by politically neutralizing the middle classes through repression and integration" (López 1978, 991).

Unlike the Chilean case, where workers' demands succeeded in strengthening a two-party system in the 1930s, the Peruvian labor movement encountered an underdeveloped state regarding its democratic openness. The differences between the political organization of the Peruvian and Chilean elites have been explored by Kurtz (2013). For Kurtz, the Peruvian state, from its independence and during the nineteenth century, emerged from a situation of institutional weakness, with elites incapable of promoting a sustained state-building agenda. This contrasts with the Chilean case, where elite factions,

> regularly alternated in power. . . . This, in turn, facilitated the construction of a strong central administrative system. And despite relying on a noncapitalist (but nonservile) agrarian system that did not generate substantial economic returns, they managed to cooperate around extensive investments in governmental institutions, public education, and military modernization and conquest. (Kurtz 2013)

By the end of the nineteenth century, the Chilean state had managed to centralize its administrative apparatus and target national integration efforts more clearly than Peru, a nation in which even in the mid-twentieth century the exclusion of rural majorities from political participation was common. In Peru, local elites did not develop strong national institutions capable of articulating the interests of the middle or working classes.

In other words, even a strong trade union movement in Peru would have had an uphill task to accomplish what its Chilean counterpart did. In Peru, there was no state capacity to bring about major changes. Therefore, I want to emphasize that in order to comprehend the ability of the working class to influence national development, the relevance of the export industry is insufficient. The political opportunity structure is also key, particularly with respect to the elites and their receptiveness to the demands of labor (Jeydel 2000; Snow Soule, and Kriesi 2004). The different political opportunity structures of Chile and Peru are important starting points for understanding the unique difficulties of Peruvian mine workers to organize strong unions at least until the end of the 1960s. As noted by Ciupa and Webber in the introduction to this volume, one element that Bergquist stresses at the end of his book is the need to comprehend the interactions between state constitution, export economies, and labor movements. The comparison between Chile and Peru illustrates the extent to which the economic relevance of mining and the potential strength of the working class also depend on the associative capacity of workers vis-à-vis the state, its laws, and repressive policies.

The end of the oligarchic state in Peru came about not because of massive mobilizations of workers and peasants, but because of a military regime with progressive attributes (Cotler 2005). Though pressed by growing popular mobilizations, it was the military regime that fostered an autonomous management of the state. This effort to carry out a revolution "from above," however, triggered conflicts with radicalized unions, which escaped the military's logic of control (Javier and Santur 2017; Gálvez Olaechea 2020). Thus Peru not only experienced progressive policies thirty years later than in Chile, but even under a progressive administration, which encouraged unionization, deadly confrontations occurred between state agents and miners (Medina 2019; Gálvez Olaechea 2021).

The situation did not improve substantially with the return to democracy in the 1980s, even when the state owned the majority of large Peruvian mines due to its aggressive nationalization policy (Thorp and Bertram 1978). There were, in these cases, no attempts to negotiate, even when workers had finally managed to organize around a national federation (Zapata and Garfias 2014). In fact, in one of the critical moments in the history of labor organizing, after months of national mobilizations to achieve an industry bargaining agreement, a paramilitary commando close to the government assassinated Saúl Cantoral, the main mining workers' leader in 1989 (Zapata and Garfias 2014). In this way, the oligarchic state in Peru was not replaced by one of a popular national character. Instead, it was followed by a weakened political organization in the midst of a severe economic and political crisis (Panfichi and Coronel 2010).

During the 1990s, economic elites reestablished more direct control of labor relations in the context of Alberto Fujimori's dictatorship (Manky 2011). Despite claims of maintaining industry-level negotiations, the Peruvian state and business associations have ignored the agreements resulting from such negotiations without major consequences. Here, contrasting the Chilean and Peruvian experiences is useful again. In the former case, labor conflicts have arisen in the mining sector, especially among contract workers (Aravena and Núñez 2009; Muñoz 2017). As they did a century ago, elites responded quickly to the mobilizations, which resulted in conventions to negotiate collective agreements with both the state-owned company Codelco and private companies such as Anglo-American (Donoso 2013; Muñoz 2017). Mining unionism in Chile has been one of the most solid spaces for the construction of working-class identities, both for regular and subcontracted workers. In Peru, on the other hand, repressive measures against workers are common even in cases where the exported product is crucial for the country, such as in the Marcona mine (where 95 percent of the country's iron ore is mined) (Manky 2019a).

LABOR GEOGRAPHIES

The second element of *Labor in Latin America* I want to discuss relates to the impact of space on collective action. Unlike political opportunity structures, this aspect does appear in Bergquist's work, although it is not always theoretically developed. Bergquist's chapter dedicated to Chile proposes reflections on the spatial mobility of the nitrate miners, suggesting that this went hand in hand with specific gender relations—the majority of workers were single— and with housing arrangements that fostered collective action. Furthermore, as noted earlier, the study also notes that the geographic isolation of the miners produced an autonomous and class-based conception of the country's development (Bergquist 1986, 38). This is not a minor topic in the historiography on mine workers, for in addition to the direct impact that these workers had on the copper miners when they arrived to their communities, subsequent studies on Chile have pointed out the spatial conditions of the "copper towns" that enabled the consolidation of a working-class culture, despite corporate attempts to control it (Klubock 1998; Zapata 2002; Cerda 2014).

Despite the wealth of these considerations, *Labor in Latin America* does not offer an analytical exploration of concepts such as space, scale, or spatial mobility. This is not surprising, as Bergquist wrote the book almost twenty years before the fruitful analysis of "labor geographies" (Herod 2001), which has shaped a body of research concerning labor organizational capacity both from a historical perspective and in the current context of globalization. In a nutshell, this approach addresses the impacts of space on collective action while also attending to how union action produces spatialities other than those imposed by the logic of capital. Based on this perspective, we can revisit the arguments concerning the nitrate miners, noting that they have specific ways of understanding the space of the Chilean north. Moreover, this approach raises questions on how their demands were anchored in an understanding of the northern space that goes beyond the sphere of production. Finally, this approach allows us to consider workers' organizing, moving from the local to the national level as more of a result of political struggles which are not known in advance (Klubock 1998).

What does this vantage point offer us with respect to the Peruvian case? Here, given the high proportion of local workers entering the mining industry early on, specific features emerge in the collective action of Peruvian workers (Flores Galindo 1974). First, the dynamics of mining production coexisted with those centered on social reproduction: the peasants of the central Andes lived with their families in community landholdings and went to the mine for specific periods of time to obtain cash (Helfgott 2013). Berquist himself notes, albeit very briefly, that this problematizes the idea of proletarianization: "How did one classify, . . . miners in highland Peru who moved in and out of traditional agriculture?" (Bergquist 1986, 8). This is not a mechanical proletarianization. It can even be argued that the company did not try to promote it, at least at first, because the coexistence with the peasant economy allowed the company to avoid paying for workers who obtained food and care in their own communities (Bonilla 1974; Sulmont 1980).

The geographical characteristics of the Peruvian central highlands, in contrast to the Chilean desert, provided a channel for collective actions that did not revolve around trade union activities, which were far from having the symbolic impact that they had in urban centers (Flores Galindo and Del Prado 2010). Hence, the defeat experienced in the face of the first attempts at unionization in the 1930s in Peru had a greater impact than, for example, the massacres experienced by Chilean miners, such as in Iquique in 1907 (Barrios, Miranda, and Castillo 2009). These defeats did not produce a collective memory as they did in the Chilean working class, partly because of the existing spatial disconnections. The miners returned to their agricultural or cattle-raising communities, finding in them spaces for survival in the midst of political and economic turmoil.

In this context, during the first half of the twentieth century, the instances of articulation between mine workers were virtually nonexistent.[1] Despite the presence of several mines around the central highlands, workers did not consolidate resilient organizations. This was a heterogeneous group, given the strength of local, communal identities in these areas (Durand 2010). Bergquist recognizes this heterogeneity as a characteristic element of export economies, but the Peruvian case is one in which this heterogeneity did not quite settle over time—at least not until the mid-twentieth century. Chilean workers mobilized in space, constructing, as the Marxist schema would expect, common spaces, interests, and identities resulting from their experience. Peruvian miners, on the other hand, returned to local communities and resisted proletarianization (Helfgott 2013). It is hard to grasp this contrast without an understanding of the spatial conditions in which they live and its effects on their social reproduction.

Besides highlighting the crucial, complex relationship between space and social reproduction, I also want to point out the need to consider different scales of coordination. The story of the Chilean miners is one where networks between workers were expanding, both internally in the mining sector through the formation of national workers' federations, and also between miners and workers in other industries (Bergquist 1986, 63). In the Peruvian case, on the other hand, this process was slow and irregular. When unions became stronger in the mid-1970s, their leaders began to dispute control of the national federations due to ideological differences (Sulmont 1985). Two mining federations emerged at that time, and they would unify after long debates only in the mid-1980s (Zapata and Garfias 2014). Scale, as a political production, is not given in advance as a consequence of a certain type of export economy. Instead, I argue that scale obeys the rhythms of political strategies that vary in each country depending on the agents and resources available (a point I develop further in the next section).

Regarding the more recent period, it is striking that the challenges of coordinating across the Peruvian territory increased during the 1990s, when new spatial difficulties emerged for mining unionism. Companies opted for a new system of space management: instead of building mining towns for workers and their families, they developed hotels in which miners would stay for specific periods of time (Manky 2017). This generated an enormous spatial dispersion in the mines, leaving only a few mines still using a traditional accommodation system. This contrasts with the Chilean case, where until a few years ago there was a very "local" dynamic in mines such as Salvador, El Teniente, or Chuquicamata. Moreover, all these mines in the Chilean case are managed by a single company, the state-owned Codelco. The neoliberal process did not result in selling the mines nationalized in the 1970s. And even when foreign investors entered the country, some bought several mining operations across the country. This corporate structure made it easier to see the national scale as the space to negotiate working conditions. It is in this context that the successful creation of a national federation of contract workers (the Confederation of Copper Workers) should be understood (Nuñez 2009). In Peru, on the other hand, along with changes in housing policies, the state promoted a radical privatization process that led to an atomization of the mining industry. Except for the mines of Toquepala and Cuajone, all large mines are owned by different private owners, making it difficult for workers to coordinate their efforts.

It is also noteworthy that indigenous and communal identities gradually became stronger within an international context concerned with the rights of indigenous peoples (Castells 1996). As a consequence, recent studies have noted the reverse of the process that occurred in the 1950s: proletarianization (from peasant to miners) gradually moved from labor-centered identities to indigenous ones (Durand 2010; Helfgott 2017). This volume's introduction notes how productive labor has been neglected in much of the literature on the region's extractive industries. This is also the case in Peru, where, in light of these transformations, most studies have focused on processes of resistance to mining (or negotiation with it) and the constitution of indigenous identities around them (Manrique and Sanborn 2021). From this perspective, the contrast with the Chilean case is critical. Most of the studies on mining conflicts in Chile have focused on labor unions (Nuñez 2009; Duran-Palma 2011; Donoso 2013; Muñoz 2017). This reflects not only the strength of the sociology of labor in the country, but also that, in fact, Chilean trade unionism is still very much marked by traditions that emphasize class as an identifying element. It is illustrative, for example, that during the mobilizations of Chilean subcontracted workers in 2006, one of their claims was that they were treated as "second class workers" (Flores 2014). Their demands focused on the need to recognize themselves as members of the working class rather than on their ethnic or local differences.

Over the last two decades, there have been conflicts between mining unions and peasant communities. These usually occur because the latter demand jobs in the mines or because they oppose their way of exploiting and transporting minerals, demanding changes or more resources to compensate them (Paredes 2016). Local actors enter into disputes with workers who are better trained but who, coming from different cities in the country, are labeled as "outsiders" benefiting from exploiting local natural resources (Manky 2020a). Sometimes this escalates when union leaders criticize local community protests, accusing them of being intransigent (*Exitosa Noticias* 2022). As scholars such as Manuel Castells (1996) and Michael Burawoy (2010) have noted, we live in a world where popular movements diverge in their demands; some are linked to more orthodox Marxist (social class) strategies, and others are rather based on social reproduction or local identities. Along these lines, I suggest that understanding the contrasts in the Chilean and Peruvian trade union experiences requires theorizing the role of space in workers' capacity to mobilize.

MILITANTS AS RESOURCE MOBILIZERS

Finally, I want to highlight a third critical element for understanding the difference between the Chilean and Peruvian cases: political militants and their role in labor organization. The chapter on Chile in *Labor in Latin America* references the importance of activists from different parties in the organization of mineworkers. Bergquist notes, for example, that they made it possible to formulate and share a radical discourse: "In their press, in public demonstrations, and weekly organizational meetings, anarchists and socialists translated their doctrinal opposition to capitalism into terms workers could understand through their daily experience" (1986, 50). Labor press, as well as the development of other cultural activities, provided workers with "the cultural tools, organizational skills, and confidence to commit themselves to collective action to change their lives" (Bergquist 1986, 52). Moreover, these militants became instrumental in disseminating the demands and perspectives of the nitrate miners to the rest of the Chilean working class (Bergquist 1986, 61).

While Bergquist gives excellent illustrations of the relevance of activists, his analyses of how they emerge, their approach to the nitrate workers, and the challenges they face in this process are rather mechanical. At least for the Chilean case, he does not raise questions that would deepen his view, which underlines, instead, the relevance of export economies as the element behind the ease and willingness to organize. Political activists appear almost entirely lacking debate among themselves, with no major tensions with the nitrate miners. For Bergquist, the particularities of the northern Chilean economy and the early emergence of left-wing parties in this country facilitated more or less automatically an early relationship between workers, activists, and a radical trade unionism.

It is beyond the scope of this chapter to discuss the limits of this interpretation of the Chilean experience. I want to emphasize, however, that the literature on resource mobilization has shown that the process through which some actors provide material and symbolic resources to social movements is far from being automatic (Edwards and Gillham 2013). On the contrary, tensions may emerge between activists and rank-and-file members when defining the goals of union organizing (Manky 2019b). Moreover, leaders and activists must learn to localize and distribute different resources on the basis of available mobilization repertoires (Ganz 2000). Finally, the capacity of civil society to facilitate activists willing to fight alongside workers is not given in advance, but obeys concrete historical processes. In other words, although in terms of productive structures Peruvian and Chilean miners enjoyed similar structural power potential, the associative power needed to realize it remained elusive in Peru.[2] Bergquist's analytical framework does not elaborate at length upon the associative power approach, but an examination of the relevance of militant activists enables a conversation toward addressing it. In the Peruvian case, workers and militants came from different economic and cultural worlds. The former came from a predominantly peasant economy, with which they maintained strong ties during the first four decades of the twentieth century (Kruijt and Vellinga 1979). The latter were not only primarily urban, but also ethnically more mestizo than indigenous (Flores Galindo 1974). As noted by Balbi (1980, 43) the miners' strikes at the end of the 1920s were spontaneous, radical but "detached from the popular movement as a whole." City and countryside were separate, although it would be more accurate to note the hierarchy between these spaces, with communist militants seeking not only to support, but to direct and control labor organizing efforts (Melgar Bao 2020). Against the backdrop of a culture that viewed indigenousness with suspicion, and work as an element that would modernize the country (Drinot 2011), these militants from the Communist Party sought to teach how to transcend economism in order to prepare those on the ground for revolution (Melgar Bao 2020, 145).

Therefore, the distance between Lima and Morococha, one of the essential mines at the turn of the twentieth century, located only a few hours away from Peru's capital, seemed more significant than the seventeen hundred kilometers that separated the nitrate fields from the Chilean capital. It is a distance that, moreover, was not shortened by the heirs of José Carlos Mariátegui (Flores Bordais 2015). While the latter proposed a framework that put forward the indigenous communities as revolutionary actors, those who followed his work in the Communist Party after his death opted for a restrictively classist approach, in which it was unnecessary to debate or even contemplate the relationship between peasant economy and proletarianization (Flores Galindo 1980). Such framing prevented Communist militants from having any impact on the mining workers' organizations during the next thirty years (Balbi 1980, 36, 97). It is an experience that clearly contrasts with the rich social life described by Bergquist in the Chilean nitrate fields. Even though mining is a key industry, and despite very poor working conditions, the relationship between activists and workers is determined not only on the basis of potential objective interests.

It was only in the late 1960s that certain groups in Peru, especially middle-class youths, approached this sector again to organize a union (Gálvez Olaechea 2021). But even then, these were isolated and small groups that confronted a government that sought to control union dynamics (Medina 2019). Thus, although mine workers were crucial to the Peruvian economy, and had some bargaining power at the structural level, the scarcity of political networks prevented the articulation of national efforts. It is a left that, with a few valuable exceptions, is incapable of engaging with the mining world. The workers, on the other hand, did not actively militate, with the exception of some leaders. These networks became weaker still during the 1980s, when mineworkers became trapped in the midst of the internal armed conflict, between the state and the terrorist group Sendero Luminoso (Shining Path). Moreover, during the 1990s an openly antipolitical discourse emerged that caused political militancy in the country to fall apart (Burt 2007).

This contrasts with the active participation of Communist and Socialist militants in the Chilean mines. This occurred clearly in the period analyzed by Bergquist, but also during the mid-twentieth century: "the strikes in the copper mines had ideological connotations that were part of the links that the unions had with the parties" (Zapata 2002, 98). As Zapata notes, however, it should be observed that this does not imply a subordination of trade unionism to the political party. On the contrary, negotiations between actors emerged, with each trying to increase its power (labor or electoral) through the other. For the most recent period, my work has analyzed the central role played by militants of left-wing parties and associations in organizing subcontracted workers in Chile (Manky 2018).

Nowadays, Peruvian mine workers have developed an outlook more focused on their specific interests—for example, their collective bargaining—than on their national organization. Although the industry has one of the highest levels of unionization in the country (25 percent), these workers negotiate at the firm level and have rarely tried to approach other working-class sectors or even more ambitious forms of national coordination (Manky 2020b). Moreover, many of the country's militants nowadays have directed a good part of their resources to the organization and defense of environmental and indigenous rights rather than labor issues. This is a change that can be understood from the emergence of "new social movements" that took place globally since the 1990s (Castells 1996). Many organizations, such as non-governmental organizations or parties traditionally close to unions, are now taking as crucial components of their work advocacy for community-based work, leaving workers with fewer resources (Manky 2019a). For example, there is a noticeable shift in the case of feminist organizations, from working closely with wives of mine workers to working with peasant women affected by environmental pollution (Amat y Leon 2015).

The background to this process has been a change in the capital intensification of mining processes, technological developments, and changes in workforce demands. This structural transformation has come hand in hand with a change in the organizational resources available to workers from other civil society organizations. However, from this point of view, the Chilean case is revealing because even though changes have also occurred there within an industry that is global, militants with more experience in political parties have been fundamental in the development of a strong mining unionism, and there are also nongovernmental organizations that are still engaged in thinking about labor issues systematically (Manky 2018).

CONCLUSION

This chapter has aimed to draw on and refine some of Charles Bergquist's central insights to explore the dynamics of the Peruvian mineworkers' struggles. To do so, I have relied on two comparisons. On the one hand, the chapter compares the Chilean case analyzed in *Labor in Latin America* to Peru, which stands out as a paradoxical case, given that despite the two countries sharing many structural similarities, Peru's labor movement did not obtain the results of the nitrate miners in Chile. On the other hand, I have charted the trajectory of mining unionism up to the most recent period. Given the ongoing relevance of mineral exports in the Peruvian economy, looking at workers and their organizational capacity from the perspective of Bergquist opens up questions about the changes and continuities of export workers' trade unionism.

Both comparisons produce counterintuitive results if we read them from *Labor in Latin America*. Why is it that in a sector so relevant to the country, workers cannot secure enough power to reform the rules of the game? I consider three elements to be fundamental. First, the strength of the Peruvian elite meant that it was not only able to refuse labor demands but also to repress and prevent unionization through the state, which it dominated with much more robust control than in the Chilean case. The logic of a state incapable of reacting to workers' demands, even in important sectors such as mining, was maintained during a large part of the twentieth century in Peru and has gained importance in the last thirty years in a scenario where it is crucial to attracting foreign investment.

Second, I drew attention to the impact of space on labor mobilization capacity. Inspired by the work of Andrew Herod, I pointed out that the Peruvian case is one in which the continuous interaction between productive spaces and social reproductive spaces has marked a proletarianization that is not only lengthy but complex and nuanced, and seems almost incomplete when compared to the Chilean case. Moreover, I showed how even if mining production occurs in locations far from urban centers, the industry has opted for new spatial configurations, which pose challenges for labor organizations, especially in terms of potential conflicts with local communities.

Finally, I drew attention to the need to address the role of political activists. These are players whose strategies are not mere reflections of structural constraints. On the contrary, they have to interpret the situation before them, and sometimes—as happened in Peru at the beginning of the twentieth century—this can result in tremendous failures. Indeed, Peruvian leftist militants seem to have been unable to understand the needs and dynamics of the mining sector and its complex proletarianization, resulting in top-down approaches and few results.

None of these arguments weaken the value of Bergquist's views. But they permit us to initiate a dialogue with his work, allowing us to refine and advance some of his arguments to calibrate their value in today's world. For example, current debates in the literature on political sociology, labor geography, and environmental issues may be crucial in illuminating the everyday challenges of trade unionism in export sectors. My intention in this chapter has not been to go into these debates, but I believe the points raised can bridge the gap between Bergquist's work and these developments. In my view, Bergquist's perspective, interested in both the material conditions of labor and the cultural struggle around it, could be helpful for a better understanding of the region. In the context of a booming extractivist development model, this conversation brings up questions as to why labor is relatively weak in most countries in the region. Or how, in the current situation, progressive governments relate to labor, and how they ignore their demands vis-à-vis other actors in civil society.

NOTES

1. I have developed this further in "Scaling The Commanding Heights Of The Economy? A Century of Mineworkers' Spatial Projects in the Peruvian Andes," a chapter of the *Handbook of Labour Geography*, edited by Andrew Herod.

2. See the introduction of this volume for a discussion of structural and associational power.

Chapter Six

Capital Accumulation and the Forms and Potentialities of the Labor Movement in Latin America

Critical Reflections on Argentina and Chile

Guido Starosta and Fernando Cazón

In his classic book on *Labor in Latin America*, Charles Bergquist attempts to bring the role and forms of the labor movement back into the study of Latin American societies and their historical trajectory. Although Bergquist's book does not offer an explicit in-depth discussion of the theoretical-methodological approach which informs his historiographical research, he does sketch out a very general framework that structures the empirical case studies of Argentina, Chile, Colombia, and Venezuela. Very broadly, his perspective postulates a causal link between the export structure of each country, the consequent potentialities for industrial development, and the features of the workers' movement (mainly, its ideological and organizational forms and its relative strength/weakness). More specifically, according to Bergquist there is an inverse relationship between the potentialities for economic diversification generated by the export structure, and the political leanings (left/right), organizational forms (independent-classist/corporatist), and strength of the workers' movement.

In this chapter, we shall critically examine Bergquist's underlying theoretical framework so as to assess its explanatory power for the study of contemporary Latin American societies. In our view, the connection that Bergquist posits between the export structure and its industrializing potential, on the one hand, and forms and strength of the labor movement, on the other, has the merit of involving an attempt at a materialist conceptualization of the relationship between the economic determinations of the process of capital accumulation and the political action of the working class. However, we shall argue that the particular manner in which Bergquist conceives of the nexus between the economic and political forms of capitalist social relations is problematic for at least two main reasons. In the first place, the connection remains utterly extrinsic. More concretely, the economic structure of society is reduced to some immediately observable "empirical" features of Latin American countries, which are then seen to coalesce into a set of external circumstances that condition the forms and scope of working-class struggles. In the second place, and more substantively, we argue that Bergquist's characterization of the "economic structure" of Latin American societies, in terms of the particular configuration of the "export sector" of each country, falls short of a rigorous explanation of the specific form of this region's national processes of capital accumulation and their role in the international division of labor. Against the backdrop of these limitations in Bergquist's framework, the chapter provides an alternative approach to the specificity of Latin American societies and the manner in which it has historically determined the forms and scope of the labor movement in Argentina and Chile on a comparative basis.

LIMITS OF BERGQUIST'S THEORETICAL APPROACH

The connection that Bergquist posits between the export structure and its industrializing potential, on the one hand, and forms and strength of the labor movement, on the other, has the merit of involving an attempt at a "materialist" conceptualization of the relationship between the economic determinations of the process of capital accumulation and the political action of the working class. However, we think that the particular manner in which Bergquist conceives of the nexus between the economic and political forms of capitalist social relations remains utterly extrinsic. More concretely, the economic structure of society is reduced to some immediately observable "empirical" features of Latin American countries, which are then seen to coalesce into a set of external circumstances that condition the forms and scope of working-class struggles, which are thereby represented as an abstractly "autonomous" and self-moving political "factor" that externally modifies or influences the potentialities and trajectory of capitalist development in each country. Yet, from a truly critical materialist perspective, the class struggle must be grasped as form-determined by the generalized commodity-form of capitalist social relations. Specifically, the class struggle actually is the most general direct social relation between collective personifications of commodities (thereby differentiated as a political form of social relations), which mediates the unfolding of the essentially indirect relations of capitalist production through the generalized commodity-form (hence distinguished as the economic form of social relations). In its simplest determination, it is the necessary concrete form taken by the purchase of labor-power at its full value and, therefore, by the attainment of the socially constituted normal material reproduction of the productive attributes of wage-laborers in a capitalistic "exploitable shape" (on average, through the cyclical oscillations of the wage, i.e., the price of labor power, around its "immanent" magnitude of value).[1]

Now, as argued elsewhere (Fitzsimons and Starosta 2018), even the most methodologically minded readings of *Capital* tend to consider that the content and definition of the value of labor-power are exhausted in chapter 6 of that book. However, those perspectives overlook the systematic-dialectical place and significance (i.e., the level of abstraction) of Marx's discussion of the value of labor-power at that stage. More specifically, those readings miss the point that this initial exposition of the latter's determination occurs in the context of the formal subsumption of labor to capital. However, the determination of the value of labor-power is not exhausted at that abstract level but involves further concretization as we move from the formal to the real subsumption of labor to capital, and from the latter to the reproduction of the total social capital.

In effect, as capital takes possession and modifies the labor process to produce relative surplus value, it transforms its requirements of qualitatively different physical and intellectual attributes that need to be set into motion to produce a mass of use-values "pregnant" with surplus value. In other words, with each cyclical renewal of the general technical basis of the valorization process, capital revolutionizes the kind of labor-power of the different organs of the collective laborer. This transformation can only result from, and be reproduced by, the mutation of the respective "norm of consumption," and so of the conditions of reproduction, of the various segments of the working class. The reason for this is that it is the consumption of those means of subsistence that (re)produces "the muscles, nerves, bones and brains of existing workers" (Marx 1976, 717) that materially bear "the aggregate of those mental and physical capabilities which he sets into motion whenever he produces a use-value of any kind" (Marx 1976, 270). Thus, the material conditions of the reproduction process of capital constitute the content of the determination of the value of labor-power, as more concretely posited by the real subsumption of labor. They do so by determining the differentiated forms of productive subjectivity that compose the collective laborer and, as consequence, the quantity and kind of means of subsistence that different workers need to consume to reproduce those variegated technical and "moral" attributes of labor-power.[2] In turn, the class struggle becomes the necessary political form that mediates the contradictory establishment of the material unity between the productive and consumptive requirements of the reproduction of the total social capital.

In sum, the organized antagonistic action of wage-workers as a class, far from enjoying "autonomy" (relative or otherwise), is the necessary political mode of realization of the contradictory economic content of capitalist social relations. Various important points follow from this inner nexus between the economic and political forms of the social relations of capitalist production.

In the first place, it goes without saying that this does not imply the denial of the transformative powers of human practice personified by workers. But it does imply that whatever transformative powers the political action of workers might have—whether capital-reproducing or capital-transcending political action—must be an immanent determination begotten by the movement of capital accumulation and not external to it. And as an expression of its simplest determination implicated in the mere existence of labor-power as a commodity, the class struggle only exists as a necessary form of capital's reproduction, but not of its transcendence. The former, let us crucially stress, is the mode of existence of the class struggle that underpins Bergquist's historical study, which mostly (if not exclusively) tends to focus on "reformist" expressions of workers' resistance, even when it appears in self-proclaimed "anti-capitalist" political and ideological forms. In this sense, it must be noted that the "measure" of the objective (progressive) transformative potentiality of a certain historical expression of the labor movement does not simply boil down to those ideological forms. Instead, it is objectively manifested in the extent to which it manages to improve the conditions of productive consumption and reproduction of labor-power in a relatively universal or undifferentiated manner across the different organs of the working class.

In the second place, this means that the determination of the class struggle as a political action is not restricted to the conquest of state power or to an action involving demands directed at the state. The political determination of the class struggle springs from the objectively general scope of the antagonistic direct social relation between capitalists and wage workers. In other words, it should be clear that this determination of the class struggle as the form of the sale of labor-power at its full value does not simply involve its "trade union" organizational expressions. Concomitantly, neither does it imply that it will always be realized through the development of mere "trade union consciousness." As a matter of fact, that determination may well manifest itself in apparently extremely radical or militant forms of the class struggle (which tends to occur in the upward swing of the cyclical oscillation of the capital accumulation process, when real wages usually rise).[3] In other words, when addressing the diverse historical expressions of the labor movement, as Bergquist intends, it is of paramount importance to grasp the "unity-in-difference" between the immanent content and the concrete mode of appearance of working-class struggles and their ideological and organizational forms. By contrast, we think the confusion between content and concrete form of the class struggle, which arguably lies at the basis of the orthodox Marxist rigid separation between economistic and political consciousness of the working class, is tacitly taken for granted in Bergquist typological "model."

Against the backdrop of these remarks on the connection between content and form of the class struggle, let us take a closer look at Bergquist's concrete application of his theoretical framework in Latin America. As we have seen, the model associates the left side of the continuum with the development of a vigorous and "independent" labor movement and "Marxist" (i.e., allegedly "revolutionary") ideological forms among leftist organizations. This would find its "material basis" in a highly concentrated and foreign-dominated export structure which blocks the possibilities for so-called import substituting industrialization (ISI). On the other pole of the continuum, a more fragmented and domestically owned export structure would give room for ISI but lead to a weaker labor movement, which thus becomes "co-opted" into "nationalist" or "populist" ideological forms. Thus, this approach implicitly measures and judges the strength and (progressive) transformative potentialities of the labor movement by the ideological forms in which most workers represent the social determinations of their existence. More specifically, Bergquist seems to suggest that the ideological forms that he sees as manifestation of a "co-opted" labor movement lacking in "cultural independence" are a sign of weakness of the class struggle. Argentina, with the "Peronist populist conservatism" as the dominant ideology of the labor movement during most of the historical period covered in his study, would be a paradigmatic case in point of this "right-wing" pole of the spectrum. Conversely, when the immediate appearance of the class struggle mostly takes the form of a self-styled "Marxist" organization, he tends to characterize the respective labor movement as "strong and vigorous" (the case of Chile is deemed as incarnation of this and as the emblematic counterpoint to the former).

Yet, paradoxically as it may seem from Bergquist's perspective, when the transformative potentiality of the labor movement is materialistically grounded as the vehicle for the establishment of socially determined conditions of reproduction of labor-power with historically changing determinate productive attributes, a different picture emerges. Where, by virtue of economic determinations and dynamics that will be discussed in the next section, the process of capital accumulation carries the potentiality to develop through a broader and deeper ISI process, the need arises for the generation and reproduction of a working class which embodies more complex productive capacities (and also of their expanded absorption as active "industrial army," i.e., through rising manufacturing employment). In turn, this will manifest itself in an overall tendency for an average higher value of labor power of the respective national fragment of the working class. Moreover, as already discussed, the necessary concrete form of the class struggle taken by the sale of the commodity labor-power at its value means that an upward trend in the latter will be realized in a stronger labor movement in its conflict against the bourgeoisie. By contrast, in countries where economic conditions did not allow for a similar degree of development of an ISI process, the material basis for such a rising value of labor-power was missing. Thus, despite the appearance of greater "radicality" and "autonomy" of the respective ideological forms, those labor movements have been actually weaker in their potentiality for attaining improved conditions of normal reproduction of labor-power. This is confirmed when one examines the most significant synthetic "empirical" expression of the transformative potentialities of working-class struggles over the conditions of their reproduction, which does not reside in the hegemonic ideological form but, fundamentally, in the historical trajectory of the average real wage. As can be seen in figure 6.1, during the period of ISI, real wages in Chile, the alleged emblematic case of a "powerful Marxist labor movement," albeit with a comparatively shallow industrialization process, have been systematically and significantly lower than in Argentina, which, according to Bergquist, is exemplary of a co-opted and weak expression of the class struggle.

To conclude this section, the critical scrutiny of Bergquist's theoretical approach shows that his "model" fails adequately to ground, and therefore

Figure 6.1.   Source: Rivas Castro (2022)

explain, the real differential strength of Latin American labor movements beyond their immediate ideological and political appearances. In our view, this shortcoming derives, first and foremost, from the external relation that he posits between the "economic structure" of capitalist society and its political and ideological forms. By contrast, we presented an alternative view based on a particular "systematic-dialectical" approach to the Marxian critique of political economy, which grasps working-class struggles as "form-determined" by the "law of value." However, we also noted that there is a further weakness in Bergquist's book; more concretely, in his conceptualization of the "economic structure" of Latin American societies inspired by Latin American Structuralist political economy. In the next section, we therefore offer an alternative approach to the specific "economic structure" of Latin American societies derived from the essentially global dynamics of the capital accumulation process and the resulting forms of the international division of labor and uneven development. On that basis, we subsequently reexamine the different forms of the Latin American labor movements in this new light (with a specific focus on Argentina and Chile), hopefully tracing the immanent unity between the specificity of the capital accumulation process in the region and the general political and ideological forms of the class struggle and its changing historical dynamics.

AN ALTERNATIVE APPROACH TO THE SPECIFICITY OF THE CAPITAL ACCUMULATION PROCESSES IN LATIN AMERICA AND THE FORMS AND SCOPE OF THE LABOR MOVEMENT

The Specificity of Capital Accumulation in Latin America

As is recognized by virtually all accounts of the history of capitalist development in Latin America, and Bergquist's book is no exception, the original subsumption of these territories to the global accumulation of capital was based on the production of agricultural and/or mining commodities for the world market. However, the developmental potentialities and dynamics of those territories was not simply determined by the use-value of those export commodities but, crucially, by the determinations derived from their value-form. As Marx remarks in *Capital*, the establishment of this "classic" modality of the international division of labor (that he labels "new"), which "converts one part of the globe into a chiefly agricultural field of production for supplying the other part, which remains a pre-eminently industrial field" (Marx 1976, 580), was determined by the production of relative surplus value through the system of machinery of large-scale industry.

In effect, the exceptional natural conditions prevailing in many of these territories allowed for a greater productivity of agricultural or mining labor, thereby resulting in the cheapening of means of subsistence and a lower value of labor-power (Starosta 2019, 671). However, this form of subsumption of Latin American territories into the global circuits of accumulation was ridden with a contradiction: if, on the one hand, the total social capital enhanced its valorization by reducing the value of labor-power, on the other this was partly offset by the drain of surplus value, otherwise available for capital's appropriation, flowing into the pockets of domestic landowners in the form of ground-rent. Moreover, to the extent that primary commodities produced in the region have been exported and consumed overseas, ground-rent has constituted a continuous extraordinary international inflow of social wealth (as opposed to the normal outflows in the process of equalization of the worldwide rate of profit emphasized by, for instance, the dependency tradition) (Iñigo Carrera 2018; Caligaris, Fitzsimons, and Starosta, 2024). Capital was thus driven to overcome this barrier to its accumulation capacity by reshaping those spaces of valorization to recover part of that surplus value, through the establishment of an "antagonistic association" with local landowners over the appropriation of ground-rent. From being simply a source of cheap raw materials and means of subsistence, those territories became also determined as sources of ground-rent recovery for global industrial capital.

The accumulation of capital through the recovery of ground-rent has taken a variety of forms (Grinberg and Starosta 2015, 242–43). More concretely, the transfer of ground-rent has been achieved through different policy mechanisms (overvalued exchange rates, export and import taxes, direct state regulation of staple food and raw material prices, etc.), which resulted in the establishment of specific domestic conditions for the circulation of capital within those national territories. Consequently, its appropriation could only be done by industrial capitals operating within those countries and whose circuit realized its final phase (i.e., the sale of commodities) almost exclusively on highly protected domestic markets of a very limited size vis-à-vis world market norms (Grinberg and Starosta 2009, 769ff). ISI, which consolidated in most primary-commodity-producing countries between the 1930s and 1950s, and which reached its peak during the "commodities boom" of the 1970s, has been the most paradigmatic and developed form through which this specific modality of capital accumulation has unfolded.

Although this has meant that individual capitals could not reach the scale needed for profitably utilizing advanced technologies, they have compensated for the resulting higher production costs by appropriating a portion of ground-rent. In this way, they have valorized at the average rate of profit despite their restricted magnitude and backward technologies. Thus, this specific modality capital accumulation has been attractive for domestic capitals that, with the exception of those producing ground-rent-bearing commodities, were not competitive enough to sustain their expanded reproduction by producing for the world market. But, additionally and fundamentally, those protected domestic markets turned out especially profitable for industrial capitals of foreign origin (i.e., transnational corporations), which were established there from the mid- to late 1950s onward.

In sum, an abundant extraordinary mass of social wealth, in the social form of ground-rent, has systematically complemented the surplus-value extracted from the domestic working class to the point of marking the very specificity of the accumulation process in Latin American countries. However, the other side of this same coin is that the scale of those processes of capital accumulation has been "structurally" subject to the markedly cyclical evolution of the magnitude of ground-rent available for appropriation. As we shall see, this explains the peculiarly pronounced "political and institutional instability" that has historically characterized most Latin American countries, with sharp ebbs and flows of the class struggle and, at the level of the state-form, with abrupt oscillations between nationalistic populist and/or developmentalist regimes and neoliberal ones. Against this backdrop, the singularity of the political and ideological forms of the labor movement in each of the four cases studied by Bergquist should therefore be seen as an expression of the specific scale and scope, cyclical dynamics, and timing of the respective national accumulation process through ISI.

The Political Forms of the Capital Accumulation Process in Argentina

Among the four case studies, Argentina arguably stands out as the one in which the ISI process developed earlier and with more breadth and depth. Its beginnings can be traced back to the 1930s or maybe a little earlier (albeit the conditions that paved its way had been germinating from at least the turn of the nineteenth century). In the following decade, mostly under Peronism, the process gained momentum through the multiplication of small nationally owned industrial capitals. Subsequently, toward the end of the 1950s, it experienced a mass inflow of foreign direct investment by virtue of which the major manufacturing transnational corporations settled in the national territory to cater for those profitable, highly protected domestic markets. In this way, global industrial capital started to partake directly as the main active partner in the recovery of ground-rent. The changing configuration of the labor movement evolved in tandem with these transformations of the productive structure of the country.

The Formation and Early Development of the Labor Movement in Twentieth-Century Argentina

Until the beginning and during the germinal stages of the industrialization process, the struggle of the wage-workers was politically and ideologically expressed through independent class organizations that, in Bergquist terms, could be seen as "non-coopted" or "culturally autonomous."[4] In the first place, these early stages of working-class struggles developed through the diffusion of anarchism among its ranks. As the renowned Argentine Marxist Aricó (1999) acknowledged, despite the apparent radicalism of its self-proclaimed "anti-capitalist" ideology and rhetoric, in actual practice most of anarchism's political efforts were geared toward typically "reformist" trade-union demands (such as full "freedom of association"). In this sense, this spread of anarchist trade-unionism was the political form taken by the emergent partial and fragmented tendency for improved conditions of sale of labor-power within particular branches of the social division of labor, as the material conditions of the specific form of valorization of capital in Argentina gradually started to require an expansion of the productive attributes of workers (hence of their "norm of consumption" and the real wage), and the restriction in the extensive productive consumption of labor-power (i.e., the shortening of the working day), to compensate for the increased intensity of labor. Later on, as this tendency became generalized across the productive structure, the political action of workers had to transcend its narrow trade-union organization and acquire an overtly political independent mode of expression at the level of the capitalist state; more specifically, at the level of its legislative power, so that the results of the class struggle could be objectively sanctioned in a universally valid and coercive manner, that is, through the legal-form. Therefore, anarchism became partly complemented by the growth of parliamentary socialism, whose mediation in the class struggle directly personified the passing of several labor laws, the extension of the franchise (given the large number of immigrants among wage-workers) and the establishment of a first, rather modest, spate of social rights (e.g., compulsory, nonreligious public elementary education). Thus, despite their outward opposing ideological rhetoric, anarchism and parliamentary socialism formed an immanent differentiated unity in this phase of the class struggle over the normal reproduction of labor-power, respectively: a "revolutionary" extra-parliamentary left and a "reformist" wing. As Iñigo Carrera (2022, 474–75) perceptively puts it, ideologically unconstrained by the state and legal-forms, the former could "hit hard" through violent direct actions and the call to general (wildcat) strikes, at a time when the regulation of the class struggle had not been fully institutionalized through the web of labor law and the corresponding bureaucratic organs. However, precisely by virtue of this, it could not politically personify the necessity for the generalization of these improved conditions of sale and productive utilization of labor-power through their sanction in the objectively binding form of the law, which was precisely the role played by the "Socialist Party" through electoral, yet class-independent, politics.

Finally, this formative stage of the labor movement culminated between the mid-1910s and early 1920s with the hegemony of revolutionary syndicalism (at the expense of and in conflict with the union branch of the Socialist Party), and its refusal for the organized working class to take any active part in the political representation of the accumulation of capital through the legislative or executive control over the capitalist state. In practice, this refusal meant that the mass electoral representation of workers fell in the hands of "bourgeois" parties (specifically, of so-called Radicalism), while their "ideologically autonomous" organization narrowed down again to its trade-union form. At first sight, this configuration of the labor movement might appear broadly to resemble the "unity-in-difference" between anarchism ("revolution") and the Socialist Party ("reform") as the necessary political forms of social mediation for the establishment a higher value of labor-power and a shorter working day, as just described. However, there are at least two significant differences. In the first place, through its mass electoral support of the Radical Party, which eventually managed to win the by then free democratic elections, the (syndicalist) working class acquired an indirect but practically effective capacity to exercise some participation in the executive branch of the political power of the capitalist state. Thus, as Iñigo Carrera (2022, 489) notes, despite its revolutionary rhetoric against "bourgeois" electoral politics, the dominant syndicalist trade-unionism did not shy away from establishing a mutually convenient nexus of clientelism with the Radical administration of Yrigoyen to "wring concessions" from capital and the state in exchange for insulation from the more intransigent and recalcitrant elements of the class struggle coming from the remnants of the anarchist movement. In the second place, the wage-workers' mass electoral support of the Radical Party meant that the labor movement's political participation in the state was no longer personified by a "reformist" yet class-independent organization (as was the case of the legislative action of the Sociality Party), but became expressed through a cross-class "populist" alliance with, fundamentally, the increasingly sizeable petty bourgeoisie.[5]

Various implications can be drawn at this juncture from this concise sketch of the formation and early development of the labor movement in Argentina. First and foremost, despite their diversity and the varying degrees of "anti-capitalism" of their ideologies and organizations, they all expressed the different changing forms in which the political action of the working class personified the development of the national process of capital accumulation and its requirements around the simplest content of the specifically capital-ist determination of the class struggle, namely the evolving material forms taken by the normal reproduction of labor-power, which reflected the chang-ing productive configuration of the capitalist labor process. In other words, despite the overtly anti-capitalist sentiments, rhetoric, and political programs of various of these manifestations of the organized working class, they were all "capital-reproducing" and not "capital-transcending" forms of political action. Fundamentally, their immanent potentiality came down to be neces-sary mediating forms for a moderate increase in real wages, the shortening of the working day, and the achievement of still rather limited social rights. Moreover, insofar as many of these economic determinations necessitated the mediation of the participation of the labor movement in different instances of the general political representation of the total social capital through the state-form, the sale of labor-power at its full value (hence the class struggle) had to take concrete juridical form through the attainment of certain political rights (extension of the franchise to all male adults, democratization of the "political regime" through the implementation of secret and compulsory vot-ing that ended so-called patriotic electoral fraud, and so on). Figure 6.2 plots the evolution of real wages that synthetically expresses this phase of capitalist accumulation and class struggle in Argentina.

On the other hand, our historical sketch suggests that there seems to be a clearly identifiable tendency underlying the development of the class strug-gle during those early stages of capitalist accumulation in Argentina. Spe-cifically, the modest yet progressive improvement in the normal conditions

Figure 6.2.   Source: Iñigo Carrera (2007)

of reproduction of labor-power asserted itself through the strengthening of the labor movement in the class struggle that, in turn, took concrete shape through the expanding scope of its organizations: they gradually evolved from one-sided (seemingly "revolutionary") trade-unionist expressions to the point of taking active part in the management of the political power of the capitalist state (firstly formally limited to the legislative branch, although later having an informal "clientelistic" channel of influence on the executive). Evidently, the ideological forms of the labor movement transformed accordingly. The more the necessary mediation of the class struggle in the upward trend and changing material composition of the "norm of consumption" entailed a labor movement with an increasingly prominent role in the personification of the general political representative of the total social capital (i.e., in the management of the capitalist state), the more the hegemonic ideology of the corresponding organizations of wage-workers took a "reformist," and eventually "populist," form. Note, however, that what might appear to Bergquist's eyes as an increasing loss of "cultural autonomy" (and thereby also of "strength" and "political power" according to his yardstick), were, in fact, changing necessary ideological forms through which the political action of the working class personified its expanding immanent potentiality to improve the normal conditions of reproduction of their labor-power. Only by idealistically grounding the objective determination and potentiality of the class struggle in the (seeming) radicality of workers' consciousness, and not in the actual form-determined practical movement of the materiality of their (alienated) social being, can Bergquist conclude that at stake in this historical process was a gradual weakening of the labor movement in Argentina (Bergquist 1986, 149–54). The labor movement, additionally, would have been already latent from its birth with a "congenital" condition of "innate debility" vis-à-vis, for instance, the labor movement in Chile (Bergquist 1986, 173–74).[6]

Thus, although the assertion of working-class power in the struggle over their normal conditions of reproduction carried an immanent limit during this stage vis-à-vis the later phases of "ISI" mediated by the formation of Peronism, we shall see, contrary to Bergquist's account (Bergquist 1986, 189–200), that the latter did not express a discrete qualitative break in the evolution of the labor movement in Argentina. Rather, it involved an ulterior continuous development of the same underlying tendency that we have just sketched out. Moreover, once we uncover the qualitative economic content that determines the specificity of the capital accumulation process in Argentina (i.e., its "structural dependence" on the oscillating inflows of ground-rent) and grasp the immanent nexus between those economic form-determinations and the political modes of existence that mediate their contradictory development, the

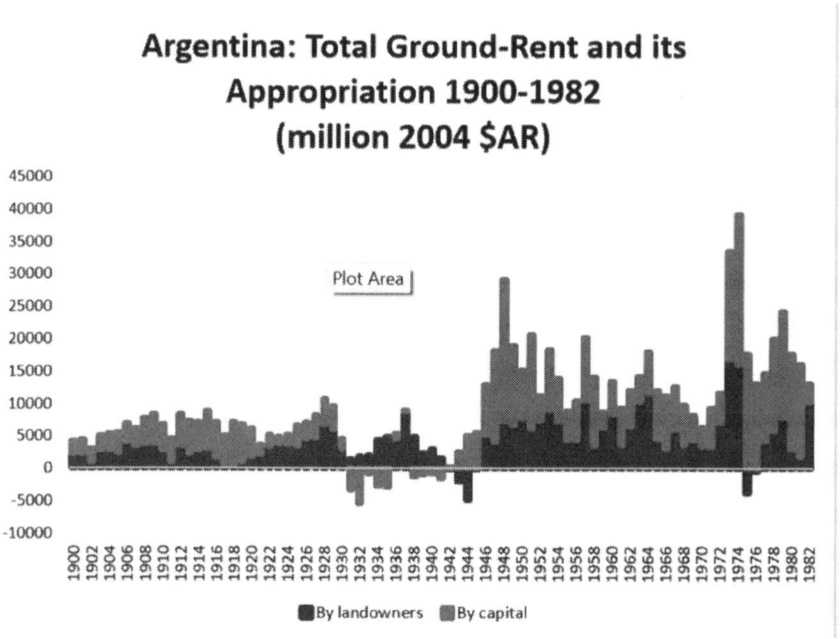
Argentina: Total Ground-Rent and its Appropriation 1900-1982 (million 2004 $AR)
Plot Area
By landowners
By capital

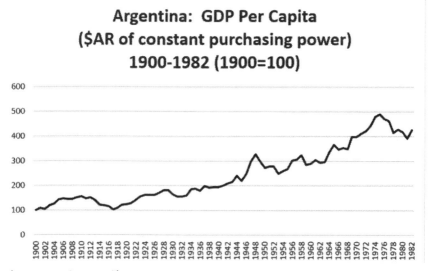

Figure 6.3. Source: Iñigo Carrera (2007)

Argentina: GDP Per Capita ($AR of constant purchasing power) 1900-1982 (1900=100)

Figure 6.4. Source: Iñigo Carrera (2007)

twenty-year hiatus of acquiescence that, according to Bergquist, separates, on the one hand, the sudden demise of a "leftist," "culturally and organizationally autonomous" first wave of working class struggles, and its resurgence after World War II in a "corporatist," "nationalistic," and "right-wing" (in sum, "co-opted") Peronist shape (Bergquist 1986, 101–2), on the other, loses its apparently enigmatic character. More concretely, as figures 6.3 and 6.4 show, toward the 1920s the inflow of ground-rent experienced a sharp contraction (and so did in particular the portion channeled to other social subjects than landowners), which led to a deceleration of economic growth and which, in turn, was expressed in a slowdown of the upward trend of real wages. In other words, those twenty years represented one of first historical expressions in the twentieth century of the highly volatile dynamics of ground-rent-fueled capital accumulation, and the consequently pronounced instability of the corresponding political mediations.

As evidenced by figure 6.3, at the turn of the 1920s ground-rent drastically plummeted and remained, on average, at historically very low levels for the subsequent fifteen years. Moreover, as has usually happened in those circumstances (Caligaris et al. 2022), most of that mass of social wealth ended in the pockets of landowners in order to sustain the scale of agrarian production, a sector that is key to the unity of the accumulation process. Thus it should come as no surprise that the general political representation of the accumulation of capital at the level of the state reverted to its old "oligarchic" forms (whether through military governments or through the resurgence of "patriotic fraud"), with a heightening of the political repression of the working class.

FROM THE GENESIS OF PERONISM
TO THE ARMED STRUGGLE

As the ISI process consolidated and gathered pace during the 1930s, the labor movement experienced three main political and ideological transformations. First, nationalism experienced a significant rise at the expense of all internationalist leanings. Second, toward the mid-1940s an internal dispute developed within the workers' movement over the political participation of unions, which, to phrase it in Bergquist's terms, brought to the fore the apparent ideological antinomy between "autonomy" and "co-option." Third, both within the organized working class and within the structure of the capitalist state, there was an emergent concern over, and search for, the legal-bureaucratic regulation of labor conflicts (Matsushita 2014; Torre 2014; Del Campo 2012; Gaudio and Pilone 1984; Cazón 2019; 2021). All these processes eventually coalesced since the mid-1940s in the institutionalization of trade unions, their growth by virtue of an accelerated mass unionization of workers, and their political participation in a cross-class, "Peronist" party that would hold office until the mid-1950s.

It goes without saying that this process of state-regulated institutionalization of trade unions did not come about in a peaceful, "judicious and orderly" manner, but took an antagonistic form, which involved the fierce repression of the more recalcitrant parts of the working class by the state. Thus, in 1943 the government decided to ban so-called National Labor Federation N°2 (CGT 2) on the grounds that it was a "communist" organization (Del Campo 2012, 181), which further involved the incarceration of numerous trade union leaders and members of the Communist Party (Matsushita 2014, 348; Iñigo Carrera 2019, 105). Unions that had formerly integrated CGT 2 were then forced into CGT 1 under the leadership of newly appointed representatives (Matsushita 2014, 350). Even under the subsequent democratically elected administration of Perón, two clearly distinct stages in the state's role in the regulation of the class struggle over conditions of reproduction labor-power can be discerned. First, between 1946 and 1948 the government supported the CGT's trade-union actions (strikes and mass demonstrations) with a view to breaking the resistance of the bourgeoisie and thus facilitating the rise in real wages. But after ground-rent dropped in 1949, the Peronist administration withdrew its explicit support of trade-union actions and actually tried to contain them through direct intervention into different levels of their institutional organization or, in some cases, through the sheer suspension or outright cancellation of their legal status (Doyon 1977; Cazón 2015).

Bergquist sees these developments as the final capitulation of the labor movement in Argentina, which relinquished all "cultural and organizational autonomy" and became fully "co-opted" by right-wing corporatist institutions and ideology, thus definitively abandoning its socialist aspirations "in exchange for" certain economic prosperity and social mobility. By contrast, we mentioned that the emergence and hegemony of Peronism was the necessary political and ideological mediation to unfold the economic developmental potentialities of ground-rent-fueled accumulation, albeit in a cyclical phase of accelerated inflows of that extraordinary mass of social wealth, and in a novel stage which involved different main modalities of its appropriation.

As can be seen in figure 6.3, the end of World War II went hand in hand with an unprecedented spurt in the flow of ground-rent into Argentina, the greatest part of which slipped through the fingers of the personifications of landed property and, with the mediation of a wide array of public policies as outlined in a previous subsection, was transferred into the pockets of industrial capital-in-general. More concretely, this diversion of ground-rent into

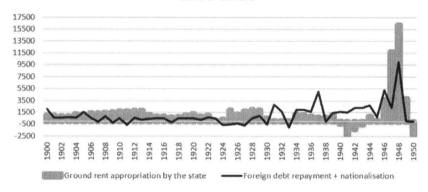

Figure 6.5. Source: Iñigo Carrera (2007)

industrial capital accumulation reached such a scale and, crucially, involved such modalities, which could only take place through the establishment of visible mechanisms such as the public monopoly over their foreign trade. Above all, this was necessary to swell the fiscal capacity of the state, whose activities would come to play a more prominent role to mediate the new modalities of appropriation of ground-rent by individual capitals (e.g., state-captured ground-rent was the main source of fiscal revenue that funded the nationalization of formerly foreign-owned public utilities, albeit usually at an overinflated price; see figure 6.5) (Iñigo Carrera 2007, 76–78).

Hence, despite being industrial capital's "hostile brothers" who also shared in the "fruits" of the expanded reproduction of this form of accumulation, landowners could no longer directly partake in its general political representation at the level of the executive branch of the capitalist state. As a matter of fact, the personifications of landed property began ideologically to appear as "enemies of the people," whose parasitic greediness thwarted the economic development and political autonomy of the "national community."

Contrariwise, enhanced political potentialities were carried by both the domestic personifications of individual capitals and the working class. In effect, although it would prove to be a transitory phenomenon which, through the consolidation of the domestic market for local manufacturing products, paved the way for the later arrival of transnational corporations as the main genuine "drivers" of industrial capital's recovery of ground-rent, this phase of ISI was led by the proliferation and vigorous expanded reproduction of small nationally owned capitals. Coupled with the resulting greater diversification of the productive structure, this stage of the national process of capital accumulation entailed a remarkable growth and upskilling of the demand for labor-power, hence of employment. More specifically, manufacturing employment increased by around 70 percent between 1945 and 1952 (Iñigo Carrera 2007, 209). On these grounds, real wages not only continued their ascending trend but notably hiked: real labor compensation (i.e., gross wages plus social security contributions) doubled between 1945 and 1952 (see also figure 6.2). Decisively, this material necessity for expanded conditions of normal reproduction of labor-power was not confined to specific organs of the collective laborer but reached across the great bulk of the working class. Against the backdrop of this greater degree of universality or undifferentiation in the "norm of consumption" of wage-workers, it proved more "economical" for the reproduction of the unity of the capital accumulation process to socialize the mass production of, and access to, certain use-values (health, education, transport, leisure, culture, etc.) through state-provision (i.e., in the juridical form of "social rights of citizenship").

In sum, the aftermath of World War II was characterized by material and social changes in the accumulation of capital that required a significant advancement and socialization of the conditions of reproduction of labor-power (alongside the nationalization of widely used industrial inputs). These economic transformations had to be politically mediated by a renewed strengthening of the labor movement in the class struggle which, in turn, had to take concrete shape through an increasing scope and effective political potentiality of its organizations. However, such was the magnitude of the change involved in the quantitative and qualitative determination of the value of labor-power, that the labor movement's indirect "clientelistic" participation in the executive branch of the capitalist state did not suffice to personify the establishment of these novel conditions of reproduction, as it did under the previous political and ideological hegemony of the syndicalist/Radical Party "antagonistic unity." Under these different historical circumstances, the Argentine working class had to become fully and directly incorporated in the active management of the political power of the capitalist state. Coupled with the growth and multiplication of small nationally owned individual capitals as the main drivers of this stage of ISI, and also with the need for directly "confrontational" mechanisms of primary appropriation of a large proportion of total ground-rent by the state to mediate its subsequent flow into the process of capital accumulation, all this meant that distinct forms of political and ideological mediation had to develop to give course to these economic transformations. In contrast to the earlier integration into the cross-class electoral constituency of the Radical Party with the petty bourgeoisie and the less "reactionary" section of landowners, the great majority of the working class converged with the petty bourgeoisie in the "Peronist Party," which crystallized as the hegemonic "nationalistic-populist" political and ideological form.

However, toward the mid-1950s ground-rent plummeted again (see figure 6.3), and so did the scale of the accumulation of capital and real wages. A military coup brought Perón's second administration to an abrupt early end. Moreover, the turn of that decade saw the mass local establishment of transnational corporations as main beneficiaries and drivers of ground-rent-fueled accumulation at the expense of domestically owned small capitals. The material bases that took the form of the Peronist Party's mediation of the general political representation of the national total social capital thereby faded away. With most of the working class, who comprised the bulk of the voting population, still leaning toward Peronism, the latter became electorally banned. Thus, reduced again down to narrowly trade-unionist expressions, the ebbs and flows of the organized collective action of wage-workers (and so the movement of real wages) would reflect, over the following two decades, the extremely cyclical rhythm of the accumulation of capital, in turn determined by the heightened volatility of ground-rent inflows. The labor movement therefore became suddenly and firmly empowered during the upswing, but only to become swiftly weakened during the downturn. Overall, however, the trend throughout this period was for a continued expansion of the conditions of reproduction of labor-power, which reflected the ongoing upskilling of the composition of the collective laborer as ISI proceeded further into more complex branches of the social division of labor.

Now, although most of the labor movement remained "loyally" Peronist during this later phase, it needs to be stressed that the "anti-capitalist" left did not just disappear. However, it did prove to remain confined to a very precise and definite role in the class struggle over value of labor-power; namely, it spearheaded the organized action of workers to personify the ascending movement of wages during the opening phases of the cyclical upswing, in order to then become overshadowed by Peronist organizations and, eventually, to end up as the scapegoat and main target of the capitalist state's violence when the time came to force down wages during the downturn. Still, with the so-called Cordobazo in 1969 as symbolic political watershed, this period saw a multifarious proliferation of (formally) socialist or communist organizations (Leninist, Maoist, Trotskyist, "Guevarist," and even a radical "Peronist left," etc.). This would inaugurate a phase of effervescence and radicalization of leftist activism, which would gather force as ground-rent hiked again in the early 1970s, and which would even lead to expressions of armed struggle.

The real wage would thus reach its all-time historic peak in 1974, only to collapse a few years later as the inflow of ground-rent brusquely slowed down upon the sudden drop of the international prices of raw materials. Against the backdrop of the prior wave of radicalization of the class struggle, a civilian-backed military government was needed drastically to force down wages, through strategically calculated mass disappearance and assassination of wage-workers (militants and activists primarily among them).[7]

Our admittedly condensed historical sketch of the formation and development of the labor movement in Argentina during the twentieth century suffices to cast doubts on the explanatory validity of Bergquist's overly schematic typology to capture the former's complexity. We cannot expand further this critical discussion into an in-depth comparative direction which includes the four countries studied in Bergquist's book. However, some brief remarks on the allegedly contrasting case of Chile are in order.

SOME CRITICAL REFLECTIONS ON BERGQUIST'S CHARACTERIZATION OF THE HISTORICAL TRAJECTORY OF THE LABOR MOVEMENT IN CHILE

At first sight, the early phases of the labor movement in Chile do not show significant differences from the course taken in Argentina. Thus, it also comprised a left-leaning "differentiated unity" between a "revolutionary" or "extra-parliamentary" anarchist wing and a "reformist" leg personified by the Communist Party (Bergquist 1986, 68ff). Moreover, despite the formally "anti-capitalist" rhetoric (in correspondingly varying degrees depending on the organization), most of their effective practical efforts and objective transformative potentialities revolved around narrowly "economic" trade-unionist demands as well. Specifically, during the 1920s working-class struggles tended to aim at certain elementary issues like full freedom of association, right to strike, and working conditions, many of which eventually materialized with the passing of the 1924 labor law, which, however, was not only rather paltry in its "concessions" but actually remained dead letter for quite a few years to come (Bergquist 1986, 69). As matter of fact, by 1928 the Chilean labor movement had suffered a resounding defeat in the heavy hands of the repressive forces of the military-controlled capitalist state, and most of the first generation of its trade-union and political organizations had been virtually wiped out (Bergquist 1986, 70). So far, then, there seems to be no significant differences in the expressions, scope, and historical pattern of the class struggle in Chile: an initial growth and effervescence with rather modest concessions motorized by a "revolutionary" anarchist plus "reformist" communist party "antagonistic dyad," and subsequent defeat and acquiescence during 1920s and most of the 1930s. At any rate, one would conclude that the improvements in the material conditions of sale and productive consumption of labor-power during this formative phase of the labor movement actually were more meager than in Argentina, and that the reflux of the initial momentum of class antagonisms was, arguably, even more pronounced.

It is in the subsequent phase of resurgence that, according to Bergquist, Chile's latent more leftist inclinations came to the fore. Thus, after a hiatus of acquiescence of about ten years, the labor movement did not resurface in a "nationalistic-populist guise," but managed to rebuild an unprecedentedly powerful radical leftist trade union federation and two Marxist mass parties whose influence would overshadow that of the Communist Party in the 1920s. This upsurge of those radical organizations reached such momentum that they took part in the center-left electoral coalition (the Popular Front) that would hold office in 1938. As Bergquist himself notes, however, the "Marxist" participation in the Popular Front was as a minority partner, a condition that would persist in their subsequent electoral "successes" throughout the following decade (Bergquist 1986, 72–73). Moreover, Bergquist further observes that this allegedly broader electoral incidence was the other side of the same coin of an "economic" weakness in the trade union dimension of the class struggle, which remained tightly constrained by the restrictive and repressive labor laws and overall system of industrial relations that had been inherited virtually untouched from the paltry legislation passed in the 1920s (Bergquist 1986, 72). Finally, he remarks that all those achievements by "Marxist" or leftist organizations came at the very high economic, political, and ideological expense of tainting their "revolutionary" credentials (i.e., by fully embracing "reformist" electoral politics). This first ascending phase of the Chilean labor movement would become eventually defeated through multiple splits and fragmentations of its diverse organizations and the systematic repression of the Communist Party in 1949 (Bergquist 1986, 73).

According to Bergquist, the combativeness of the Chilean labor movement resurfaced in the 1950s. Thus, only at this arguably rather late stage did it engage in a determined and vigorous attempt at challenging the long-standing repressive and restrictive system of industrial relations. Still, at a broader political level the left remained committed to an "electoral road" to socialism. All in all, however, and as Bergquist's own narrative attests, the improvement in the conditions of reproduction of labor-power during this period remained comparatively modest. In effect, albeit with strong oscillations, average real wages would continue experiencing a rather moderate upward trend at least until the end of the 1950s (Rodriguez Weber 2014). Crucially, average real wages in Chile gravitated persistently around 15 percent of Argentina's

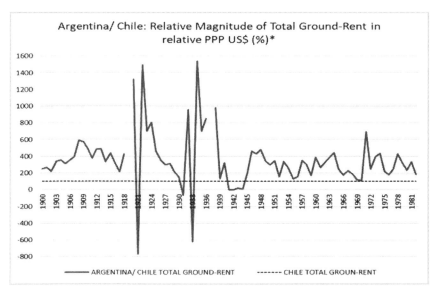

Figure 6.6.　Note: Data for 1919 and 1937 have been removed to preserve the scale of the chart Source: Iñigo Carrera (2007) for Argentina; Rivas Castro (2022) for Chile

purchasing power parity, equivalent between 1946 and 1958, actually standing below the relative levels that they had reached before 1945 (see figure 6.1). This, Bergquist continues, was the expression of a faltering and high inflation economy "as export production stagnated and the limits of import substituting industrialization were reached" (Bergquist 1986, 78). Yet he does not consider this to be an expression of the comparatively weaker developmental potentialities for capital accumulation, derived from lower inflows of ground-rent available for appropriation in the Chilean national space (see figure 6.6). Instead, in what we think is an overly contentious and untenable "voluntarist" view, the stagnation of capital accumulation is explained as the outcome of the "withering political and ideological offensive by the left against capitalism in general, and foreign capitalists in particular," which "jeopardized dependent capitalist development" (Bergquist 1986, 74).

Be that as it may, Bergquist submits that this wave of intensified militancy of organized labor and "Marxist" parties led to "increased support for their policies among workers and the electorate" during the 1960s. Eventually, this leftist ideological turn among the population at large crystallized in their hegemony within, and electoral victory of, the Popular Unity coalition, which "managed to elect Socialist Salvador Allende to the presidency" (Bergquist 1986, 74). The labor movement thus eventually assumed a direct active role in the general political personification of the national total social capital. However, as it transpires from Bergquist's own historical sketch, despite the "formal anti-capitalism" of the Popular Unity's ideology and rhetoric, both its organic electoral base and political program hardly differed from Peronism's in Argentina: a cross-class coalition between "progressive" and "nationalist" elements of the petty bourgeoisie and the great bulk of the working class, with "reformist" public policies aimed at the expansion and socialization of the conditions of reproduction of wage-workers, which, nevertheless, lagged far behind those of the Argentine workers in the same period.

Yet there is one noticeable difference. In Chile, the Popular Unity's nationalization program did include the copper export sector (i.e., the main ground-rent-bearing commodity). However, we do not think that this is self-evident proof of an unbridgeable ideological gulf between a powerful and "culturally autonomous" Chilean left, and a weak labor movement co-opted by corporatist populism in Argentina. As argued elsewhere in relation to the oil sector (Caligaris, Fitzsimons, and Starosta, 2024), due to the peculiar material conditions prevailing in mineral extractive industries, the latter are similarly prone to lead to the joint personification of capital and landed property, with a consequent tendency for a greater capture of ground-rent by mining individual capitals themselves. Thus, in a phase characterized by the need for a larger primary appropriation of ground-rent by the state prior to its subsequent channeling into the valorization process of the generality of individual capitals, the nationalization of copper companies emerged as the concrete form that gave "room to move" to the "antagonistic association" between capital-in-general and landed-property. In this sense, the nationalization of the mineral export sector was not a partial measure in the "electoral road to socialism," but a particular concrete form taken by the reproduction of the specificity (and "backwardness") of ground-rent-fueled accumulation in Chile. So much so that it would remain untouched by Pinochet's "neoliberal" military coup that overthrew Allende's government in 1973.

It seems to us that this brief critical reconstruction of Bergquist's own account of the historical trajectory of the Chilean left shows that there are no substantive differences of qualitative content vis-à-vis the Argentine case. It has also been an oscillating development which, beyond the anti-capitalist ideological rhetoric, had no transformative potentiality other than being a concrete form of the simplest determination of the class struggle as the necessary mediation in the establishment of the normal material conditions of reproduction of labor-power (i.e., it had a "reformist" content). In turn, the latter have been shaped by the developmental dynamics of the specific modality of capital accumulation based on ground-rent recovery by capital. As a matter of fact, this is where the essentially quantitative differences are to be found: the magnitude of the immanent potentialities of ground-rent-fueled capital accumulation in Chile have been arguably smaller, thus leading to a narrower and shallower ISI process. This means that the material basis for a steadier expansion of the conditions of reproduction of labor-power developed both later and to a lesser degree: the productive attributes of the collective laborer acquired a less complex configuration, the absorption of manufacturing employment was lower, and, therefore, the reproduction of a rural latent relative surplus population was larger. In brief, capitalist development in Chile generated a much more modest, fragmented (i.e., not universal), and unstable objective ground for working-class power, which has been synthetically manifested in the comparatively weaker upward historical trend of the real wage.

As a matter of fact, we think that the outward appearance of greater resilience of "culturally autonomous," leftist ideological, and organizational forms of the Chilean labor movement, rather than expressing a greater transformative potentiality of the class struggle, actually manifests the opposite content: it has been the form taken by the greater objective impotence of the working class to overcome the continued reproduction of harsher conditions of exploitation of their labor-power by capital. They were, to put it bluntly, expressions of "desperate resistance." In this sense, it could be argued that the longer-lived ideological or formal "anti-capitalism" of Chilean trade-union organizations manifested a more enduring and longer-lasting phase of the more restrictive and narrowly institutionalized modalities of managing class conflict, which delayed the universalization of unionization levels and the crystallization of effective legally sanctioned recognition of labor rights until significantly later. In a similar vein, until the late 1960s or early 1970s the electoral gains of Chilean "Marxist" parties were always with a minority share in ideologically very broad and "flexible" cross-class electoral coalitions alongside the more progressive elements of the urban petty bourgeoisie (Aggio 2008). Although this might have meant the preservation of a more pristine "cultural and institutional autonomy," in practice it meant a weaker incidence over the general political representation of the executive power of the capitalist state than the also cross-class, yet labor-led, populist Peronist Party in Argentina (Grinberg 2022).

CONCLUSION

The first conclusion that can be drawn from our discussion is that the comparative historical trajectories of the labor movements is much more complex and intricate than Bergquist's overly schematic model allows. For instance, "ideological autonomy" versus "co-option" is not a mutually exclusive dichotomy that can be easily applied to different countries but actually expresses distinct moments of the unfolding of the class struggle in its synchronic and diachronic unity, as it obtained throughout the highly cyclical movement of capital accumulation in both Argentina and Chile.

Nevertheless, we acknowledged that, to some extent, the contrast that Bergquist makes between the respective institutional and ideological forms of the labor movement in Argentina and Chile does make some sense. However, our own explanation of that phenomenon is at odds with Bergquist's. Thus, we argued that the alleged greater "cultural and institutional autonomy" of the Chilean labor movement, which Bergquist sees as a sign of its superior strength, has been in fact an expression of the less developed material basis of the capital accumulation process that, in turn, has led to weaker transformative potentialities in the class struggle over the normal conditions of reproduction of labor-power.

Paradoxically, the connection between a weaker material basis and a more radical ideological expression of the labor movement is acknowledged by Bergquist himself. Thus, he links "the failure of the export economy to promote capitalist expansion and economic development even indirectly" with the "strength and Marxist commitments of organized labor and the Left" and the broader predisposition of "more social groups . . . to share the Marxist vision of national problems" (Bergquist 1986, 78). By contrast, we have seen that he considers the farther-reaching material gains of the labor movement in Argentina as the "culprit" for the greatest ideological and organizational disappointment in the history of the Latin American working class. In our view, this amounts to making virtue out of necessity: the glorification of harsher conditions of exploitation for the sake of the preservation of an alleged ideological and institutional "purity." In sum, this seems to be an idiosyncratic version of "defeatism" applied to the class war, captured in the old political formula: "the worse, the better."

Still, the bottom line is that both "Peronism" and the Chilean "Marxist left" have been political and ideological forms of the reproduction of the specific Latin American modality of "ground-rent-fueled" accumulation, which, as we have argued, has allowed capital to retard the development of the productive powers of social labor and, therefore, the development of its own historical supersession through the conscious revolutionary action of the global working class.

NOTES

1. For a more in-depth discussion of the historically specific simplest determination of class struggle in the capitalist mode of production, see Starosta (2015, chapter 7).

2. By "moral" attributes of labor-power, we mean the aggregate of determinate forms of consciousness, self-understanding, attitudes, and dispositions that, coupled with the narrowly defined "technical" attributes, *also* need to be "set into motion whenever the workers produce a use-value of any kind." See Fitzsimons and Starosta (2018) for an in-depth discussion of this issue.

3. As we shall see in the next section, this statement merits a caveat, as the radicalization of the class struggle over the value of labor-power can actually embody the *opposite* content. Thus, under certain circumstances, it can express the *impotent* desperate resistance to the deterioration of the conditions of reproduction of wage-workers.

4. For the account of the content and form of these initial political and ideological expressions of the class struggle in Argentina, we fundamentally draw on Iñigo Carrera (2022).

5. As a matter of fact, the electoral base of the Radical Party was organically comprised of some segments of landowners and of the most concentrated agrarian capitalists, and, to a large extent, of the massively expanding petty bourgeoisie (Sigal and Gallo 1963). The latter expressed not only the multiplication of small capitals and petty commodity producers generated by the limited scale of the national process of capital accumulation, but also the mass of wage-workers employed as civil servants in the expanding state bureaucracy.

6. Admittedly, those expanded potentialities were limited to the simplest determination of the class struggle as a necessary form of the reproduction of capital and, more concretely, of its specifically "backward" modality in Argentina. However, as we have already mentioned, this is the only relevant determination as far as the critical assessment of Bergquist's contribution is concerned, whose effort is chiefly concerned with the comparative task of making sense of the respective degrees of "ideological and organizational autonomy" in the different national labor movements that comprise his study.

7. As a matter of fact, the disappearance and assassination of workers and activists already started under the Peronist administration through the state-sponsored creation of a brutal parapolice force called Argentine Anti-Communist Alliance.

Part III

EXTENDING THE FRAMEWORK

Chapter Seven

Labor/Nature in (Late) Capitalist Mexico[1]

Anna Zalik and Aleida Hernández-Cervantes

Ricardo Flores Magón, Mexican anarcho syndicalist, is respected even among liberal elites as a key figure in drafting Mexico's post-revolutionary constitution. His name adorns streets, schools, and cultural institutions across the country. But conventional analysis pays limited attention to his life as a radical organizer imprisoned in both Mexico and the United States for sedition. A fellow traveler of such individuals as Emma Goldman, he and his brother and their comrades—the "Magonistas"—were central to the Cananea miners' revolts suppressed by both Arizona rangers and Mexican Rurales (federal troops) in 1906, and subsequently of the Rio Blanco textile workers strikes of 1908. In 1912, he took part in a brief invasion of Baja California advanced by anarchists working alongside the Industrial Workers of the World. Flores Magón's organizing was thus internationalist and spanned what today are sometimes reified as extractive and productive (manufacturing) sectors. Ultimately, in the aftermath of the Mexican revolution, and in a set of processes that crushed its more radical branches, Flores Magón died in a Kansas prison cell in 1922. As a watershed in the oppression of labor movements in Mexico, the 1906 Cananea miners' oppression was a spark in the Mexican revolution. But in the aftermath of these movements, a crackdown on leftist revolutionaries occurred both south and north of the Mexican-US border. A century later, Cananea was once again the site of a major labor standoff, this time with the firm Grupo Mexico—where in 2010 striking Mineros were attacked by federal and state police. Thereafter, along with Los Mineros at Taxco (Guerrero) and Sombrete (Zacatecas), Section 65 of Los Mineros has remained in an ongoing strike against Grupo Mexico for fifteen years.[2]

A consideration of the life history of Mexican revolutionary Ricardo Flores Magón suggests the importance of these miners' struggles within the sweep of Mexican revolutionary history, a position that counters some conventional

US historiography of Mexico. Reexamining long-standing debates on the Mexican Revolution, including its outcomes for reformism and radicalism, one recent account centers Flores Magón's early student activism linking peasant uprisings to urban discontent (Lomnitz 2014). As a student journalist, Flores Magón revealed a massacre by Mexican federal troops of a peasant uprising in Chichahuaha in 1892 (Lomnitz 2014, 59–60). His subsequent writing stressed collusion between Mexican elites and US imperialism, including in perpetuating the abysmal conditions faced by mine workers, particularly on the Mexican side of the border at Cananea. Mexican radicals were especially threatening to elites in both Mexico and the United States because they did not focus on Mexican urban labor alone; rather, they were explicitly anti-imperialist and favored alliances with campesino sectors.[3] They also received support from American radicals.

We depart from Flores Magón's legacy to argue that in Mexico the control of national as well as transcontinental labor power and solidarity in extractive production has been central to shaping capitalist reregulation both within the Mexican state and with relation to external trade in the twentieth and early twenty-first centuries. Following Bergquist (1986) methodologically—as Kristin Ciupa and Jeffery R. Webber stress in the introduction to this volume—this chapter attends to the specificities of the Mexican context that distinguish the trajectory of twentieth-century Mexican state formation from the case studies—Argentina, Chile, Colombia, and Venezuela—central to Bergquist's (1986, 9–14) analytic in chapter 1. Near the end of the book, Bergquist (1986, 380) raises the contingency of the Mexican setting and suggests ways that the framework might be extended to Mexico by incorporating the peasantry as a branch of labor. While we welcome this general departure from Eurocentric Marxism in his account, we note that methodologically and conceptually the features unique to the Mexican context are gestured at but not discussed in this section. In particular, even in Mexico's nationalized energy-extractive sector, subsistence agriculture continues to act as a subsidy to capital (industry), with many campesinos also working shifts in oil and mining (Bergquist 1986, 380). Berquist largely references conditions in the nineteenth century, prior to the revolution, writing that a systematic demonstration is still to be undertaken of the

> extent to which the workers' struggle can illuminate much broader issues in modern Mexican historiography; most generally the ideological trajectory and institutionalization of the revolution itself over the next several decades . . . (and its role in) the dynamics of the economic "miracle" in the decades after 1940, and the origins of the grave crisis of contemporary Mexican political economy. (Bergquist 1986, 381)

It is to labor's role in key twentieth-century events in Mexico, although not precisely to those developments identified here by Bergquist, that this chapter attends.

Accordingly, in our analysis and in an attempt to write in consonance with Berquist's model of nuanced, historically driven discussion, we draw attention to key events that differentiate the Mexican setting, starting first with the Mexican Revolution and the 1917 constitution that emerged from it—one of the most progressive in the world—that distinguished the country from the rest of Latin America in the first two decades of the twentieth century. Second, the Cardenista period of the 1930s, during which the expropriation of Mexico's previously foreign-dominated, export-production oil and gas industry was accomplished. We would note that Bergquist indirectly refers to Mexico in this period in reference to the 1944 international worker's meeting in Venezuela that led to the ouster of communist groups from the Venezuelan worker's movement. Here Berquist (1986, 251) refers to the important presence of Mexican labor leader Vicente Lombardo Toledano— of the Confederación de Trabajadores de América Latina (Federation of Latin American Workers)—in encouraging Venezuelan worker unity in this period. But Berquist's reference to Lombardo Toledano does not lead to a discussion of Cardenismo, which Toledano supported. As a consequence of expropriation, production of (extracted) hydrocarbons was subsequently geared toward domestic developmental priorities rather than export, a process accompanied by state-labor corporatism as a key means of mediating social tensions. Third, the 1980s and the onset of neoliberalism crystallized in the North American Free Trade Agreement (NAFTA) signaled a major shift in Mexican labor regulation, initiating the beginning of the end of labor corporatism in energy and extractives. This shift was co-constituted with the reorientation of Mexican production toward the export of labor-power and the country's increasing structural dependence on imported staple crops, namely maize and, more recently, energy. From the angle of state reregulation the export of labor is manifest in (a) migrant workers returning remittances and (b) the hyperexploitation of frequently female, maquila workers subject to what may be understood—given its relationship to the overall wasting of (re) productive labor power—an extractive form of neoliberalism (Wright 2006; Killoran-McKibbin and Zalik 2016).

Although both Mexico's twentieth-century revolution and the foreign oil industry's expropriation by Mexico in 1938 were continentally and internationally distinctive events—with expropriation seen as a threat to the interests of the oil majors across the Global South—they also hold certain parallels with Bergquist's analysis. The radical, anti-imperialism of the oil workers in Mexico's foreign-owned petroleum sector during the revolutionary and immediate post-revolutionary era, first, was precisely central to making the expropriation possible. Here the Mexican context runs parallel to Bergquist's observations concerning labor radicalism occurring in export-oriented production complexes that are, among other things, owned by foreign capital. As per Bergquist's observations regarding owner nationality (Bergquist 1986, 11), labor radicalism among oil workers continued to be high in the post-revolution, pre-expropriation period. Second, following the shift in the oil and gas production complex away from foreign ownership and export orientation, radicalism was quelled through labor corporatism under the parastatal sector, also squaring with Bergquist's observations; this labor corporatism suppressed worker mobilization in both energy/extractives and manufacturing, but also fomented national development. And finally, under NAFTA's export-directed "race to the bottom" neoliberalism—the focus of our discussion in the second half of this chapter—rising, autonomous labor mobilization against foreign and private firms made possible significant gains for labor in the new millenium. These gains are expressed in Mexico's recent labor reform and accompanying revisions to the NAFTA 2.0 agreement (Canada-US Mexico Accord [CUSMA]) two decades subsequent to its first ratification in 1995. But for those gains to be achieved, and here revising and updating Bergquist's analysis for the neoliberal NAFTA era explicitly, transnational labor solidarity turned out to be a highly salient factor.

To conceptually situate this position, we draw attention to the relational nature of what may be described as the extractive-productive binary (Killoran and McKibbin 2016). Adhering, in part, to the overall position on nature and open dialectics with regard to capital, labor, and land that the editors—following Fernando Coronil—adopt in the volume, we nevertheless more centrally emphasize the intertwined dynamic of humans—as part of, and embedded in—extra-human nature, and thus integrate labor/nature as a conjoint category into our analysis. This is an approach that arises in indigenous ontologies and feminist political economy, and via conjoint understandings of human-labor-as-nature (Moore 2015). We thus adopt an approach to extraction that incorporates into its understanding of extracted material not just more-than-human nature, as it is conventionally understood, but also human labor.[4] As described by Sonja Killoran-McKibbin and Anna Zalik (2016), the hyperexploitation of (re)productive labor under neoliberalism is itself subject to extractive, export-oriented processes. Human labor in Mexico's maquila sector (both waged and/or, as conceptualized in feminist scholarship, subject to a double and triple reproductive workday), also experiences extreme gender violence in the sphere of reproduction. A discussion of this dynamic through the lens of a feminist analytic animates the penultimate section of this chapter. Under conditions of late neoliberal hyperexploitation, human labor is conceived by capital as waste (Wright 2006), and as wasted nature may thus be situated as part of the extractive complex.

Organizationally, we begin with the twentieth-century history of the hydrocarbon-energy and mining sectors, their position in Mexico's revolutionary and immediate post-revolutionary period, and end with the demise of state corporatism under neoliberal globalization crystallized in the NAFTA accord, an accord updated as CUSMA in the second decade of the twenty-first century. Prior to neoliberal reforms, Mexico's parastatal Pemex—the outgrowth of the expropriation of holdings of what would today be Shell, Chevron, and Exxon subsidiaries—employed more workers per barrel than any other oil company in the world. But accelerating from the late 1980s, as a prerequisite to neoliberal production, trade policy, and integration of Mexican oil and energy sectors into North American continental markets, Mexican oil and energy worker unions previously central to the corporatist state were crushed. This process spanned from the late 1980s through to the early 2000s, ultimately culminating in the 2014 energy reform. In the manufacturing (including maquila) sector—a sector that mushroomed alongside the demise of parastatals in energy and extractives—the problem of the hyperexploitation of frequently migrating women (Wright 2006) workers has been partially offset through the increasing strength of autonomous labor organizations. Over three decades of neoliberalism, the growth of transnational labor solidarity culminated in Mexico's 2019 labor reform and the re-ratification of NAFTA 2.0, now CUSMA. While these two periods differ substantially from one another, they suggest that even under labor corporatism workers can achieve gains, but that, indeed, under conditions of foreign ownership workers are most radicalized. Gains are also augmented under conditions of transnational labor organizing, as manifest in the context of twentieth-century globalization. In the late twentieth-century neoliberal era, democratic workers' movements—distinct from those affiliated with Institutional Revolutionary Party (PRI) corporatist structures and buttressed by continental labor solidarity shaped through, and consolidated after, struggles over the first NAFTA accord—have been key. Despite advances for some workers, however, women in the maquila sector and in the context of reproductive labor have remained subject to alarmingly high levels of violence in this same period—as discussed in the latter sections of this chapter. Indeed, in recent years, dangerous circumstances facing women, as well as student activists, in private and public life—including in the workplace, in domestic care work, and informal and formal labor—have spurred the country's most significant mass protests. These protests followed on the mobilization against rising fuel and commodity costs (the so-called gasolinazos) that resulted from the 2014 energy reform.

ON ENERGY AND EXTRACTIVE SECTOR WORKERS

The opening discussion on Flores Magón also underlines a problem in elite scholarship, which tends to obscure the importance of anarcho-syndicalism, radicalism, and labor mobilization in general to twentieth-century Mexican state formation. As per Bergquist's critique of mainstream interpretations, the fundamental role of workers and autonomous labor organizing to the development of the twentieth-century Latin American state remains hidden in much of the conventional writing on Flores Magón. For instance, Mexico's business daily *El Financiero* refers to Flores Magón as a founder of the "Partido Liberal Mexicano" without elucidating the politics of that party's name at the turn of the twentieth century[5] and his identity as an anarchist. Mexican historians offer an important corrective not only on Flores Magón, but on the agency of radical labor movements in shaping the contemporary Mexican state. This discrepancy in interpretation between left and conventional analysis is present in historiographical debate concerning the nationalization of the petroleum sector as well. On this subject, the role of labor and anti-imperialist mobilization to the expropriation of what would today be Shell and Chevron/ Exxon subsidiaries—a major event in Mexico's relationship with imperial powers—is deemed less salient in the American literature (Grayson 1988; Brown 2010). In contrast, the classic accounts of the expropriation by Mexican scholars (Meyer and Morales 1990; Silva Herzog 1964/2010)—and a more recent generation of historians of Mexico (Dwyer 2008)—emphasize the importance of popular mobilization, including labor-campesino alliances, to the expropriation of the oil sector and US lands in the 1930s and to ongoing state restructuring in Mexico throughout the twentieth century.

It is precisely the strength of labor-campesino alliances, and in accordance with Bergquist's framework, nationalist anti-imperialism (Bergquist 1986, 11) that brought to fruition the Mexican revolution. Among the outcomes of that revolution, for which Flores Magón is partially credited, is the 1917 constitution. Recognized as one of the first in the world (along with the Constitution of the Weimar Republic) to incorporate social rights in its text, an outcome of social movements struggles in the decade leading up to its promulgation, its Article 3 mandates the right to public, secular, and free education; its Article 27 acknowledges the rights of the peasantry; and its Article 123 recognizes the rights of the working class. Over subsequent decades, however, more radical branches of the revolutionary movements were betrayed in the interests of the liberal pacts that ensued, leading to state-corporatist mechanisms to quell radicalism. Here the labor charrismo[6] unfurled via the Partido Nacional Revolucionario, a party founded by Populist president Plutarco Calles after the assassination of Álvaro Obregón, was key. The Partido Nacional Revolucionario, which became the PRI in 1929, remained in power for seventy-one years and continues to hold significant political control in many parts of Mexico. Among significant features of social control exercised by the PRI are corporatist labor bodies and bosses unions that suppress autonomous and radical elements among both workers and campesinos. These bodies were strengthened in the period following the revolution, facilitating precisely the "institutionalization" of the revolution. National organizations enrolled in these processes have included the Confederacion de Trabajadores de Mexico, the Confederación Revolucionaria de Obreros y Campesinos, and the Confederación Regional Obrera Mexican, as well as the Sindicato Mexicano de Electricistas, Sindicato de Trabajadores Petroleros de la República Mexicana (STPRM), and los Mineros in the energy-extractive sector.[7]

The expropriation of the Mexican petroleum industry in 1938 was the first case of a southern nation taking significant control over subsoil resources,[8] long before the creation of the Organization of the Petroluem Exporting Countries. Significantly supported by oil workers' movements, President Lazaro Cardenas was heroized for the nationalization of the industry; people of all classes deposited their most prized possessions in Mexico City's central square to finance the costs of expropriation. Cardenas' later support for the Cuban revolution foreshadowed his son's political career as leader of the left-wing of the PRI which then split off to form the Partido Revolucionario Democrático (Party of the Democratic Revolution) in the 1980s. More recently, under Andrés Manuel López Obrador, a personality-driven split led to the formation of the Movimiento Regeneración Nacional (Movement for National Renewal, MORENA), which historically came to power in 2018, following a succession of fraudulent elections that had allowed elites to retain power throughout the twentieth and twenty-first centuries.[9]

After the expropriation of the foreign oil companies in 1938, the consolidation of the PRI-affiliated oil workers union, the STPRM, served as a fundamental pillar of the PRI's corporatist state apparatus for fifty years.[10] But the expropriation also widened an opening for popular claims on state institutions wherein capitalist regulation remained contested and challenged by social conflict. By constituting the subsoil, in both a legal and figurative sense, as the property of "los Mexicanos," the extractive resources of the nation were made a public good whose redistribution via the provision of well-compensated employment and social programs, or lack thereof, remain to date the site of significant autonomist movements.

LABOR HISTORIOGRAPHY AND HYDROCARBONS

Many nationalist histories of the Mexican expropriation of US and UK oil firms in 1938 center on oil worker mobilization. These accounts, part of (post)revolutionary Mexican historiography, center upon cross-class solidarity in the expropriation. Such historiographical interpretation formed part of solidifying Mexican national identity as at once anti-imperialist, yet compliant with domestic social stratification (Morton 2010; Mallon 2003). As an expression of anti-imperialism, the expropriation of these firms was crucial to (temporarily) solidifying a modified social democratic approach to national development promoted by parastatal industry, which would also serve the interests of Mexican national capitals against imperial capitals.

From the 1970s onward, accounts emerged concerning the antidemocratic tendencies of a Mexican polity dominated by PRI corporatism and the ways in which perverse incentives in the oil sector favored corruption in the STPRM and prompted environmental degradation in Mexico's Gulf region (Moreno Andrade 2007). But even with this partial shift in focus from imperialist oil agents to corrupt government and labor bureaucrats as impediments to social progress, labor remained front and center in analysis.

Indeed, an extensive political-popular literature, written in part by aspiring PRI politicians between the 1950s and the 1970s, depicts the nationalized industry as one of the party's great triumphs and portrays the intricacies of British and American intervention in Mexican national development—with the PRI ultimately triumphant (Silva Herzog 1964/2010). A more radical branch of this literature criticizes the Mexican state for failing to deliver on the promise of nationalization and counters the dominant discourse that "petroleum belongs to the nation," with the refrain that the petroleum in practice "belongs to a few." The overtly PRI partisan literature shares some features with the apologia and racism that Bergquist identifies in Justo Sierra's interpretation of the treatment of workers and Indigenous people in Mexico under the Porfiriato (Bergquist 1986, 238)—a term of referring to the government of General Porfirio Diaz and its alliance with foreign capital—against which the revolution was mobilized.

In contrast, some analyses of the expropriation by US-based historians render social mobilization and revolutionary organization of lesser consequence (Brown 2010; Grayson 1988), reflecting dominant anglophone interpretations of industrial relations in Latin America that Bergquist sought to correct.[11] The conventional US view held that foreign companies were able to extract oil only due to their previous investment of millions of dollars in the construction of roads, pipelines, and pumping stations. From this perspective, the United States "permitted" American-owned holdings to be expropriated because of

(a) the declining significance of Mexican production as a proportion of global availability/reserves and (b) the relatively limited US interests in Mexico when compared to British interests in Mexico—at a time when the United States was pleased to see the sun setting on the British empire. For what could be described as the US nationalist/imperialist stance, that Mexican nationalism came to target US imperialism had less to do with the violence of imperialism and more to do with Mexican authoritarian populism, which used nationalist ideology as a means to control diverse forces (Brown 1993/2022).

Leading Mexican studies of the history of the expropriation, among them that of Lorenzo Meyer (1972), tend to emphasize the extractivism of the industry prior to nationalization. In addition to siphoning profits to foreign firms, private capitalists in the oil and gas industry secured their operations violently, a subject critiqued on the pages of publications put out by the Flores Magón brothers and their fellow travelers. In the early twentieth century, foreign firms' activities were protected by *guardias blancas*, a general term describing the activities of private militias who subdued/terrorized campesino populations during the pre- and post-revolutionary period. The Anglo-American, Huasteca, and El Aguila companies, subsidiaries of Royal Dutch Shell and Standard Oil, employed these guardias blancas "to assassinate peaceful campesino proprietors of . . . small pieces of land" (Ros and Monsivais 1987, 290) and to suppress labor.

> The petroleum companies were always enemies of the unions. If they had managed to take their immense territory from under state sovereignty using mercenaries, criminals and soldiers, it was even easier to control workers and employees through the creation of "white unions" (company unions). The companies, like all colonial powers, ruled through corruption and abuse; these abuses generated more abuse and corruption that affected everyone from the highest levels of managements to the lowest rung of workers. (Benitez 1984, 117).

The foreign oil industry's negative environmental impact has also received attention, documented in Myrna Santiago's (2006) environmental history of the expropriation. Santiago also describes the pressures put on the widows of Mexican men who had died violently after resisting foreign oil companies' attempts to purchase their land. Under these conditions, the nationalist push for expropriation of foreign industry sought to simultaneously protect workers and local land tenure rights as well as conserve land and petroleum for future generations of Mexicans (Santiago 2006; 2009). Competing narratives of the development of the Mexican oil industry thus consist on the one hand of the promotion of US and UK entrepreneurs as positive influences on the national economy—the kind of interpretation countered by Bergquist and Lomnitz in their distinct ways—versus an anti-imperial description of the windfalls these private, foreign operators earned within Mexican borders, through the conjoint exploitation of labor/nature.

When Cárdenas came to power, 98 percent of the Mexican petroleum industry was controlled by foreign companies (sixteen in total), primarily El Aguila and the Huasteca. By 1934, the unions, particularly the independent-democratic ones of the Tampico area, had won wage increases through strikes. After founding the STPRM in 1936, the workers sought a collective agreement for labor control over operations, a forty-hour work week, and further increases in salaries and benefits. But the expropriation had implications far beyond Mexico in that it could serve as an example of resource sovereignty for other areas of Latin America. In this sense, the strategic and historic significance of the Mexican expropriation was equally important as the direct material implications of expelling the companies, given fears on the part of Royal Dutch Shell that the expropriation would set a precedent across Latin America. The nationalization also led to a significant departure from the case of the Venezuelan foreign-owned enclave. In Mexico regardless of socio-ecological critiques one can make of the sector, expropriation contributed to both the growth and development of the national economy (see in contrast, Bergquist 1986, chapter 4).

PRI corporatism solidified throughout the heyday of Keynesian policies, and in the context of the developmental state in Latin America. But as economic winds shifted toward a reregulation of global and state economies in the context of the oil shocks and their aftermath, transnational firms sought reentry once again into the Mexican hydrocarbon sector (Zalik 2006). Ultimately, the contradictions in global economic regulation made manifest in the debt crisis shaped the conditions for the demise of corporatist workers unions in Mexico and informed the 1988 neoliberal constitutional reform that resulted in agrarian displacement as well.

THE UNDOING OF ENERGY AND EXTRACTIVE LABOR UNDER NEOLIBERALISM

Concurrent with the oil shocks, the liberalization of Mexico's oil industry became a rising objective for US capital and global finance. The debt crisis provided an important opening in that the subsequent Mexican bailout involved collateral in Mexico oil. But a broader undoing and reform of the energy sector required that the corporatist bodies surrounding the nationalized industry be dismantled. Carlos Salinas's neoliberal presidency (1988–1994) in Mexico eroded the STPRM's power, a major turning point being the 1989 arrest of "La Quina," Joaquín Hernández Galicia, the charro leader of the STPRM. The creeping denationalization of the oil industry was advanced under successive pieces of oil industry restructuring that began in the 1970s in the Gulf of Mexico, among them the creation of "multiple services contracts" that allowed foreign firms autonomy in the Mexican offshore (Barbosa 2003; Shields 2003; Uribe Iniesta 2008).

In the energy sector more broadly, the dissolution of Mexico's former central power company entailed the 2009 layoff of forty-four thousand workers in a day (Cypher 2014; Arroyo and Zalik 2016). The Mexican drug war facilitated deepening extractivist relations, with affiliates of drug cartels in Northern Mexico selling stolen oil to US companies on the other side of the border. Facilitated by compliant or threatened oil workers, this contraband trade has been made possible via a violent protection racket along the lines of the pre-expropriation *guardias blancas* that controlled the oil workers. With this heightened cartel-associated violence as the backdrop, the 2014 Mexican energy reform significantly accelerated the privatization and denationalization of the oil and gas industry that began in the 1970s. In the lead-up to it, the US business press frequently identified state workers as an obstacle to "efficient" (read neoliberal) reforms of the country's oil sector given that Pemex had previously employed more workers per barrel than any other oil company in the world. After the implementation of NAFTA in 1994, and particularly with the 2014 energy reform that for the first time since the expropriation allowed foreign firms hydrocarbon production leases, ongoing privatization has advanced alongside reductions in labor in the nationalized sector and increased private subcontracting, while secure employment has significantly diminished (Arroyo and Zalik 2016). The *gasolinazo* protests against rising fuel and basic commodity costs of 2017 further drove the popularity of the opposition López Obrador's MORENA party. But even once the MORENA came to power in 2018, and in the context of López Obrador's discursive performance of energy sovereignty, labor's strength in the oil sector has not improved. This is particularly notable in the petrochemical corridor in the southeast.[12]

Thus, in the decades previous to the 2014 energy reform, and co-constitutive with the neoliberalism enshrined in the 1994 NAFTA, corporatist oil and extractive workers were laid off, while campesinos were displaced from their livelihoods. Mexico's declining sovereignty in food and energy via NAFTA led to the parallel decline of the variable capital (that is, human labor) quotient in agricultural and energy production. Continentally, this benefited predominantly US and, later, Canadian capital blocs (Grinspun and Shamshie 2007). As part of this process, Mexican state workers and campesinos were increasingly displaced into the maquila sector, away from both subsistence agriculture and the social security offered through protected jobs in national firms such as the oil company Pemex and the federal power company.[13] The exploitation of maquila workers, which—as we have theorized—may be understood through an extractive lens, was accordingly a result of a reregulation of a shift of labor out of parastatals and campesino livelihoods and into low-wage manufacturing, delivering returns to the maquila sector. Concurrently, Mexican and foreign capital took advantage of the growing reserve army of workers to crush labor in private extractive sectors as well. The long-standing strikes against Grupo México by Los Mineros referenced earlier, leading to the president of the Mexican Mineros Napoleon Gómez Urrutia seeking exile in Canada, offer a clear example. This long-term standoff is just one of many that demonstrate the resilience of workers' movements—whether engaged in agrarian livelihoods or formal employment—characterizing Mexican history. As discussed in the next section, with the movement of labor into the maquila sector, the possibility for solidaristic organizing there—in conjunction with labor "continentalism" (read internationalism)—has significantly increased.

ON MEXICO'S 2019 LABOR REFORM
AND THE MAQUILA SECTOR

What we will refer to as the late neoliberal period, following upon the 2008 global financial crash, overlapped with the demise of extractive-energy sector labor in Mexico. As per the previous discussion, the implementation of NAFTA was mutually constituted with the end of corporatist labor protections in Mexico's parastatal energy sector—both the STPRM and the Sindicato Mexicano de Electricistas—as well as for more advantaged PRI-affiliated unions in the private sector, including the Mineros. This crushing of organized, if corporatist, labor was a prerequisite for the further privatization and denationalization of an energy-extractive sector to which US and Canadian capitals successfully sought entry via NAFTA (see Hernández Cervantes and Zalik 2018). But the labor struggles that ensued due to NAFTA, notably through international/continental solidarity challenging global neoliberal pacts, marked a shift from previous dynamics. Poor working conditions in Mexico increasingly affected the material interests of American and, further afield, Canadian workers. Simultaneously, NAFTA's agricultural chapter led to the importation of corn and beans to the country, seriously undermining the Mexican campesino sector.

Thus, despite the layoffs and diminishing strength of parastatal unions as a consequence of NAFTA, the power of organized labor persists and has even redoubled as a key feature in the reregulation of capital in Mexico—via cross-continental labor and solidarity organizing. The January 1994 Zapatista uprising was a reaction precisely to the deepening dispossession wrought by neoliberalism. Over subsequent decades, and in the context of weakening sovereignty with respect to nature and natural resources, organized labor has sought and achieved greater autonomy—in part due to workers' pressures for wage protection across the continent. By the time that CUSMA came into effect twenty-five years later, gains had been achieved, notably those enshrined in Mexico's 2019 labor reform discussed in the following section. Despite increasing union autonomy and wage floors, however, the broader context of worker precarization continues; the rising wave of Central American and global migrants fleeing the violent aftermath of neoliberalism forms part of these conditions.

NAFTA AND NAFTA 2.0: LABOR STRUGGLES UNDER A CONTINENTAL MARKET

The original 1994 NAFTA was embedded within broader neoliberal trends in global trade architecture and financial regulation, crystallized in the 1995 World Trade Organization. Under NAFTA, Mexico's central commitment was to modify state regulatory and industrial structures toward a trade regime based on a logic of export, to modernize and make more "efficient" its industrial sector—entailing a reduced proportion of labor costs—and ultimately to market itself as a provider of cheap workers to the manufacturers. The growing reserve army of wage labor has drawn from those laid off from employment in parastatals, alongside the aforementioned "liberalization" of Mexican corn markets. The automotive and electronics sections of the maquiladora export industry were the most advantaged by this growing precarity. Following the implementation of NAFTA, the United States became Mexico's major trading partner, representing 80 to 90 percent of the Mexican export market. In this relationship, lower labor costs, weaker environmental regulations, and tax breaks have improved US firms' competitiveness against Asian and European imports. This was a boon to US capital given the intensified global competition accompanying the World Trade Organization. For Mexico, national subcontractors to the United States in the north of the country have been the main beneficiaries.

NAFTA truncated Mexico's economic modernization in that it oriented the national market to export. The export maquila sector was consolidated, and alongside it, infrastructural development favoring the transport of goods. The maquila sector's main structural advantage has been its low-wage structure and proximity to the United States, reflecting the spatial/

geographical features raised in Berquist's account elsewhere on the continent. International labor solidarity led to some improvements in working conditions, which went hand in hand with the crisis of that sector at the turn of the millenium as a result of a redirection of capital toward Asia (de la Garza Toledo 2007). The maquila sector continues to deliver a considerable volume of poorly remunerated jobs, contributing more than 10 percent of the members of the Mexican Social Security Institute that provides health-care coverage to private sector workers. But the sector's overall contribution to national revenues remains small; in its largest proportion, it consists of low-wage labor in modern enterprises. For Mexico, NAFTA's profits ultimately have remained in the hands of a few large maquiladora companies given that enormous asymmetries with its northern neighbor have prevented effective competition in other sectors.

In this context, the United States, Mexico, and Canada signed a renegotiated trade agreement on November 30, 2018, after López Obrador was elected, but a day before he assumed office. Following legislative debates in all three countries, and ultimate ratification, CUSMA entered into force on July 1, 2020. A number of key changes were implemented with particular resonance for Mexico—new percentages on rules of origin requirements for the automotive industry, a nominal fight against corruption, the protection of intellectual property, the environment and digital trade, and—crucially for our argument here—improved protections for labor.

Like the previous agreement, CUSMA emphasizes the transit of goods and capital between the signatory partners, without considering the unequal economic and social conditions among the treaty countries. The conditions arising from the agricultural chapter of NAFTA discussed earlier—which spurred considerable response in Mexico including the 2007 Sin Maíz No Hay País/Without Corn There is No Country movement in defense of food and agrarian sovereignty—have not altered under the new agreement. Likewise, while the controversial Investor State Dispute Settlement was removed for Canada and the United States—a major target of civil society criticism in those countries—it remains in force over Mexico's energy sector. The threat and use of international arbitration against Mexico was clearly in evidence in the 2022 standoff on energy/hydrocarbon sovereignty between the Mexican government on the one hand and the United States and Canada on the other. Nevertheless, the labor chapter of the accord represents a major step forward for manufacturing workers producing for continental markets. Buttressed by Mexico's 2019 labor reform, this advance is the result of three decades of solidarity work in the shadow of NAFTA.

COMMITMENTS TO LABOR RIGHTS FROM THE CUSMA: CHAPTER 23 AND LABOR REFORM IN MEXICO[14]

A key outcome of CUSMA is the dismantling of Mexico's labor corporatism, a system that the PRI had built, which enabled the proliferation of so-called *collective agreements for employer protection*. These prevent substantive collective bargaining and consist of formal legal contracts signed by a person claiming to represent workers, prior to their employment, and an employer who chooses a "union" with whom they need not genuinely negotiate. Similar to employer-protection unions, in Mexico approximately 90 percent of collective agreements prior to the negotiation of CUSMA were in fact *collective agreements for employer protection*. For decades, such agreements curtailed meaningful negotiations over working conditions.

Structurally, CUSMA's key variation from the first NAFTA agreement is its labor chapter, a departure from the "labor side agreement" of the 1994 accord. In Chapter 23 and an accompanying Appendix 23 A for Mexico—entitled "Worker Representation in Collective Bargaining in Mexico"—the parties commit to key International Labor Organization (ILO) principles, including the freedom of association. As opposed to CUSMA's environmental chapter, which various commentators describe as window dressing and/or contradictory, the labor chapter is praised by labor advocates. Chapter 23 establishes the obligation of the three signatory countries to respect and enforce internationally recognized labor rights in ILO declarations and conventions. The parties also agreed to the ILO principles for fair globalization—extending social services, social security, and worker protections; promoting social dialogue and tripartism; and implementing fundamental rights at work. If substantively realized, such commitments will continue to stymie the corporatist system that privileged bosses unions/charrismo and prevented meaningful labor action.

Extending and updating Bergquist for the new millenium, then, the conditions facing Mexico under CUSMA suggest the need to move beyond a comparative nation-state framework toward one that integrates the role of labor transnationalism to our understanding of Latin America under late neoliberalism. An outgrowth of decades of continental labor solidarity, the entire Annex 23A of the new agreement hinges on the country carrying out labor reforms to guarantee collective bargaining by the working class. Mexico's labor reform was in fact made a condition for CUSMA's entry into force (see paragraph 3 of Annex 23A). CUSMA requires that Annex 23A stipulations be incorporated into constitutionally protected national legislation in Mexico, presumably to prevent discretionary public policy at substate levels or technical guidelines that would allow for circumvention.

Mexico's broad-spectrum labor reform was approved by the Mexican Congress and published in the *Official Gazette of the Federation* on May 1, 2019. In the lead-up, Mexico ratified, in September 2018, ILO Convention 98 on the Right to Organize and Collective Bargaining; Mexico's signature had been pending since the convention came into effect in July 1949. Also of significance, the new "rules of origin" entail particular expectations for worker remuneration. Commentators such as academic and labor activist Alfonso Bouzas Ortíz (2022) argue that this is the most important modification to labor protection since the 1917 constitution given that the right to collective bargaining is now recognized in the constitutional text, putting into effect democratic unions of the working class (Bouzas Ortiz 2022).

The labor transnationalism that shaped CUSMA and the labor reform were significantly impelled in Mexico by the Frente Auténtico de Trabajo (Authentic Labor Front), in alliance with progressive unions in Canada and the United States, among them the United Steelworkers. This labor transnationalism facilitated Gómez Urrutia's exile to Canada and occurred in parallel with deepening trade relations between the two countries, especially in extractives and energy (see Hernandez-Cervantes and Zalik 2018). As Laura MacDonald (2020) explains, the Canada-Mexico relationship and Canadian investment that was understood as of minimal import prior to the first NAFTA accord—despite longer-term Canadian investment—grew significantly in import over the subsequent decades (see Gordon and Webber 2016), placing both parties in a somewhat allied position when Trump threatened to withdraw from the agreement. Ironically, although the worker protection provisions in the new agreement emerged from decades of labor internationalism through which Canada became a proponent of the Mexican labor reform, renewed protectionism under the Trump government ultimately made this palatable to conservatives via its compatibility with a "national jobs first" discourse that sought wage floors, notably in the automotive sector. These advances in labor protections, however, were also prompted by the overall conditions of violence in the workplace (including the domestic workplace) that has affected women as formal, informal, and reproductive labor under neoliberalism. We return here to Wright's theorization of how womens' labor is consumed in maquiladora industries, with "managers developing strategies to extract the maximum amount from the feminized workforce while externalizing all costs of social reproduction. In this manner, the women move from forms of value to waste, and this fluctuation is precisely part of their appeal to employers" (Wright 2006, 470). Wasting human labors parallels the generation of revenues through natural resource waste in extractive processes, separating the valued commodity from that which is considered useless. Here, workers themselves move from value forms to waste forms, which signals the adept processes of extraction at play in securing labor power (Killoran-McKibbin and Zalik 2016, 632).

GENDER AND EXTRACTIVE (RE)PRODUCTION
UNDER CONTINENTAL MARKETS

Despite some legislated advances, the conditions facing women in the maquila sector and elsewhere in the country remain very dangerous—an issue that drew global attention throughout the 1990s due to the femicides in Ciudad Juárez. Women remain subject to rising levels of gender-based violence, a problem that deepened alongside the steep increase in human trafficking globally over the past two decades, and which has greatly affected Mexico and Central America.

Gender rights are incorporated only to a limited degree in CUSMA, through articles asserting nondiscriminatory employment. The Trump administration strongly resisted the incorporation of transgender rights. Yet labor transnationalism under NAFTA was in part facilitated by transnational feminist solidarity. Women's working conditions—in formal, informal, and domestic labor—underline the importance not only of incorporating organized labor (as per Bergquist) and the labor of extraction (see Atabaki, Bini, and Ehsani 2018), but also the importance of considering questions of extraction from labor in Mexico. This point is clearly embedded in the organizing strategy and movement writing of the Magonistas, among whose key US supporters was a US suffragette (Lomnitz 2014). Considering the interconnectedness of the exploitation of labor and the exploitation of land/subsoil/nature draws attention to how hyperexploitation is derived from gender categories. It asks scholars to adopt a conjoint understanding of labor/nature in lieu of the binary approach that has largely situated extraction and wasting from human workers, and extraction and wasting from the more-than-human environment as distinct, rather than deeply relational, processes (see Killoran-McKibbin and Zalik 2016; Moore 2015).

Among Organisation for Economic Co-operation and Development countries, Mexico continues to have one of the largest employment gaps by gender; of the women who work, many do so in the informal sector, with little or no social protection, high insecurity, and low wages. The sexual division of labor and minimal services to support social reproduction continue to limit the options of Mexican women and girls, who account for more than three-quarters of unpaid domestic and care work. Women are thus marginalized in the formal economy, although they largely carry out the work that supports biological and social reproduction. Hours spent on unpaid work either restrict the time available for paid work or else contribute to the double or triple workday—involving reproductive and productive work in the former, with the addition of campesino/agrarian work in the latter. Feminist and gender and development scholars have widely analyzed and theorized these conditions. The culture of long working hours in Mexico, which affects a broad range of social classes, makes it difficult for parents to reconcile work with family life. Women as well as transgender people have suffered extremely high rates of violence in the home and public space, with their access to justice conditioned by socioeconomic status (Espino and Salvador 2013; Organisation for Economic Co-operation and Development 2017). Such conditions are at the root of massive women's protests over the past five years, among the most important social mobilizations in Mexico since the gasolinazo referenced earlier.

Consequently, it is apt to consider why the question of gender is largely absent from CUSMA's labor chapter (Chapter 23). Arguably, the rights of working women must be protected and guaranteed within the framework of production and commercial exchange so as to match the labor floor available to women and men. But as a category of differentiation, gender, like race— or, as Bergquist notes, ethnic composition—allows for a further offsetting of capitalist contradictions. Although the category of gender does not enter his analysis, differentiated ethnic composition, for Bergquist "complicated efforts (of workers) to achieve unity as a class and to meld nationalist sentiments . . . and class perceptions in a collective struggle to improve their lives" (Bergquist 1986, 11). The asymmetry of spatial relations across North America—with some resonance with Bergquist's geographic analysis but on the continental scale—is mirrored continentally and within Mexico in the asymmetries in power, the wage gap, discrimination, and violence against women in the world of work. This asymmetry ultimately cushions women in the middle classes—whether in the United States and Canada or in Mexico or elsewhere internationally—from the kinds of (re)productive labor that many Mexican and Central American women are compelled to take on for limited pay (Vergès 2019).

FROM LABOR TO (RE)PRODUCTIVE LABOR/ NATURE IN LATE CAPITALIST MEXICO

Just as the spatial asymmetry in power between CUSMA parties is mirrored by the inequality and wage gap on the basis of gender, so the varied coverage of labor radicalism in mainstream versus radical analyses of Mexican history is mirrored in the limited attention those histories have paid to gendered exploitation. For example, in a 2018 article, Óscar Alzaga, a Mexican democratic labor lawyer, writes:

> Strikes and major social struggles are an integral part of Mexican history, they have played a decisive role in that history, but they have been little studied. The official history (holds) the right . . . to deliberately downplay the importance of the workers' deeds. Ideologically, it is inconvenient for workers to become aware of their role in society and of the changes that their struggles generate in the political reality, in which they have left a deep mark despite everything. (Alzaga 2018, 412)

Akin to Bergquist's consideration of ethnic composition, Alzaga's essay contemplates the racialized nature of worker exploitation and the ways in which indigenous and Afro-descendant populations are particularly subject to such exploitation historically. Gender differentiation and discrimination, however, do not figure in the analysis—one that remains relegated largely to feminist scholarship.

In this chapter, we have adopted a view that sutures nature/labor under extractive-export-oriented production in part by attending to the co-constitution of reproduction/production under neoliberal regulation and by highlighting extractivist parallels across energy/mining and manufacturing/maquila sectors. This requires attention to how capitalist exploitation shifts to hyperexploited segments of labor, including humanity differentiated on the basis of both race and gender. A conjoint focus on the hyperexploitation of at once productive and reproductive labor allows us to see labor (human workers) and nature (mined, nonhuman material) as concurrently and necessarily simultaneously subject to extractive processes—labor/nature. Ultimately, on the basis of this approach and the specificity of Mexican history, we argue that the (organized) labor of extraction/(re)production continues to be central to capitalist regulation in twenty-first-century Mexico, just as it was throughout the twentieth century. But in addition to the conditions arising from labor radicalization in Mexico that parallel Bergquist's (1986) conceptualization, under early twentieth-century, pre-revolutionary, and early twenty-first-century neoliberal globalization, the role of transnational labor solidarity is highly salient to shaping working conditions in the energy-extractive sector and to "extracted" labor's achievements. Transnational solidarity has been central to the achievement of certain gains for workers since NAFTA and now CUSMA—just as such solidarity was salient in the early twentieth-century revolutionary period when the Magonistas were active.

As we have discussed, the nationalized oil industry in Mexico was co-constituted with a project of labor corporatism. The revolutionary constitution, and subsequently the expropriation of the oil industry under Cárdenas, partially decommodified labor and land/nature. This was a consequence of placing the means of production nominally in the hands of labor through the labor rights and entitlements that decades of social struggle by workers and radicals managed to enshrine in Article 123 of the 1917 constitution. But social reregulation under neoliberalism was shaped by disadvantaging extractive and energy sector workers and by the hyperexploitation of women as wasted labor in the maquila sector. Via an increasing organic composition of capital in energy/extractives—machinist technology replaced human labor or variable capital, while human labor/variable capital shifted into manufacturing—the highly precarious maquila sector is profitable precisely because of its low wage structure. Into this picture, twenty-five years of grassroots labor organizing and continental struggles, including among women engaged in simultaneously productive and reproductive labor in Mexico, ultimately bore legislative fruit in CUSMA's Article 23.

Given the tendency of mid- to late-twentieth-century social movements to reformism, it is important to return to the vignette with which we opened this chapter. Flores Magón's trajectory indicates that the transcontinental solidarity that secured achievements in CUSMA existed one hundred years previously. It is by no means the outgrowth of late-twentieth- and early twenty-first-century neoliberalism. The recently institutionalized labor solidarity expressed in CUSMA is built atop the legacy of transnational, radical, and, indeed, armed revolutionary movements of the past century and more— a history that liberal capitalism and indeed reformist solidarity deliberately obscures or conveniently forgets. The institutional reformism of today was also foreshadowed in the earlier period. The Magonista legacy indicates how radical branches of Mexico's revolutionary movements and intracontinental organizing were increasingly subject to incorporation, revealing the "growing limits on transnational grassroots movements in Mexican-American relations and their progressive subordination to intergovernmental channels" (Lomnitz 2014, 10).

With this history to guide us, we can thus center the role of labor organization in progressive change and in labor/nature-exporting complexes, as a countermovement to capitalist regulation but one that tends toward reformism rather than transformational outcomes. As opposed to accounts centering US authorities refusing to repatriate Ricardo's body to Mexico, Flores Magón's comrades in fact refused to allow his body to be used as a state symbol:

> The image of what had happened at Peter Kropotkin's funeral in Russia was fresh in the minds of the Mexican anarchists: a state funeral, orchestrated by Lenin, had been a nail in the coffin of Russian anarchism, which first had suffered implacable Communist persecution and now had to live with the state's

symbolic appropriation of its most revered leader. Similarly, President Álvaro Obregón had already wrenched control over a key sector of Mexico's labor movement from the anarchists, and now, they feared, he would use Ricardo's body to the same effect as Lenin had used Kropotkin's. . . . Enrique (Ricardo's brother) wrote telegrams to the press stating "We will not turn Ricardo's body in to any government, only to the workers." (Lomnitz 2014, 495)

Thus, coupling Coronil's open dialectics and Berquist's focus on labor organizing, Ricardo Flores Magón's legacy underscores the exploitation of the human body/labor and nature/society as deeply relational, conjoint processes, materially and symbolically.

NOTES

1. The authors thank Jeff Webber and Kristin Ciupa for careful feedback as well as participants in Toronto's Political Ecology Action Network for insightful comments on earlier drafts of this chapter.

2. Discussion on the consequences of this strike and recent moves to resolution are available via IndustriAll at https://www.industriall-union.org/los-mineros-wins-workers-their-share-of-profits-from-grupo-mexico and in recent press on Sonora at https://www.jornada.com.mx/notas/2023/01/08/sociedad/mineros-piden-intervencion-de-amlo-en-conflicto-laboral-en-cananea/.

3. This resonates with Bergquist's position emphasizing the role of both urban and rural workers. As he writes, "sometimes more industrial and urban sometimes more agricultural and rural, sometimes pure wage workers, sometimes not" (1986, 8), although his focus on export workers is more salient to Mexico before the revolution and less after.

4. Similar arguments appear in Arboleda (2016) and Mezzadra and Neilson (2019).

5. https://www.elfinanciero.com.mx/nacional/2022/01/03/quien-es-ricardo -flores-Magón -y-por-que-es-una-figura-relevante-en-la-historia-de-mexico/.

6. In Mexico, a reference to government-imposed business side union bosses known as "charros."

7. For a full theorization of this dynamic, see de la Garza Toledo (1993).

8. Bolivia, in fact, nationalized Standard Oil's small concessions in 1937, prior to Mexico, but this represented a tiny fraction of global reserves. China and Burma nationalized their oil industries in the late 1940s.

9. Here we refer specifically to the 1988 and 2006 election results—as well as the biased media coverage of 2012 that spurred the YoSoy132 student movement. The extent to which MORENA represents a transition from elite rule is itself the subject of contestation.

10. The STPRM, like the Confederación Revolucionaria de Obreros y Campesin and the Confederación Regional Obrera Mexican, was among the key PRI-affiliated labor unions.

11. See for instance Bergquist (1986, 205) on the central role of Venezuelan working class, and oil workers in particular, in shaping the "liberal economic and political order that has distinguished Venezuela's history from that of the majority of its Latin American neighbours. The central role of the labor movemet in this remarkable social process has been systematically ignored in U.S. scholarship on the subject."

12. Fieldwork and interviews 2019, 2022.

13. Formerly Luz y Fuerza del Centro (now the Federal Electrical Commission). In 2009, the Mexican government laid off forty-four thousand of its workers in one day.

14. This and subsequent sections of the chapter draw from Hernandez-Cervantes (2021).

Chapter Eight

From *Sindicalismo* to *Cooperativismo*

The Fragmentation of the Bolivian Miners' Movement

Andrea Marston

Driving through much of the Bolivian altiplano, one has the impression of a single, neverending mining operation. Heaps of discarded stones, chemically glossy tailings ponds, and variously sized holes appear frequently and without securitized fanfare. Numerous men and the occasional woman can be seen hauling sacks of ore, crushing ore under cement rollers, and filtering ore slurries through artisanal concentration systems. Semi-trucks carrying the refined product to merchant houses rattle down the road at an alarming speed, while the country's handful of smelters seem to operate nearly constantly.

Despite appearances, these mining operations do not belong to same company. Instead, most of them are run by mining cooperatives, or associations of small-scale independent miners. Varied in terms of target mineral, production capacity, and membership size, mining cooperatives are united by what they lack: corporate structures, significant capital inputs, and salaries. They are also united politically by the National Federation of Mining Cooperatives (Federación Nacional de Cooperativas Mineras [FENCOMIN]), under the auspices of which they exert considerable pressure in the national political arena. Although it is notoriously difficult to track the number of cooperative miners in Bolivia, a recent government report suggests an increase from sixty thousand in 2008 to more than 135,000 in 2021 (Viceministerio de Cooperativas Mineras 2021). These statistics, moreover, do not include either dependent family members or people whose jobs depend indirectly on cooperative mining—such as those working as mineral merchants or in miners' markets—meaning that the number of people economically reliant on cooperative mining is significantly greater. Regardless, the number of cooperative miners is exponentially greater than the number of miners for either the state mining corporation or the private sector, which in 2020 hovered around six thousand and forty-seven hundred, respectively (Zaconeta 2022).

Where did all these cooperative miners come from, and how are they connected to Bolivia's once-famously militant miners' unions? From the early twentieth century to 1985, tin mining was Bolivia's most profitable industry, and unionized tin miners were at the radical helm of the country's labor movement. Influenced by Marxist—especially Trotskyist—theories, tin miners led the charge during Bolivia's 1952 National Revolution and proceeded to struggle against a series of right-wing dictatorships from the mid-1960s onward. By the time that Charles Bergquist published *Labor in Latin America* (1986), however, Bolivia was in the throes of a dramatic political, economic, and labor transformation. In the decades since then, mining cooperatives have numerically and—at least as far as influence is concerned—politically surpassed the unions. Recently, mining cooperatives have also become the greatest ore producers in the country, producing 47.5 percent of total mineral value compared to 46.5 percent from the private sector and 6 percent from the state sector—although they contribute far, far less to national coffers (Ministerio de Minería y Metalurgia 2021).

The fragmentation of the Bolivian miners' movement, by which I mean the shift from a labor scene dominated by unions (*sindicalismo*) to a labor scene dominated by cooperatives (*cooperativismo*), progressed over three periods. First, from around 1960 to 1985, an unstable tin market and post-revolutionary economic contractions forced the Bolivian government to turn to foreign lending agencies for assistance. These loans were conditional on layoffs in the Mining Corporation of Bolivia (Corporación Minera de Bolivia [COMIBOL]), and the state began creating mining cooperatives to absorb excess—and potentially revolutionary—miners. Second, from 1985 to 2000, the global tin sector collapsed, and the Bolivian state introduced a series of neoliberal austerity measures that eviscerated the unionized mining sector. In this context, the state dramatically increased the number of mining cooperatives as a means of mollifying laid off workers, and these newly "cooperativized" miners made use of abandoned deposits, favorable political conditions, and their own organizing experience to cement their presence on the national political stage. Third, from roughly 2000 to 2020, the global commodity boom encouraged many people to seek employment in resource sectors at the same moment that a newly leftist government was refocusing its efforts on natural gas production, which has comparatively low labor requirements. The state supported mining cooperatives throughout this period in part because cooperatives absorb surplus labor, which is advantageous to capital, but more importantly because cooperative miners agitated collectively and often violently when their demands were unmet.

Using this history as an organizational device, the core question explored in this chapter is how the structural shift from *sindicalismo* to *cooperativismo* transformed the mine workers' labor movement, in terms of both their political goals and their ability to leverage their collective power to achieve these goals. Drawing on Bergquist's analysis of labor politics in Latin America's export-oriented industries, I argue that this shift triggered a major change in miners' political orientation even while the associational power once cultivated by the unions remains preserved within the cooperatives. While mid-twentieth-century Bolivian tin mining closely paralleled Bergquist's characterization of the Chilean nitrate and copper mining in the late nineteenth and early twentieth centuries, in terms of both the industries' structural features and their workers' political objectives, contemporary Bolivian mining (of tin and other metals) more closely resembles Bergquist's characterization of Colombian coffee cultivation, again in terms of both the industries' structural features and their workers' political objectives. In the earlier moment, Bolivian tin mining was a capital-intensive and technologically sophisticated enterprise that involved significant foreign investment, while tin miners were mostly Bolivians working in a handful of geographically isolated mining towns; in the contemporary moment, capital requirements for mining have decreased (in part because cooperative miners continue to employ existing technologies), cooperative miners are themselves in charge of the mining operations, and these operations are geographically dispersed across the country. In terms of their political objectives, unionized tin miners were stridently anti-imperialist and sought workers' control over mining operations, whereas cooperative miners typically demand more work areas, lower taxes, and reduced regulatory oversight. Despite all this, cooperative miners differ in practice from coffee growers and other workers in structurally similar locations in that they enjoy significantly more associational power, or the ability to behave as a collective actor (Ciupa and Webber, this volume). The main reason for this, I argue, is the legacy of the miners' unions. Many of the unions' organizing and mobilizing strategies have been transferred, along with the miners themselves, into the cooperatives, where they have been used for different purposes but to great effect. While the cooperatives' capacity to absorb surplus labor lends them some structural power, it is their inherited associational power that matters most.

Given that Bolivia was not a major focus of Bergquist's original analysis, I begin this chapter with an overview of the structural conditions of, and labor organizing within, the Bolivian tin mining sector since 1965. In this section, I also discuss the early history of cooperative mining, from its roots in colonial k'ajcheo (customary ore theft) to its adoption as a labor management strategy during the Cold War era. I then examine the period of neoliberal restructuring and the initial substantive explosion of mining cooperatives that started in the 1980s, focusing on the emerging relationship between the cooperatives, the unions, and the state. In the penultimate section, I explore the continued growth of mining cooperatives since the early 2000s, during decades marked by a global commodity boom, the election of left-leaning president Evo Morales, and renewed interest in state-led resource extraction, particularly natural gas. Finally, I conclude by reflecting on very recent developments in the Bolivian mining sector (2020–2022) and on the importance of understanding historical labor movements to adequately interpret their contemporary counterparts.

TIN MINING, LABOR ORGANIZING, AND COLD WAR COOPERATIVES, 1900–1985

Bolivia is famous for its silver mines, which underwrote Spanish imperial advances from the mid-sixteenth century onward and provided the nascent republic of Bolivia with much-needed foreign exchange throughout much of the nineteenth century. For labor movement scholars, however, the more relevant industry is the tin mining sector, which began at the turn of the twentieth century and quickly came to dominate Bolivia's economy. Buoyed by new applications for tin in Europe, Bolivia's tin sector seemed to enjoy limitless growth for the first several decades of new century, and its labor force expanded accordingly (Almaraz Paz 1980; Mitre 1993).

Bergquist's analysis suggests that radical political consciousness among workers is more likely in the presence of a "class and national dichotomy, one of national labor versus foreign capital" (1986, 11), in which export workers could mobilize patriotic sentiment to garner widespread support of class interests. In the case of Bolivia, this dichotomy was present but not clearly so: although workers were mostly Bolivian, company owners—at least from the 1920s onward—were Bolivian too. While early claims were made by a variety of foreign prospectors, especially Chilean and British, three Bolivian "tin barons" were ultimately able to edge out most foreign companies. By 1940, Carlos Victor Aramayo, Moritz Hochschild, and Simón I. Patiño had formed a small oligarchy who collectively controlled 80.9 percent of all Bolivian tin mines (Granados 2014, 50). The richest of these mines belonged to Simón I. Patiño, who became one of the wealthiest men in the world after finding tin in the departments of Potosí and Oruro.

Yet this focus on ownership masks the degree to which the tin barons relied on foreign banks, infrastructure, and technology to construct their tin mining empire. Patiño was particularly adept at building networks with commercial banks such as Anglo-South American Bank, which was headquartered between London and Santiago. This bank supported Patiño with the extension of credit lines and by assisting him as he stealthily purchased the majority of shares from the Chilean-controlled Compañía Estañifera Llallagua (Mitre 1993). Patiño also processed his ores in the British smelter Williams Harvey, incorporated his company in Delaware in 1924, and kept his profits in foreign banks (Saunders 2016). Finally, he and the other tin barons moved their ores along railroads that had been mostly paid for with British capital. It was through the railroad system that Britain in particular was able to cement its power in Bolivia at the turn of the century (Lora 1977). For instance, in 1904, as part of the formal peace treaty for the War of the Pacific (1879–1884), Chile agreed to build a railway between La Paz and Arica on the Chilean coast, but this railway was built by British companies and funded by the Anglo-South American Bank (Granados 2014). Similarly, in 1906 the Bolivian government signed the "Speyer contract," a joint venture with the National City Bank of New York and the Speyer Company to build railway lines that would connect major mining towns and cities; when Bolivia could not repay the loan, the foreign partners sold their shares to a British firm (Thomson et al. 2018, 193).

Tin miners were aware of foreign interests in the tin sector, and they were even more acutely aware of their shared structural position in the national economy. In line with Bergquist's model, the geography of the industry likely encouraged the development of this kind of class consciousness among tin miners. With the exception of a few mines within the boundaries of the city of Oruro, tin deposits were located relatively far from urban centers, and most workers were migrants from other regions of Bolivia, especially silver mining zones and the agricultural valleys (Oporto Ordóñez 2007). The settlements that sprang up around tin mines were classic company towns in that workers relied on the pulpería (company store) for staples such as bread and meat, lived in company housing, made use of company-provided medical services, and sent their children to the company-run school. For all these reasons, miners tended to develop stronger ties to distant mining zones, to which they were connected via railroad, than they did with nearby communities. Moreover, the railroads became conduits for political theory as well as tin ore, since the railway workers had already been politically radicalized in conversation with their Chilean counterparts (Smale 2010).

Particularly after the Chaco War (1932–1935), which pitted Bolivia in a losing struggle against Paraguay, miners also began to link their class struggle to the emergent sense of "popular nationalism" that, many historians have argued, was fostered on the Chaco frontlines (Zavaleta Mercado 1986). Returning to the mines at the war's end, miners used underground meeting and storage rooms, known as pauwiches, to share new ideas and debate political strategies. Unlike the alluvial tin deposits that were contemporaneously being discovered in Malaysia and Indonesia, Bolivian tin ores were found within hard-rock, vein-like lode formations, and the hollow spaces left behind once the ore was mined were known only to the miners who walked or crawled through them. As Mitchell (2011) has argued about British coal miners, Bolivian tin miners developed a sense of themselves as revolutionary proletarian nationalists while working in subterranean places with relatively little managerial oversight.

Aboveground, however, one of the most important factors in the tin labor movement was the unpaid, social reproductive labor of nonmining women organized as *amas de casa* (housewives). Bergquist's narrow focus on productive labor ruled out explicit inquiry into social reproductive labor, but in Bolivia at least it is difficult to understand the associational power of the miners' unions without attending to women's organizational efforts. Since they could not be directly penalized by the company for missed work or public protest, the amas de casa organized and participated in direct actions across the country (Barrios de Chungara 1978; Nash 1979). Most famously, in 1977, when leaders of the miners' unions had been incarcerated, a group of women and children led a hunger strike in downtown La Paz. This incident gained international visibility in a moment of fierce state oppression and resulted in the prisoners' release (Galeano 1997). Moreover, the presence of families—most of whom spoke Quechua at home—worked to integrate indigenous communal practices into the labor unions, strengthening the latter and contributing to workers' sense that they were doubly oppressed, both as proletariat and as indios (Rivera Cusicanqui 1987). While Bergquist found that the unmarried status of Chilean nitrate miners is what permitted their hypermobility and strengthened their power as laborers—so much so that Chilean companies tried desperately to hire married men instead (1986, 39)—the integration of kinship networks into the Bolivian tin miners' unions meant that organizing happened in community spaces as much as it did in the mines. Indeed, contra Bergquist, other authors have identified mutually supportive linkages between households and unions in Chilean copper mines as well (Finn 1998; Klubock 1998).

With these support systems, unionized tin miners in Bolivia led the charge during the 1952 National Revolution, which united campesino militias, workers' unions, and urban intellectuals against the country's traditional elites. Foremost among these traditional elites were the tin barons, whose hold on the country's resources had tightened following the ups and downs of the global tin market. When prices collapsed in the late 1920s, smaller firms went out of business; when Bolivia became a founding member of the first international tin cartel in 1931, the tin barons spoke on behalf of the country (Mitre 1993). Although business was constrained by events of World War

II—Bolivia became the only supplier of significance to the Allies and was forced to ship its product to smelters in Texas, where prices were kept artificially low—it remained the most valuable industry in Bolivia (Dunkerley 1984). Therefore, one of the central rallying cries of the National Revolution was the nationalization of the tin industry, which had clearly made some people very rich while failing to contribute to widespread economic growth—an imbalance that tends to contribute to radical worker consciousness, according to Bergquist's analysis. Shaped by both their interpretations of Marxist political philosophy and growing nationalist sentiment, unionized tin miners believed that it was not only their surplus labor but also their country's patrimony that had been accumulated in few hands. Although the largest mining companies were Bolivian in name, miners saw that the benefits of these enterprises were enjoyed far beyond Bolivian borders. In response to their demands, the newly established government nationalized the tin barons' holdings and created COMIBOL in October 1952.

The corporation's financial troubles, however, started almost as soon as the post-revolutionary dust had settled. Headed by Juan Lechín, the Syndical Federation of Bolivian Mine Workers (Federación Sindical de Trabajadores Mineros Bolivianos [FSTMB]) had won "workers' control" over the new state mining corporation, which meant that they were involved in decision-making processes and even had veto powers. One of the FSTMB's core demands was that COMIBOL hire back all the miners who had been fired for political or medical reasons. The salaried workforce swelled from twenty-four thousand in 1952 to 35,660 in 1956 (Espinoza 2013, 56). In a context of falling tin prices, this threw the country's economy into disarray. However, this financial crisis was also the result of policies enacted by the center-left government, which had chosen to "nationalize" the mines via forced sale rather than expropriation without compensation, which is what the workers had demanded. In its early years, COMIBOL had to keep paying former mine owners in annual installments that were a huge blow to profit margins (Canelas Orellana 1981, 60–61). All these internal problems were exacerbated by changes in the international market after World War II, when trade embargos lifted and military demands diminished.

In the face of COMIBOL's mounting debts, the new Bolivian president, Víctor Paz Estenssoro, approached the international community for financial assistance. In 1961, his diplomatic efforts crystallized in the Triangular Plan, a sixty-two million US dollar program funded by the Inter-American Development Bank and the governments of West Germany and the United States (Burke 1987). Conceivably a precursor to later neoliberal policies, the Triangular Plan aimed to "rehabilitate" the flagging COMIBOL, but the funds were conditional on a series of massive worker layoffs. Melvin Burke highlights that the unions were initially amenable to the layoffs, since it was clear that some workforce reduction was needed, and the compensation packages were generous. Their attitudes, however, changed as the plan progressed and the government's methods grew violent.

By 1965, more than five thousand miners had been laid off, but COMI-BOL was still not generating a profit. At this point, General René Barrientos Ortuño, who had come to power via a coup in 1964, launched another round of worker cutbacks—this time without generous compensation packages. Instead, the Barrientos government created "mining cooperatives" and "subsidiary organizations" that could mine independently from the state corporation, absorbing laborers and relieving the corporation of the burden of paying salaries. The unions fought back against the new austerity measures—with the most violent confrontation occurring in Llallagua on June 23, 1967, when soldiers were dispatched to attack miners during the nighttime festival of San Juan—but Barrientos's plan continued apace. When the Triangular Program ended in 1970, COMIBOL's property was dotted with forty-eight cooperatives which collectively had five thousand official members and four thousand associate members (Burke 1987, 33). By not only legalizing but actively institutionalizing mining cooperatives, COMIBOL reduced its expenses and neutralized the unions. The cooperatives thus crystallized as a strategy adopted by the Bolivian government to preserve the profitability of its failing state corporation in the post-revolutionary period.

At the same time that COMIBOL was creating cooperatives from scratch, it also began formalizing preexisting groups of independent and small-scale miners who had always worked on the margins of mining properties. According to most historical records, the oldest cooperative in the country was founded in the city of Potosí in the immediate aftermath of the global economic crash of 1929 (Mariobo Morena 2007). But this group was not technically a cooperative when it first formed; rather, it was a "union of free workers" claiming a lineage with k'ajcheo, a practice that began as organized ore theft by miners in sixteenth century and slowly evolved into a customary right in the seventeenth and eighteenth centuries.[1] During the economic crisis of the 1930s, however, many unemployed miners turned to k'ajcheo as a full-time livelihood strategy, and they formed the collective K'ajchas Libres y Palliris to combine their extractive efforts and avoid the commitment of selling their ore to a single processing plant. They did not become a cooperative until 1958, when the Bolivian government passed the General Law of Cooperative Societies (#5053), after which they functioned as something of a template for the many autonomous societies and cooperatives that began in earnest in the 1960s.

For most of the twentieth century, Bolivian tin miners enjoyed significant structural power: as productive workers in the country's most important industry, they were capable of disrupting the accumulation of capital with relatively local actions, including work stoppages. Moreover, tin mining was capital intensive, involved significant foreign (especially British) control of capital, took place in geographically isolated locations that were connected to one another by railroad, and relied on mostly Bolivian labor—a series of structural factors that Bergquist identified in the Chilean copper and nitrate mining industries, and which he associated with a strong and progressively oriented labor movement. As in Chile, Bolivian mine workers not only became a powerful collective actor but also found widespread support among other Bolivians by articulating their demands with an emergent popular nationalism. The state began establishing mining cooperatives in the 1960s and 1970s as part of a deliberate effort to undermine the powerful miners' unions, but during this period the cooperatives remained a relatively small and politically demobilized percentage of the mining workforce. This changed in the mid-1980s, when more dramatic restructuring efforts permanently broke the miners' unions.

NEOLIBERAL RESTRUCTURING AND THE RISE OF MINING COOPERATIVES, 1985–2000

The Latin American structural economists of the 1960s and 1970s, whose work Bergquist analyzes in *Labor in Latin America*, developed theories of global dependency and contributed to the widespread adoption of import substitution industrialization across Latin America. Akin to Keynesianism in the United States, import substitution industrialization involved the subsidization of domestic industries, government-funded construction projects, and import regulation, though it put more emphasis on holistic state economic planning than its northern counterpart. But with the global debt crisis of the 1980s— which was in turn spurred by the irresponsible recycling of "petrodollars" as loans to governments in the Global South, followed by a sudden hike in interest rates by the US Federal Reserve—import substitution industrialization was no longer a viable option. The only financial relief for debt-stricken countries came with golden handcuffs: in exchange for their help, the World Bank and International Monetary Fund required strict economic structural adjustments of indebted countries. These conditions forced open national borders to "free" trade, drastically reduced state services, and privatized state industries—a recipe that has since been described as economic neoliberalization. As state institutions and industries were shuttered or winnowed down to size, state employees had their salaries frozen or were laid off altogether (Gowan 1999).

In Bolivia, this global economic challenge was exacerbated by crisis in the tin sector. During and after World War II, the United States had stockpiled 350,000 tons of the metal, equivalent to world consumption for two years (Mallory 1990, 839). In the 1980s, however, when tin was no longer as "strategic" a metal as it had once been, the United States began dumping its stockpile, which dramatically depressed global prices. The International Tin Council—the tin producers' cartel that had expanded since its formation in the 1930s—tried to buy all the tin off the market to stabilize prices, but this involved extensive borrowing from commercial banks. The International Tin Council hit its credit limit in 1985, which triggered such a rapid collapse of tin prices that the metal was delisted from the London Stock Exchange for about three years (US Geological Survey 2013, 181). Coupled with hyper-inflation in the wake of the global debt crisis, the collapse of the tin market constituted an economic disruption severe enough to force through neoliberal austerity measures.

Against this backdrop, Bolivia had the misfortune of being one of the first Latin American countries subjected to economic "shocks" coordinated by the World Bank and International Monetary Fund. Less than a month after having been sworn in as the country's first democratically elected president in two decades, Víctor Paz Estenssoro—ironically, the same man who had established COMIBOL after the 1952 National Revolution—signed Supreme Decree (Decreto Supremo [DS]) 21060 on August 29, 1985. Much more than a single policy, DS21060 targeted hyperinflation by allowing the currency to float against the dollar, ended protectionist regimes, and privatized state-owned enterprises (Perreault 2006). In one fell swoop, this decree seemed to undo three decades' worth of political organizing by workers' and peasants' unions across the country.

More than any other sector, DS21060 explicitly targeted COMIBOL's operations. Today, neoliberalism in Bolivia is nearly synonymous with relo-calización (relocalization)—a euphemism for the massive layoffs of union-ized tin miners. Most miners, however, prefer to call it the masacre blanca (white massacre) because few were able to turn their severance packages into viable new careers. Truckloads of miners began to leave mining towns across the highlands, transforming them into ghost towns nearly overnight.

Yet many miners soon returned. They came following the 1987 passage of another decree, DS21377, that permitted the formation of mining coopera-tives in COMIBOL's abandoned properties. The impetus for this decree was that many laid-off miners had gone to cultivate coca in the Chapare, a low-land valley outside of Cochabamba, and the explosion of coca and its refined product—cocaine—was a political problem for the Paz Estenssoro administration, which was relying on the goodwill of the United States to negotiate its way out of debt. As it had in the 1960s, the Bolivian state once again began creating mining cooperatives to disrupt the power of export-oriented labor; in this case, however, the laborers in question were linked both to the formal tin mining sector and the much newer and more illicit coca growing sector.

Former miners flocked back to mining towns. Between 1986 and 1990, the number of mining cooperatives in Bolivia jumped from 325 to 586, with the new ones all located in the former holdings of COMIBOL (Poveda Ávila 2014, 97). Rather than a one-to-one ratio—or one mine being transferred to one cooperative—mines that had been treated as a single operation were often divided among several cooperatives that took control of different sections of the mine, including above- and belowground, holdings. For example, one of Patiño's ex-holdings, the Llallagua tin mine, was divided among seven cooperatives: four working in different subterranean sections, two processing ore sands through surface-level artisanal systems, and one operating a Patiño-era ore refining plant (Marston 2020). In cases where mines were only partially opened up to cooperative mining, the cooperatives typically received exhausted or unproductive work areas, while richer sites were retained by private companies and/or a much-reduced COMIBOL. In these cases, the relationship between these mining cooperatives and companies varied wildly. For instance, while several mining cooperatives were established in both the Huanuni tin mine and Colquri silver-tin-zinc mine in the 1990s, COMIBOL continued small operations until private companies were interested in taking over, which happened in Huanuni in 2000 with the British company RBG/Allied Deals and in Colquiri in 1999 with the Bolivian company COMSUR (Poveda Ávila 2014). In both these mines, the relation between cooperativistas and salaried miners was tense, as I elaborate in the next section. On the other end of the spectrum, in the famous Cerro Rico in the city of Potosí, mining cooperatives that predated neoliberalization by many decades formed partnerships with the private companies that started entering in the 1990s (Francescone 2015). Regardless of variation, however, it was generally the case that mining cooperatives were allotted the least lucrative deposits with the lowest possibilities for development.

In technical terms, mining cooperatives are collective tenants within COMIBOL concessions. As analysts have pointed out, however, government policies since the 1990s have increasingly favored cooperative miners (Francescone and Díaz 2013). First, cooperative miners pay relatively little in rent and royalties and no formal taxes to speak of. What they do pay comes in the form of three small income deductions: one for exploitation rights, one for the use of abandoned COMIBOL machinery, and one royalty that varies depending on mineral market prices. As legally nonprofit entities, mining cooperatives do not pay any taxes beyond royalties, and the royalty amounts (which are different for each metal) are capped at rates that made sense in the 1980s, when all metal prices were low, but cannot adequately deal with current high prices. Second, several support systems were put in place for mining cooperatives, including technical assistance from COMIBOL and financial support from the Central Bank of Bolivia. Third, although mining cooperatives are supposed to adhere to principles of cooperative organization as well as general Bolivian labor standards, neither of these conditions are enforced in practice. Outside their collective agreements with COMIBOL, few mining cooperatives have genuinely collectivized operations. In most instances, cooperatives subdivide their contracted areas into dozens or even hundreds of parajes, or work areas, each of which is operated by a work crew, or cuadrilla, that might be composed of between two and thirty people. Profits and expenses are not redistributed across the cooperative as a whole, and they are hierarchically redistributed even within a single cuadrilla. Each cuadrilla brings their own ore concentrates to market in a commercial warehouse, and it is at this moment that deductions are calculated. This system means that some cuadrillas grow wealthy while others work for years at a loss. Indeed, in some regions of Bolivia, such as the city of Potosí, the uneven accumulation of wealth has resulted in a kind of tercerización (outsourcing) whereby some cooperative members accumulate enough capital to become stakeholders and employers rather than workers. Cooperative miners cannot legally hire third-party workers at all, and those who do so anyway rarely respect labor laws, often paying below the minimum wage or hiring children to work alongside adults.

The structural position of mining cooperatives within Bolivia's mining sector, as well as their own internal operations, has had a contradictory impact on the organizational capacity and political objectives of workers in Bolivia's mining sector. On the one hand, the absorption of so many recently laid-off workers transformed FENCOMIN from a relatively low-profile organization into a coordinator of major protests and political actions. Although it was founded in 1968, at the height of the Triangular Plan, FENCOMIN only began organizing nationwide roadblocks and releasing lists of demands—two strategies long practiced by unionized miners—in the late 1990s. On the other hand, cooperative miners made very different demands than those of their salaried counterparts. Without formal employers, they could not logically demand eight-hour workdays, better housing, higher wages, or better safety equipment—all of which were demands made by the unions. Instead, they called for expanded work areas, relaxed environmental and labor standards, lower royalty rates, and expanded lines of credit. Although they did not technically own their means of production, as their subterranean deposits and most of their machinery was rented from COMIBOL, their demands were nevertheless more suggestive of the petit bourgeoisie than the proletariat. They inherited their mettle from the unions, as well as their general conditions of impoverishment, but not necessarily their political orientation. More specifically, they have taken the organizational strategies and protest tactics used by the unions and deployed them for very different ends: they are highly organized, but are no longer using their associational power to disrupt the accumulation of capital.

Thinking with Bergquist's analysis of export-oriented workers, Bolivian mining cooperatives might be imagined as similar to Colombian coffee growers, since both industries wound up favoring small and dispersed instead of large and concentrated forms of ownership, and in both cases this sectoral orientation led to a relatively conservative workers' movement. Yet tin mining is distinct because of its history: it began as a highly concentrated industry, it required substantial investments in infrastructure and machinery to become operational, and it used to house one of the continent's most militant labor movements. Mining cooperatives could not operate at all if the initial investments in mining infrastructure and technology had not already been made; just as importantly, they would not enjoy their current associational power if not for the social relations that they inherited from the unionized tin miners.

COMMODITY BOOM AND NEW LEFT GOVERNMENT, 2000–2020

In both the 1960s to 1970s and the 1980s to 1990s, mining cooperatives were created to manage the unruly social effects of a large reserve army of workers in times of economic contraction. In both cases, tin prices were unreliable, falling unsteadily in the first period and collapsing completely in the second period. Starting in the early 2000s, mining cooperatives also grew, but for different reasons. Instead of falling prices, the first few years of the new century were marked by a major global commodity boom, spurred mostly by China's rapid industrialization. In this context, Bolivians who had never before been miners began forming or joining mining cooperatives, since it had become a much more lucrative business than in years past. The influx of people into the cooperative sector, moreover, was supported by the political and economic agendas of President Evo Morales, whose 2005 election marked a decisive turning point for the cooperatives.

The protests that proceeded Morales's rise to power—such as the 2000 Cochabamba Water War, the 2003 nationwide Gas War, and the 2005 El

Alto-La Paz Water War—were all influenced by the organizing expertise of ex-unionized miners who, after having been laid off in the 1980s, moved to the peri-urban areas of major cities and got involved in neighborhood associations (juntas vecinales). Although no longer organized as workers, these ex-miners continued to shape political outcomes (Gill 1997). Meanwhile, the (much-reduced) federation of unionized miners, the FSTMB, joined urban social organizations, campesinos' unions, and indigenous federations as early supporters of Morales, an intersectoral coalition that resulted in the victory of the country's first ever indigenous-identifying president.

Although their involvement is less well-documented, mining cooperatives also supported Morales's rise to power. Most of this support took the form of public demonstrations: cooperative miners are notorious for their militant—and sometimes violent—commitment to public protests and roadblocks. For instance, they showed up en masse at the 2003 Gas War blockades, which were protesting the construction of a natural gas pipeline through Chile, a country widely understood to be Bolivia's enemy since the War of the Pacific (1879–1883). Still articulating the nationalist sentiment for which the unions were famous, mining cooperatives protested imperialism in the gas industry—an ironic position, given that much of the ore extracted by cooperatives—all except what is sold to the state-owned smelter, Vinto—is exported by private commercializers to the Chilean coast. Cooperative miners also supported Morales electorally; although they do not constitute a voting bloc in and of themselves, they are overrepresented in rural municipal governments, where they run campaigns and have an outsized influence over electoral outcomes.

As if to mark his allegiance to the cooperative sector, Morales chose Walter Villarroel, a cooperative tin miner from the town of Huanuni, as his minister of mining and metallurgy, which marked the first time a cooperative miner had been elevated to such an important position. Conflicts between the cooperative and state mining sectors began, however, just a few short months into Villarroel's term—and they began in Villarroel's hometown. The Huanuni mine had been shared between four cooperatives and the British company RBG/Allied Deals since 2000. In 2002, RBG/Allied Deals was charged with fraud in the United Kingdom after it was discovered that the company had been operating a global mining Ponzi scheme. Upon hearing this news, the salaried miners in Huanuni expelled the company from the mine, and Bolivian authorities began the process of dissolving the joint venture contract. On the other side of the ocean, however, the British judicial system granted the consulting company Grant Thornton responsibility for liquidating RBG/ Allied Deal's assets, and Grant Thornton made an agreement with Huanuni's mining cooperatives that allowed them to buy the concession outright. The

Bolivian state, however, refused to recognized this agreement. In retaliation, on October 4, 2006, the cooperativistas took the mine by force, exchanging bullets and dynamite with salaried miners in a conflict that lasted three days and left seventeen people dead (Howard and Dangl 2006). The solution introduced by the Morales government was a full nationalization of the mine, including both its privatized and cooperativized workers, in a formal reactivation of COMIBOL. Altogether, more than four thousand cooperative miners and eight hundred ex-employees of RBG/Allied Deals became COMIBOL employees in the Morales government's first "re-nationalized" mine (Ruiz Arrieta 2012). Villarroel, meanwhile, was removed from his post.

This nationalization happened at an interesting moment for the Morales government, which had also just announced that it would be nationalizing natural gas production through its state corporation YPFB. Although the degree to which this latter was a "true" nationalization is debatable, given that the state only purchased the majority of the company's shares rather than expropriating any of its holdings (Kaup 2010), the nationalization of natural gas nevertheless had a huge impact on Bolivia's economy. Rents from natural gas quickly became the state's main source of income, which it redistributed in the form of social grants, rural infrastructure, and universal pension plans. Given events in Huanuni, commentators wondered if a similar nationalization was also coming to the mining sector. But such hopes slowly dissipated: to this day, Huanuni remains the only profitable mine to have been fully nationalized.

This is not to say that other nationalizations have not occurred, but rather that they have been either more partial or significantly less profitable. In 2012, a conflict reminiscent of Huanuni occurred between mining cooperatives and private company employees at the Colquiri silver-tin-zinc mine, and it was resolved with a nationalization that incorporated only some of the mine's cooperative miners rather than all of them (Noticias Fides 2012). Although Colquiri, along with Huanuni, is one of COMIBOL's most important holdings at present, the number of cooperative miners has continued to grow and is once again equal to the number of salaried miners, suggesting the possibility of a future conflict on the horizon. Another nationalization also occurred in 2012 in Mallku Khota, where the Canadian junior mining company South American Silver had been exploring a massive silver and indium deposit. On this occasion, the nationalization was responding to a conflict led by regional indigenous groups who claimed their consultation rights had been violated and who were interested in forming a community enterprise to continue mining (Garces 2012). Given that community enterprises are not constitutionally recognized in the mining sector, however, protestors shifted gears and instead demanded the right to form a cooperative to exploit the deposit (Le

Gouill 2016). Against both sets of demands, the Morales government opted to nationalize the mine. Because it had still been in the exploration phase at the time of nationalization, however, very little infrastructure had been put in place, and the mine remains inactive to this day.

What this means is that, although COMIBOL has been "reactivated," it has not become a major productive force, nor has it created many jobs. The private mining sector is significantly more productive, and mining cooperatives incorporate significantly more workers. Of course, it would have been very institutionally and politically challenging to nationalize the entire mining sector after decades of neoliberalization (Kohl and Farthing 2012). There are dozens of private companies and thousands of mining cooperatives operate across the country, and displacing them would have resulted in lawsuits—as in the case of Mallku Khota, for which the Bolivian government was required to pay twenty-eight million US dollars in compensation to South American Silver (Da Silva 2018)—as well as massive protests. Indeed, in early 2007, twenty thousand cooperative miners launched a massive protest against the nationalization of the mining sector, since many of them would have earned less working as salaried miners, while others would not have been employed at all (Webber 2011, 111).

In comparison to the mining sector, natural gas production is geographically confined to a few lowland sites and, because of the massive capital inputs required to pump and refine it, few companies were involved in its development prior to Morales's nationalization. Moreover, mineral prices, while historically high, were nothing compared to windfall profits from natural gas. Given Bergquists's arguments about the importance of high capital requirements and geographic isolation for fomenting worker consciousness, one might expect a fresh labor movement to emerge from within the natural gas sector. But natural gas production creates few jobs relative to mining (or at least, relative to mining in the 1980s), and particularly few blue-collar jobs. Although YPFB workers are unionized and affiliated with the Bolivian Workers' Central, they do not represent a particularly large or vocal force for social change. Instead, FSTMB continues to helm the Bolivian Workers' Central despite the comparative economic insignificance of mining.

Mining cooperatives, meanwhile, are technically affiliated with the Bolivian Workers' Central but are in practice disinclined to participate in the broader workers' struggle. They are not "workers" in the sense of their counterparts in FSTMB, in that they have no employers or wages, which means that they have a different structural location and different political demands. Structurally, they cannot disrupt the accumulation of capital through work stoppages, and indeed they would not be interested in doing so, given that they are the direct benefactors of their own labor. To the degree that mining cooperatives have structural power in the Bolivian economy, it is in their capacity to absorb an apparently endless number of surplus workers, which is desirable for capitalists since cooperatives can reduce the number of anti-extractive protests and buffer against political upheaval in moments of labor reduction. But cooperative miners do have significant associational power, and increasingly they have a numerical advantage, as ever more people are becoming cooperativistas.

Cooperative miners exercise their growing power in the legislature and in the streets; often, their participation in the former arena is backed by the threat of a mobilization in the latter arena. They participated in writing the new constitution, which came into effect in 2009, and they succeeded in obtaining constitutional recognition of mining cooperatives as one of three actors in the mining sector (alongside COMIBOL and private corporations). Because of this victory, representatives from FENCOMIN were invited to participate in drafting a new mining law. When a draft of this law was circulated in early 2014, analysts almost universally agreed that it was favorable to mining cooperatives, in that it kept royalties, rental rates, and health-care contribution rates extremely low and continued to excuse mining cooperatives, as nonprofit entities, from paying formal income tax. In the Bolivian senate, however, the bill's progress ground to a halt when senators took issue with Article 151, which stated that mining cooperatives could form partnerships with private companies. This, the senators argued, was unconstitutional: mining cooperatives should not be able to maintain their protected status as nonprofit entities when partnering with a for-profit company.

The Senate's decision was immediately challenged by cooperative miners, for whom the right to private-cooperative partnerships had been a core demand throughout the process of drafting the law. As the situation escalated, cooperative miners erected roadblocks across the country to disrupt the circulation of commodities and force the state's hand. These roadblocks ended after a standoff with the police left two miners dead and more than sixty people injured, but they did not have much of an impact on the new Law of Mining and Metallurgy (#535). Finally passed on May 28, 2014, the law explicitly forbid cooperative-private alliances without supervisory involvement of COMIBOL. Nevertheless, many such partnerships persisted long after the law's passage; perhaps deterred by the threat of a longer roadblock, the state never actually enforced the ban.

In 2016, a new conflict emerged that echoed many of themes of 2014 but with more violent overtones. This struggle started with a proposed modification to the General Cooperative Law (Law #356, originally passed in 2013), which was slated to recognize the right to unionization for workers employed by all "cooperative societies." This change was targeted at the service cooperatives, which provide things like water and phone connections; as productive entities, mining cooperatives had never been legally allowed to hire third-party workers, except for administrative and technical support (Law #356, Article 17). Despite not being targeted, however, cooperative miners adopted the struggle as their own, and used it as a platform to release a ten-point list of demands, only one of which was related to the General Cooperative Law. The other demands included relaxed environmental standards, the extension of electrical lines to all mining cooperatives, and a modification of Article 151 of the Mining and Metallurgy Law. The 2016 protest devolved into chaos when cooperative miners murdered the deputy minister of the interior, Rodolfo Illanes, who had gone to the roadblock to negotiate its end. His body was discovered the next day, wrapped in a sheet and dumped on the side of the road. In the uproar that followed, Morales announced five supreme decrees designed to limit the cooperatives' political and economic activities, which were later elevated to the status of law (#845). All this was a serious blow to the cooperative mining sector, which had lost not only its privileged relationship with the government but also all the public support (or at least public obliviousness) it had ever enjoyed.

Still, mining cooperatives did not go away, and they slowly regained their position of relative political influence. The reason for this is likely connected to their associational power, bolstered by their growing membership: cooperative miners are militant, numerous, and potentially violent (as demonstrated by the murder of Rodolfo Illanes). Fear of a mobilization led by mining cooperatives is often enough to deter people from passing or enforcing unfavorable legislation. Moreover, given the fact that cooperative miners had been running Morales' campaigns in many rural mining districts, concerns about the impending election of 2019—already a contentious race, given debate over whether Morales should have been constitutionally allowed to put his name on the ballot for a fourth consecutive term—likely encouraged a slow rapprochement between mining cooperatives and the state. This arrangement did not end well for Morales, who was forced to resign after accusations of voter fraud and a coup led by right-wing elites, but mining cooperatives held on. After a yearlong reactionary interim government, Morales' party returned to power under the leadership of Luis Arce, and mining cooperatives began to grow again.

CONCLUSION: LEGACIES OF LABOR MOVEMENTS PAST

Although the commodity boom that underwrote much of Morales's economic success wound down in the mid-2010s, the number of cooperative miners is climbing once again. The slow but perhaps accelerating global move away from hydrocarbons has favored the metal market, given the material needs of renewable energy (Månberger 2021). At the same time, watchdog organizations indicate that the COVID-19 pandemic has counterintuitively encouraged mining (Coalition Against the Mining Pandemic 2022); this tendency has been especially evident in the gold sector, given that the price of gold has soared as central banks and investors around the world hedge against a declining US dollar (Poveda Ávila 2021). Yet the number of jobs directly within the mining sector has not risen alongside mineral prices, in large part because industrial mining operations are increasingly dependent on large-scale technology rather than human labor—a trend that has been accelerated by the pandemic (Ramdoo 2020). Instead of seeking formal employment, therefore, many people have looked for alternative ways to benefit from the most recent boom in mineral prices.

In Bolivia, the number of mining cooperatives has exploded. For every ten new jobs created in the Bolivian mining sector, nine are in cooperatives (Zaconeta 2022). Much of this growth is in the gold mining sector, which is based primarily in the eastern lowlands and the northern reaches of the department of La Paz. According to a recent government report, in 2020 gold surpassed natural gas to become Bolivia's primary export, and 97 percent of Bolivian gold is produced by cooperatives (Villegas Flores et al. 2021). Researchers consider gold cooperatives to be more environmentally and socially damaging than their traditional counterparts (tin, silver, zinc, and lead) because cooperative gold miners use large amounts of mercury, contaminate rivers in their search for alluvial deposits, displace lowland indigenous communities, and form illicit partnerships with wealthy foreign investors (Bell, Evers, and Burton 2021; Poveda Ávila 2021). But mining cooperative growth has not been constrained to the gold sector. While the number of mining cooperatives in the traditional sector has not seen significant increases, membership within each cooperative has been creeping up (Zaconeta 2022). Moreover, the influx of people into gold mining has strengthened the cooperative mining sector as a whole, including its more traditional actors, since the groups share similar political interests. Already a historically layered institution—an amalgamation of colonial-era *k'ajcheo*, Cold War union-busting tactics, neoliberal restructuring, and more recent extractivist dynamics—cooperative mining has now become an even more influential, widespread, and divisive sector.

More precisely, the contemporary growth of mining cooperatives, both gold and traditional, depend on both the existence of the legal category "mining cooperative"—a category invented to manage layoffs in the formal, state-owned sector—and on the organizational work done by ex-unionized miners to ensure that mining cooperatives are not politically marginalized.

The movement of miners from unions into cooperatives, which was slow in the 1960s to 1970s and rapid in the 1980s to 1990s, implied a transfer of political knowledge and organizational experience from the formal to the informal sector. The techniques deployed by mining cooperatives in political standoffs with the government, such as nationwide roadblocks, are strikingly like those practiced by the unions. While unionized tin miners influenced many social sectors, both by example and when laid-off miners migrated to other regions of the country, mining cooperatives might be considered their most direct descendants. Even if most twenty-first-century cooperative miners are operating in the gold sector with no personal or familial links to either tin mining or the miners' unions, they are nevertheless occupying a position made possible by the long history of tin mining labor in the twentieth century.

This should not be taken to imply, of course, that cooperative and salaried miners have similar or even compatible political objectives. Mid-twentieth-century tin miners read Marxist political theory closely and understood themselves to be part of the global proletariat, producing surplus value for a few Bolivian elites and much of the Global North bourgeoisie; accordingly, their political strategies were aimed at increasing the percentage of profits returned to workers, on the one hand, and increasing the surplus value that remained in Bolivia, on the other hand. In short, they organized around class-based and national interests. Cooperative miners, by contrast, are often described by leftist commentators as political opportunists or—even less flatteringly—as "savage capitalists" because they work hard to minimize their own contributions to national coffers and rarely act in solidarity with the working class.

Animosity between the unionized and cooperativized mining sectors, as demonstrated by conflicts such as those at the Huanuni mine (2006) and the Colquiri mine (2012), not only makes trans-sectoral political action difficult to achieve; it also makes investment in the formal sectors (state-owned and private) more challenging. For instance, conflicts brewing at the Porco mine, where cooperatives exist alongside a private operation, make investors nervous about avasallamiento, or an illegal occupation, either by cooperatives or community members. In a very different instance, ex-cooperative miners who were incorporated into the newly nationalized Huanuni mine following the 2006 conflict have fought to maintain a "selective" labor system, in which they are paid relative to the quantity of ore they extract rather than the number of hours they work. This system is very similar to the cooperative labor approach and it prevents the company from adopting a more systematic or economically sustainable extraction method.[2] Both cases demonstrate how mining cooperatives have been able to influence mining practices and infrastructures across the mining sector as a whole. The state might have created mining cooperatives to manage unruly miners, but today's cooperativistas are far more politically disruptive than their unionized contemporaries.

Thinking with Bergquist's examples, Bolivian miners' unions were most similar to Chilean miners' unions, whereas the mining cooperatives more closely resemble Colombian coffee growers in their structural organization and political orientation. Where cooperatives differ from the coffee growers is in their associational power, which is a legacy they inherited from the miners' unions. In the conclusion of his book, Bergquist (1986, 367) notes that a shortcoming of his model is its limited treatment of political systems and state formation; extending his point, this chapter shows the hand that the Bolivian state has had in shaping and obstructing the labor movement, and the ongoing effects of this history. Indeed, the post-revolutionary Bolivian state (after 1952) increasingly consolidated itself in relation to foreign governments and in opposition to unionized tin miners (Field 2014). Mining cooperatives were the mechanism of this consolidation, but they have since become a force in their own right. *Cooperativismo* could not have taken its current form without the historic struggle between *sindicalismo* and the state, and this history continues to inflect the dynamic that Bergquist theorized between class consciousness in the export sector and Bolivia's structural position in the world economy.

NOTES

1. There are several excellent historical accounts of the *k'ajchas*, but foremost among these is Tandeter (1992). See Barragán Romano (2017) for specific connections between *k'ajchas* and cooperatives.

2. These two examples come from interviews conducted with salaried miners in Huanuni on June 23, 2022, and in Potosí on June 24, 2022.

Chapter Nine

The Extraction of Migrant Labor-Power

Chris Little

Charles Bergquist's analysis in *Labor in Latin America* focuses on the politically determinant role of labor in extractive export industries across four case study countries. This chapter builds on Bergquist's methodological and theoretical prioritization of the structurally bounded agency of labor by explaining circuits of labor migration as a form of extractivism. I propose that Bergquist's approach can be deployed to understand the political economy of migrant labor and its role within states and across borders. This entails a partial inversion of the focus of Bergquist's analysis, shifting from labor in extractive export to the export of labor-power itself. In distinction from the narrower definition offered by Kristin Ciupa and Jeffery R. Webber in the introduction to this volume, this chapter draws on recent scholarship proposing expanded understandings of extractivism whereby the extractive logic operating in the utilization of natural resources under capitalism extends into other spheres of accumulation (Chagnon et al. 2022; Gago and Mezzadra 2017; McKay, Alonso-Fradejas, and Ezquerro-Cañete 2021; Ye et al. 2020). In contrast to both Bergquist and Ciupa and Webber's tight focus on productive labor, this chapter shifts our attention explicitly to social reproductive labor, because it is ultimately in this realm that the process of extracting migrant labor-power takes place.

This chapter builds upon Bergquist's contention that his approach has "heuristic value," whereby directing our attention to workers in export production and the structuring of said production in a given state opens up a vital perspective on the political importance of labor to that state's development (Bergquist 1986, 376). I propose that Bergquist's heuristic can be extended to apprehend the importance of the export of labor-power itself, and that our understanding of the political economy of this export can be aided by adopting an expansive understanding of extractivism. The central argument of this chapter is that the export of labor-power can be considered a form of extractivism when it takes place under certain combined conditions of uneven development, accumulation by dispossession (often related to other forms of extractivism), and the externalization of the costs of social reproduction by receiving states. The value of this perspective is that it can explain how labor migration appears to play a positive developmental role while in fact being reproductive of an uneven, hierarchical international system that distributes wealth upward, reinforcing the relative positions of richer and poorer states alike. The export of migrant labor-power in contemporary global capitalism reflects the subordination of workers' agency and structural power to the demands of the world economy.

I aim to demonstrate the usefulness of Bergquist's approach in understanding the political economy of migrant-sending states and their position within the world economy through attentiveness to class formation across, as well as within, nation-state borders. His approach is valuable because it offers a tool to understand the position of labor in relation to the structural forces of the world economy while not losing sight of its agency or potential structural power. At the same time, it acknowledges the profound constraints placed upon this agency by the operation of global capitalism, especially with regards to migrant labor. Yet constrained agency does not negate the political importance of labor, migrant or otherwise. As such, where Bergquist contends that "the primary object of early-twentieth-century Latin American labor history should be workers in export production" (1986, 8), in the same spirit I argue that one of the primary objects of contemporary Latin American labor studies should be migrant workers and the export of labor-power.

This chapter proceeds as follows. First, I situate Bergquist's methodological and theoretical approach within the contemporary world economy and propose utilizing it beyond the original scope of his studies in *Labor in Latin America*. Second, I draw from the literature on expanded extractivism to propose how Bergquist's approach can be utilized to understand the export of labor-power. Third, I elaborate on this in the context of theorizations of uneven development, migrant labor's agency, and social reproduction. Finally, I situate this expansion of Bergquist's methodology in relation to some brief examples of literature relating to migration and extraction in Central America's "Northern Triangle"—El Salvador, Guatemala, and Honduras—gesturing toward the fruitfulness of further research employing this approach.

FROM LABOR IN EXPORT PRODUCTION
TO THE EXPORT OF LABOR-POWER

Labor in Latin America focuses on the undertheorized political role of labor in Latin American development. Bergquist considers workers in export production to be fundamental to understanding development in Latin America. By placing labor at the center, he contends that we can both better understand the political economy of the region and states within it, and also empower labor as the subject of analysis, recognizing the decisive political role of its struggles (1986, 386). His focus on workers in export production is grounded in the importance of this sector for the development of Latin American economies over the course of the nineteenth and twentieth centuries, with the specialization of national economies in the production of particular commodities for export within a world economy. Many of the commodities produced for export were extractive commodities. In some cases, in the strictly traditional sense with natural resources extracted from the earth for further processing and utilization elsewhere, as in the nitrate industry in Chile and the petroleum industry in Venezuela. In other cases, the commodities were agrarian in nature, and their extractive character more figurative, with meatworkers in Argentina and the coffee farmers in Colombia as key examples. This chapter attends to the varying definitions of extraction in the following, but for now it is sufficient to note that the labor forces Bergquist studies were engaged in work that involved marshalling natural resources in some form for export.

The production of such commodities for export remains a vital part of national economies across the Latin American region, including in the form of neoextractivist national development strategies. While questioning just how "new" neoextractivist policies are, Liisa L. North and Ricardo Grinspun describe them as "a focused intent on using extractive activities—not only mining and petroleum but also new agro-exports for food, feed and energy markets . . . to finance public policies that advance social well-being" (2016, 1484). This developmental model traces a lineage back to the "colonial formula for generating wealth . . . which generated the patterns of dependency that the first wave of developmentalist policies were designed to overcome" (North and Grinspun 2016, 1484). The literature on extractivism within this context seeks to understand the political economic context within which a return to, or retrenchment of, extractive exports has taken place across the region. Over the course of the twentieth century, another export commodity has risen in importance both at a regional level and for particular states within the region—that of labor-power.

A proxy for this increasing importance is the rise in the proportion of gross domestic product (GDP) in the region accounted for by migrant remittances.

Remittances accounted for just 0.2 percent of GDP in Latin America and the Caribbean in 1979, but as of 2021 they accounted for 2.7 percent, the highest proportion on record (World Bank 2023a). The figures are significantly higher in certain states. For the Northern Triangle states of El Salvador, Guatemala, and Honduras, the 2021 proportions of remittances to GDP were 26.1 percent, 17.9 percent, and 25.3 percent, respectively, also the highest proportions on record for all three states. By comparison, in 1979, the figures were 2.9 percent, 0.03 percent, and 0.3 percent, respectively. If we take migrant remittances as being the return on the export of labor-power, this particular commodity emerges as a central pillar of these three economies. Indeed, the rents from extraction when understood solely as fossil and mineral extraction pale in comparison for all three countries in the most recent data, ranging from 0.5–1.9 percent of GDP in 2021 (World Bank 2023b).

We can account for the way in which the export of labor-power unfolds within national economies and flows into the circuits of the world economy through an expanded conceptualization of extractivism. This will allow us to understand the connection that can be drawn between labor in extractive export production, as in Bergquist's analysis, and the export of labor-power.

AN EXPANDED CONCEPTUALIZATION OF EXTRACTIVISM

To establish the grounds on which Bergquist's approach can be utilized to analyze circuits of migrant labor as being part of an extractive export process, we must unpack what we mean by extractive. A key contemporary theorist of extractivism is Eduardo Gudynas, who defines it as the "appropriation of natural resources," taking "diverse forms with very different dynamics" (2018a, 62). It is important to note the distinction between extraction and extractivism. Gudynas sets out a framework for determining when an extractive activity becomes a form of extractivism, defining this as "appropriation of natural resources in large volume and/or high intensity, where half or more are exported as raw materials" (2018a, 62). Activities that are extractive but do not meet this definition in full, such as the extraction of material for construction at the national level, food production for national use, or lower-intensity agriculture such as organic export production, are not considered extractivist. Activities that are both high intensity in their extraction, and destined for export, such as mineral and hydrocarbon extraction as well as industrial export agriculture, are what constitute forms of extractivism for Gudynas (2018a, 62). He cautions against extending the concept of extractivism to "other ways of appropriating natural resources that have high social and environmental impacts" but do not meet the conditions of both volume/ intensity and export destination (2018a, 63).

Can the logic of Gudynas's conceptualization of extractivism be maintained while extending its scope to encompass the export of labor-power? First, it cannot be assumed that positioning the export of labor-power as extractive necessarily makes it a form of extractivism. The analysis can at first proceed by identifying the features of export of labor-power than can be understood in the same, or similar, terms as the extraction of other commodities for export. This involves a degree of abstraction, as we move away from the visceral physical reality of natural resource extraction—be it open-pit mines, vast clearcut forests, labyrinthine petroleum infrastructure, or monocrop plantations—to a focus on the exploitation of the human potential to labor. Here, the extraction of labor-power can be usefully understood as a form of extractivism under certain circumstances, precisely because of its potential to meet Gudynas's credentials of intensity and destination and, crucially, because of its linkages to wider processes of extractivism and its centrality to certain national economies.

Expanded understandings of extractivism and their application have proliferated in recent literature (Riofrancos 2020). This expansive terrain of analysis is well explored by Christopher W Chagnon et al., who note that "[w] hile natural resource extraction remains an important focus, the processes, and conditions of extractivist practices have been abstracted and applied to entirely new areas" (2022, 2). Extractivism thus becomes an "organizing concept" (Chagnon et al. 2022, 2), departing from the more restrictive account of extractivism offered by Gudynas, as well as the approach established by the editors in the introduction to this volume. Yet I believe that it is analytically fruitful to pursue this line of thought in order to understand the contemporary political economy of migrant labor. Within this mode of analysis, we can identify and explore common logics that structure both patterns of accumulation and the options available for export for subordinated states within the world economy. The approach is particularly useful in terms of agrarian political economy (Chagnon et al. 2022), offering a means of addressing the relationship between agrarian change and labor migration, a dynamic of particular relevance for states of Central America's Northern Triangle.

Another key recent explanation of the possibilities inherent to expanded conceptualizations of extractivism is Jingzhong Ye et al.'s (2020) elaboration of key features that constitute a system of extractivism. Of particular relevance is the organization of the system into a chain along which extracted commodities are "transported from places of poverty to places of richness, where high prices can be obtained for them" (Ye et al. 2020, 156). This wealth is accumulated in these places of richness, resulting in extractivism being "constituted by, and through, inequalities" while further creating and deepening them. Part of this wealth may be utilized to support developmental policies, as in neoextractivism (North and Grinspun 2016)—not a necessary condition but rather a feature of certain forms of extractivism. The final crucial element here is that extractivism "centres on the use of the already available resources, it does not invest in the material reproduction of these resources" (Ye et al. 2020, 157).

Extractivism understood as such departs from the most restrictive definitions, situating the definitive aspect as being "control" rather than the involvement of a particular type of resource (Ye et al. 2020, 160). For example, using mining in a broad, quasi-metaphorical sense, Ye et al. (2020) apply the term beyond narrowly defined natural resources to include the mining of social resources as well. This approach to the commodity is the same with the natural resource as it is with the social resource—control is exerted over it, and it is appropriated, without regard for its reproduction. This element of control is crucial because it is where extractivism takes on its specificity. It differs from the appropriation of surplus value in general terms because it is not rooted in (although can involve) direct ownership and control of the means from which the commodities are produced, but rather the primary feature is control over the flows of extractive commodities (Ye et al. 2020, 162). For extractive commodities that are not labor-power, this is a relatively simple contention. But to establish that labor-power can be an extractive commodity, it is necessary to consider how that commodity is produced and what constitutes the means of production in this particular case. This leads us into the realm of social reproduction and to consider its relationship with labor migration, as well as the way control is exerted over migrant labor and how that relates to its reproduction.

Extraction in these terms becomes a logic that can be discerned beyond the intensive extraction of natural resources for export, sharing key elements in common with these processes yet not being restricted to specific commodities. In this sense, it becomes "a logic of valorization" rather than simply a procedure for exploiting natural resources (Gago 2021, 667). Verónica Gago and Sandro Mezzadra argue that this expansion "can help us more systematically define the fundamental features of the logic of contemporary capitalism's functioning" (2017, 577). Expanded extractivism as a concept does not seek to undermine the analysis of extractivisms focused on natural resources, nor to diminish the specific and profound impacts that these processes have had on societies in Latin America and beyond. However, what it does do is open up the possibility that the logic underpinning these processes that have been so successful for capital accumulation through natural resource exploitation might be found elsewhere. Extractivism then transcends a focus on natural resources and turns toward other avenues for value extraction including labor and life itself (Gago and Mezzadra 2017, 579). In this sense, it is a reiteration of Marx's original logic of primitive accumulation, whereby there is a move from the violent extension of commodification into the non-capitalist world to "the violent reorganization of spaces and societies already subsumed under the logic of capitalist valorization" (Gago and Mezzadra 2017, 585). Here, again, we find both a logic and a process of (re)organization guided by that logic.

Extractivism has an important interrelationship with dispossession, and as such David Harvey's (2003) concept of "accumulation by dispossession" can be applied (Gago and Mezzadra 2017). For the study of labor migration as a form of extraction, the concept offers insight through Harvey's contention that it is necessary to understand how the original logic of primitive accumulation as described by Marx persists in a variety of forms, and that it occurs inside of capitalism. The extractive logic represents a corollary of accumulation by dispossession as a mode of accumulation that relies on the operation of structural and coercive forces alongside the market relation between capital and labor. Dispossession is a key example of these forces, in that it involves the creation of new markets and new processes of commodification in order to secure grounds for accumulation. Gago and Mezzadra note that their analysis differs from Harvey's in that they do not see dispossession and exploitation as operating in isolation from one another (2017, 586), but rather the ongoing processes of dispossession open up a question as to how the basis for labor exploitation is secured and reproduced under historically specific circumstances. This conceptualization of the extractive logic, with dispossession as a part, allows an understanding of how labor forces are (re)produced and shaped in particular ways for accumulation.

Dispossession often unfolds in the agrarian context, and as such it is important to consider how agrarian extractivism operates. Ben McKay, Alberto Alonso-Fradejas, and Arturo Ezquerro-Cañete's account of agrarian extractivism travels beyond more restrictive versions focused on monocultures or raw materials "to the inherent logic and underlying workings of a mode, based on the appropriation of commodified and non-commodified forces of production" (2021, 2). Understanding extractivism in this manner draws our attention to the impact of extractivist models of agriculture in social terms, and the relationship that this has with labor. As such, agricultural transformation has "not only resulted in biophysical contradictions and inefficiencies, it has also altered the social relations of production, property, and power in the countryside" (McKay, Alonso-Fradejas, and Ezquerro-Cañete 2021, 5). An expanded concept of extractivism allows investigation of how the logic underlying the appropriation of raw materials then metastasizes across sectors and throughout economies. We can then attend not only to processes of uneven development engendered by these forces, but also the profound and destructive nature of their social consequences (McKay, Alonso-Fradejas, and Ezquerro-Cañete 2021, 7).

Two key dynamics emerge from this perspective. First, the social consequences of extractivism include dispossession and displacement, driving those dispossessed and displaced to migrate in order to survive. Second, there is also the extraction of labor-power itself, operating in combination with other forms of extractivism. Labor migration cannot simply be considered as a consequence or side effect of extractivism, but rather in certain cases it becomes a form of extractivism itself. In the agrarian context, questions relating to extraction, social reproduction, dispossession, and labor migration coalesce within the analysis of extractivism. With regard to labor, extractive agrarian capitalism operates by "(hyper-)exploiting, exhausting or outright displacing [it]" (McKay, Alonso-Fradejas, and Ezquerro-Cañete 2021, 16). In fact, it both exploits and exhausts in combination with displacement, with that displacement acting as an important enabling condition for the extraction of migrant labor-power.

Under an extractive logic, beyond dispossession it is necessary to exercise control over the commodities that are then extracted. Here, extractive commodities are analytically distinct in the nature of their appropriation; or, in the case of migrant labor-power, its exploitation followed by the appropriation of the surplus value it generates. Given this, we must focus on processes of control and their drive to avoid contributing to reproduction. One way this manifests is that extraction does not develop the productive forces and instead merely drains value from one area to another without any corresponding progressive role for capital (Ye et al. 2020, 163). Here, we can establish a point of cohesion with more traditional understandings of extractivism focused on natural resources, in that there is a reproduction of a position of (under)development through the logic of extraction. While inequality itself is not the sole condition for expanded extractivism to operate as a mode of accumulation, it is a crucial one. The concept of expanded extractivism, both in general and specifically where it is applied to the extraction of labor power, is most analytically useful when bolstered by a focus on uneven development and unequal exchange. Furthermore, with the extraction of labor-power we can locate a key aspect of this unevenness in processes of social reproduction and their geographical separation from the site of labor.

UNEVEN DEVELOPMENT AND EXPANDED EXTRACTIVISM

To argue that there is a logic of extraction underpinning the operation of the world economy is to advance a particular position on how that economy is structured. Unevenness and inequality are implicit to the existence and operation of a logic of extraction. As described earlier, extraction is rooted in flows along axes of inequality and the movement of extracted resources from poorer regions to richer regions (Ye et al. 2020). Bergquist situates his account in relation to the contributions of world-systems theory and dependency theory while expressing caution regarding their focus. His study shares their contentions that underdevelopment is rooted in the "cultural, political and material consequence of unequal exchange and specialization of function in a world division of labor that disproportionately benefits core capitalist nations" (Bergquist 1986, 384). However, he critiques what he sees as a single-minded focus "on the global structural 'logic' of the world system," neglecting both the actuality of class struggle within societies as well as "human consciousness and agency." He seeks to address this neglect through a focus on the meaning of export structure for the working class, and by expanding "the question of economic development by linking it to the related issues of social and political transformation" (Bergquist 1986, 385).

Having set out the logic of expanded extractivism and contended that it can be determined in the export of labor-power, I will now situate it in relation to Bergquist's exhortation to focus on more than just structural logics. Expanded extractivism is reliant on a structural unevenness in the world economy that is reproduced over time and across geographies through the operation of capitalism on a global scale. This returns us to questions of development as well, crucial to understanding both the abstract logic of capital accumulation as well as the ideological justifications sometimes given for extractivism as a means of bolstering development. Bergquist's study seeks to determine not just the relationship between particular export orientations and paths of national economic development, but the pivotal role of labor and its agency within these dynamics. A theory of uneven development can help us become attuned to this, as it necessitates identifying the stratifying features that constitute and reproduce paths of uneven development throughout the world economy. A central stratifying feature here is labor-power, the variegated characteristics of its bearers across borders and the way it is commodified and operationalized.

Fouad Makki describes "development" under capitalism as "a product of the differential but interactive (uneven but combined) processes of capitalist expansion" (2015, 485). This approach to understanding the nature of capitalist development centers on the interaction between unevenness and combination rather than the content of these terms individually (Makki 2015, 483). We can relate this back to expanded conceptualizations of extractivism and accumulation's grounding in the exploitation of social differentiation across borders. In the search for new grounds for commodification and through the cultivation of relations of inequality, it relies on difference and variation. This approach complements Bergquist's concerns regarding structural overdetermination in world systems theory and dependency approaches. For Makki, "instead of conceptualizing development in terms of ineluctable progress or catastrophic arrest . . . it makes better sense to think of development as a relational global process" that can be both analyzed structurally as well as being understood in relation to "its concrete conditions of existence in particular social formations" (2015, 490). For understanding extractivism in an expanded sense, this means being attentive both to the structural dynamics that underpin extraction and its positioning as a model of development, as well as its operation within differentiated social formations and the particularities that result from this variation.

Understanding development through emphasizing its unevenness and its combination challenges approaches to development that privilege the national context. Methodological nationalism is incompatible with analyses of extractivism on the terms being pursued here. Extractivism is structured by the uneven relationship between national economies. Its nature, both in more restrictive but especially in expansive terms, is found in the interrelation between these national economies and the flows between them, structured by unevenness. This attention to both the world historical and the local allows us to delve deeper than a homogenous understanding of capitalist accumulation on a global scale (Makki 2015, 490). An approach attentive to unevenness situates "the flow of local events in wider interactive contexts [avoiding the] reductive view that social processes are delimited by discreet territorial boundaries," (Makki 2015, 490) while giving due weight to overbearing global structures and human agency within them. Theorizing uneven development to retain a focus on human agency means that the impact of an extractive logic can be emphasized while not dehumanizing those who bear the commodity labor-power.

An expanded understanding of extractivism also allows for situating the dynamics of extraction in a world economy defined by imperialism and marked by increasing complexity in a variety of forms. Imperialism in the "complexly stratified world system" of contemporary global capitalism "is characterized by deep structural inequalities among regions and countries of the world" (Gordon and Webber 2020, 119). This is particularly relevant to the extraction of labor-power, due to the centrality of delineated nation-states and their borders in how labor-power as a commodity flows throughout the world economy. The patterning of global capitalist dynamics today constitutes "a system in which global interdependence, rather than national independence, becomes a necessary starting point for comprehending the specific trajectories of different societies" (Gordon and Webber 2020, 119), of particular relevance for the interrelation between uneven development, extractivism, and migrant labor. This returns us to the need for a theoretical prioritization of the interrelationship between states while recognizing the persistence and importance of states as an organizing unit within the world economy.

Increasing integration of the world economy alongside the maintenance and reproduction of unevenness as an inherent quality of the capitalist system is a seemingly contradictory yet essential feature of contemporary capital accumulation. Given this, Todd Gordon and Jeffery R. Webber note that the maintenance of the "environmental prerequisites for accumulation across the distinct levels of the scalar hierarchy is more important than ever" (2020, 113). The indispensable prerequisite for accumulation under capitalism is the commodity labor-power. There are, of course, a multiplicity of forms by which this commodity is made available for use in capital accumulation. One central form in contemporary capitalism is through flows of migrant labor and, under certain conditions, these flows of migrant labor operate through a logic that matches that of the extraction of commodities other than labor-power. The complexity of the contemporary world economy requires an array of approaches to securing labor-power, and within this the extraction of migrant labor-power occupies an increasingly important role, although not one without historical analogue in previous flows of labor across borders. The character of states and the nature of their economies is defined by their relationship to, position within, and dependence on, the world economy, its circuits and its flows (Dale 1999, 13). A crucial element within this relationship is labor migration, and in the world economy "all varieties of transnational interlinkages, of deprivation and oppression, of aspirations, provide the bases for unprecedented flows of international migration" (Dale 1999, 14).

Migration is central to capitalism's function and the ordering of the world economy. As Adam Hanieh describes, it forms "a movement of people that is relentlessly generated by the movement of capital, and which, in turn, is constitutive of the concrete forms of capitalism itself" (2019, 52). It is here that we can apprehend the complexity of labor's agency when that labor is migratory. Bergquist's analyses of labor in export production highlighted the impact of dispersal and concentration of labor in its capacity to exert structural power, and with migrant labor the process of movement and dispersal takes center stage. While migrant labor is disempowered by the process of movement and attendant marginalization within receiving states, its agency and potential for exerting structural power nevertheless persists amid over-bearing structural constraints. Perspectives that consider migrant labor resistance, such as the history of migrant worker strikes in the United States (De Genova 2010; Robinson 2006), those that look at migrant worker organizing to resist the imposition of precarity (Vosko 2019), and those that categorize migration itself as a form of social movement (De Genova and Mezzadra 2020), are instructive in this regard.

An extractive understanding of the export of labor-power offers a way of understanding labor migration as a form of accumulation within the world economy rooted in unevenness, considering its vital importance to the trans-national circuits of economic life. It asks: What is the specific role of the extractive logic within the wider operation of capitalism across an uneven, differentiated system? In which specific areas is the presence of the extractive logic most apparent, and in what manner does it unfold across particular sectors? Exploring the interrelation of the extraction of labor-power with other iterations of extractive logics allows us to develop a deeper understanding of the persistence of unevenness.

LABOR MIGRATION AS THE
EXTRACTION OF LABOR-POWER

Extractive processes can be understood as taking place through uneven social relations, structured at the level of the world economy and in relations between nation-states as well as in specific local conditions. A fundamental feature of this is the creation of the need to migrate in order to survive (North 2021) due to a deteriorating ability to reproduce oneself or one's family at home. Yet a corresponding feature of this is the social cost of migration in the place of origin. By understanding labor migration as a potentially extractive process, we have a framework for understanding these costs. The focus on the "return" or benefits from labor migration, in particular remittances, must be accompanied by a thorough understanding of the social forces that compel labor migration in the first place, as well as the consequences of labor migration that accompany this "return." One of the primary manifestations of an extractive logic in circuits of labor is the externalization of social reproduction.

Aaron Jaffe describes social reproduction theory (SRT) as shifting "our gaze to concentrate on those agents and forms of work through which abilities to satisfy life's needs are produced, set in motion, and reproduced" (2020, 2). SRT allows the development of an adequate account of the capital-labor relation and capital itself, moving beyond an abstract understanding of value production to account for "the evolving cycles and social circuits that capital moves through as it valorizes" (Jaffe 2020, 20). Furthermore, it allows analysis of the structural forces through which capital accumulation operates "while directing our gaze to research on the specific ways that gender, race, sexuality, immigration status, and other oppressions form the particular social paths through which valorization takes" (Jaffe 2020, 21). To apprehend extractive logics at work in labor migration, this attention to the social forces through which valorization takes place is essential to transcending a mechanistic logic of supply and demand in analyzing circuits of labor migration. SRT attunes us to the historically specific conditions related to the separation of workers from the means of production and how that separation is reproduced over time (Jaffe 2020, 22), "with particular attention to the way our embodied labor powers are made and sustained" (Jaffe 2020, 26). In a similar vein, Susan Ferguson and David McNally contend that theorizing in this regard "requires a multi-dimensional analysis that, while acknowledging the decisive role of waged-work and other monetized practices, situates these within a nexus of practices through which working-class life is produced and reproduced" (2015, 2). On this account, attention to social reproduction must accompany an exploration of logics of extraction, especially when applying that logic to labor-power.

The production of unevenness in the world economy is channeled in part through processes of social reproduction; as Isabella Bakker and Stephen Gill describe it, social reproduction is "variegated and uneven across scales, locations and jurisdictions" yet "increasingly shaped by the power of capital in a global process of accumulation that is, in turn, premised on the commodification of labor, society, and nature" (2019, 504). This holistic conceptualization of social reproduction supports an analysis of extractivism on expanded terms because it makes clear the interdependence of various processes of commodification, including for labor-power. It must also be noted that commodification is ongoing and not totalizing, with processes of commodification requiring a noncommodified outside to draw from and expand into (Fraser 2014, 66). These processes also draw attention to the agency of labor, and in utilizing SRT to analyze the capital-labor relation, we can capture the breadth of terrain for agency and struggle. As Nancy Fraser puts it, "even as these 'non-economic' orders make commodity production possible, they are not reducible to that enabling function" (2014, 69). Determining the operation of an extractive logic in the export of labor-power means being attentive to the complex of social relations from which that commodified human potential is drawn; SRT assists us here because it attunes us to the full gamut of extraction as well as the possibilities for resistance and alternatives to it.

In extending Bergquist's analytical prioritization of labor's agency and politically determinant role in export structure, we must investigate the social relations in which labor is enmeshed and through which its agency is exercised. With SRT, we can understand the shaping of workers' agency under the shadow of capital (Jaffe 2020, 26). SRT attunes us not only to gender but to other processes of differentiation and stratification within the working class, from the local, specific context to the transnational level. A combination of SRT and an expanded understanding of extractivism means being able to comprehend the interplay of these forces across scales. Labor migration, or the export of labor-power, in combination with the extractive logic presents a compelling example of this dynamic unfolding across multiple scales. Migrant labor has a unique vantage point in transnational accumulation and processes of social reproduction. It has taken on a specific role within neoliberal capitalism as a result of an epochal shift in the character and size of the global working class on account of intense dispossession and displacement, unleashing vast new reserves of labor-power (Ferguson and McNally 2015, 9). It is through this relationship, embedded in unevenness and the potential for drawing from poorer areas to support accumulation in richer areas, that an extractive logic takes hold in circuits of migrant labor.

Migrant workers engage in movement because of the potential to materially improve their economic situation, not because they are inanimate commodities pulled between locations by inexorable structural forces. However, this element of choice and agency is most fruitfully investigated in conjunction with the structural forces ordering the possibilities for labor migration. SRT helps us understand the nature of this integration into the world economy by overcoming the ideological myopia of approaches positioning labor migration as a "triple win" for migrants—migrant-sending and migrant-receiving states alike. In this perspective, advanced in publications such as the International Organization for Migration's *World Migration Report 2008*, the relationship between these three parties is one of mutual benefit, with each having a complementary need met through labor mobility, albeit on highly regulated terms (International Organization for Migration 2008). Some scholars acknowledge that these benefits are not (yet) fully realized, arguing for policy fixes to unlock the full benefits of "circular migration" (Angenendt 2014; Rahim, Rayph, and Ruyssend 2021). These policies are positioned as a means of addressing the geographical and regulatory barriers that exist between the type of workers needed in receiving countries, and the type of jobs needed in sending countries, as though it were at its root a form of transnational commuting. Yet the "triple win" philosophy does not adequately address the full balance sheet of labor migration, assuming a coherence of interests between the three parties that does not adequately account for the structure of the world economy within which labor migration takes place (Castles and Delgado Wise 2012; Delgado Wise 2015, 39).

With the approach advanced in this chapter, grounded in SRT, we can make the extractive logic at play visible. This draws our attention to both what is "left behind" in the receiving state when a migrant remits their wages, and the costs of producing that labor-power in the first place, ultimately borne by migrants, their communities, and the (typically highly constrained) social expenditure of the sending state (Delgado Wise 2022a). This relationship is fundamentally rooted in, and reproductive of, patterns of global uneven development. Ferguson and McNally acknowledge the dual form of the capital-labor relation in which while capital exploits labor, it is also the source of the wages that enable reproduction, a relation that is of course "massively unbalanced and exploitative" (2015, 11). This takes on a specific character with regard to migrant labor because "much social reproduction occurs at sites significantly separated from the spaces of capitalist production—and frequently by way of geographic separations that involve cross-border movements" (Ferguson and McNally 2015, 11). Thus the movement of workers and the return of their wages as remittances benefits capital in each instance, with precarious, low-wage labor flowing one way and remittances flowing to support social reproduction in a poorer, cheaper location to replenish the global labor reserve (Ferguson and McNally 2015, 11).

Saskia Sassen's (1990) seminal study of the relationship between the internationalization of production and labor migration analyzes the incorporation and positioning of states within the world economy. She contends that the way these processes restructure the economies of both sending and receiving states has crucial implications for the options available to migrant labor. In sending states, this involves the disruption of traditional, agrarian economies and the incorporation of new wage workers into the labor market (Sassen 1990, 118). Further disruption involves labor force feminization and shifting labor market compositions, as well as the development of ideological and cultural links between sending and receiving states through circuits of capital and corresponding circuits of labor migration. Sassen focuses on how these circuits interact and intersect, reproducing one another, with borders acting not as boundaries but as mechanisms of systemic reproduction (1990, 34). One element underpinning these circuits is that of social reproduction, and its unevenness is central to transnational capital accumulation through the utilization of migrant labor.

The claimed "return" on labor migration central to the idea of the "triple win" is partly found in the idea that remittances both support social reproduction and drive national development (International Organization for Migration 2008; UN Network on Migration n.d.). This view, however, is contested—Raúl Delgado Wise, for example, argues that the "costs of social reproduction, education and training" are assumed by both families and, to an extent, the sending state, and that "these costs, compared with the accumulation of remittances . . . tend to be much more onerous" (2022b, 9). In this sense, remittances are not "a North-South subsidy but rather exactly the opposite: A South-North subsidy" (2022b, 9). This subsidy is part of the process of externalization and is extractive in its logic. There is an added layer of complexity to this position in that the sending state itself can be seen as being extractive of its migrating citizens, with remittances forming part of national development strategies, making up for shortfalls in public provision and state capacity to meet social needs (Phillips 2009, 241).

As would be echoed by Ferguson and McNally's (2015) analysis, for Sassen the geographical separation between sites of productive labor and reproduction activities "allow[s] the receiving country to externalize renewal costs" when utilizing migrant labor-power (1990, 37). Michael Burawoy also focuses on this externalization, noting that "costs of renewal, normally borne by the employing state and economy, are to a considerable degree borne by another economy or another state or a combination of the two" (1976, 1053). This process is supported by the precarity and temporariness of migrant labor in a vast array of contexts. Unlike the extraction of natural resources, the extraction of labor-power through circuits of migration is rooted in the temporariness of the workers in the receiving state. It is defined by the maintenance of transnational relations of dependence between productive labor and reproductive labor (Burawoy 1976, 1053). Burawoy also notes that this export of labor-power serves to defuse domestic political tensions, releasing the pressure caused by underdevelopment through securing a wage via labor migration and associated geographical dispersal of members of the working class (1976, 1068).

Focusing on social reproduction develops the full picture of the extractive logic at work in the export of labor-power: it is dependent upon renewal in the sending state, and upheld by precarity and temporariness for migrant labor in the receiving state. An example of this relationship is investigated in the Canadian case by Tyler Chartrand and Leah Vosko (2021). They describe the externalization of social reproduction in the case of agricultural workers in Canada's Temporary Foreign Worker Program and the reliance on the temporariness that secures this source of vulnerable labor for Canadian capital accumulation. Astutely, they tie this to Canadian capital accumulation overseas with Canada's "robust investment and ownership relations" in Latin America and the Caribbean matching the sending state of many participant agricultural workers (Chartrand and Vosko 2021, 95). It is notable that not only is Canadian capital invested in sending states, but a significant degree of this investment is in extractive industries, and that Canadian finance is a global leader "in investment in mining throughout Latin America, which entails the ongoing dispossession of land and livelihoods" (Chartrand and Vosko 2021, 94; Gordon and Webber 2016). Here we see an interrelation between various extractive activities, with the extraction of natural resources being generative of the conditions for labor migration and thus the extraction of labor-power.

EXTRACTIVE DYNAMICS IN THE EXPORT OF LABOR-POWER IN THE NORTHERN TRIANGLE

It is complicated to analyze the export of labor-power in the same spirit in which Bergquist focuses on the agency and political determinacy of labor in export production. Much migrant labor is defined by compromise and constrained agency, be it in the sending state with the need to migrate and secure the basic conditions of sustainable existence, or in the receiving state under conditions of precarity, temporariness, and low wages. Expanded extractivism as a frame of analysis for the export of labor-power can help address the implications of this, while leaving room for the exercise of agency under conditions of profound disadvantage both at an individual migrant worker level and for sending states in the world economy. Exploring the operation of extractive logics also allows an analysis of agency that acknowledges its constraint by forces of unevenness in the world economy. This is particularly valuable for addressing migration from the Northern Triangle states of Central America, as the extractive logic is clearly present within their wider economies—especially in mining and agriculture.

The underlying dynamics of displacement and migration in the Northern Triangle crystallized with the region's civil wars and continue through to the neoliberal restructuring transforming the economies of El Salvador, Guatemala, and Honduras today (North 2021). Neoliberal transformation dismantled what redistributive policies existed, leading to the retrenchment and redoubling of land concentration, as well as the favoring of extractive monoculture export agriculture (North 2021, 50). Because migrant remittances form a substantive part of the GDP in these states, the "expulsion of the poor . . . turned into a principal source of foreign exchange for the Northern Triangle economies and a substitute for public social programs" (North 2021, 58). The connections between all of these factors underpinning "survival migration" from the Northern Triangle is demonstrative of an extractive logic behind the export of labor-power. This export of labor-power is catalyzed by displacement, dispossession, and a lack of other options, common features of the neoliberal era in particular for rural populations and agrarian labor

(Vergara-Camus and Kay 2017, 250), resulting in a fundamental constraint of agency.

In Guatemala, the social relations engendered by, and supportive of, extractivism are in need of greater scholarly attention (Alonso-Fradejas 2021). Agrarian extractivism in the form of monoculture crops generates an enormous "surplus" population with limited job prospects in an extractive sector with minimal labor requirements. National development is also undermined by the peasant dispossession associated with extractivism, given that "[p]easant-farmed crops generate up to 10 times more 'local wealth' than corporate sugarcane and oil palm," key agro-extractive crops in Guatemala (Alonso-Fradejas 2012, 517). The deterioration of rural conditions through extractive activities undercuts the conditions for survival at home, laying the basis for "survival migration."

The relationship between labor migration and debt is one key aspect of the extractive export of labor-power—an example of the centrality of financialization in expanded understandings of extractivism (Gago and Mezzadra 2017). We can see this at work in the impact that migration has had on land distribution in rural Guatemala. Debt plays a central role in migration, with the financing of illicit journeys from Guatemala to North America involving leveraging land and homes as collateral (Johnson 2021). Briefly, this is notable in extractive terms because it demonstrates the use of remittances to finance not just social reproduction but debt repayment and the costs of migration itself, complicating simplistic narratives about remittances as a productive, developmental return on labor-power's export.

In Honduras, the environmental consequences of natural resource extraction have been linked to labor migration by Garifuna people (Wrathall 2012). The combination of natural resource extraction, its environmental consequences, and disruption to human communities is definitive of the unfolding of expanded extractivism. The root causes of migration from Honduras are not solely the frequently cited proliferation of violence, but also the lack of infrastructure and "human capital" in the form of education (Quijada and Sierra 2019)—echoing Delgado Wise (2015; 2022b) and Phillips's (2009) contention that migration serves to pick up the slack from inadequate social provision. In El Salvador, the economic predominance of remittances has been a means of cementing ruling class control, with dependence on them constraining the agency of the working class and reorientating the economy in favor of the elites (Warnecke-Berger 2020). Climate change and environmental degradation are also linked to extractive industries as part of the driving force behind migration out of El Salvador (Lakhani 2019)—again demonstrating the interrelationship between forms of extractivism when conceptualized expansively.

CONCLUSION

The analysis of extractivism needs to be accompanied by an analysis of the extractive export of labor-power, a frequent corollary of these processes definitive of the experience of vast swathes of labor throughout Latin America and in particular in the Northern Triangle. However, there is a risk in taking this approach that the experience and agency of migrant labor could be written out of the analysis altogether, or instrumentalized and subordinated in an effort to demonstrate a structural logic. This is a particular problem with regards to workers whose agency is profoundly constrained and compromised while engaged in labor migration on account of precarity, temporariness, and geographical dislocation from both one another and communities of origin. I have argued that an expanded understanding of extractivism can contribute to an analysis of contemporary circuits of labor migration because of a shared logic underpinning accumulation across various commodities, including that of labor-power. To combine this approach with Bergquist's prioritization of labor in analyzing the production of commodities for export offers a unique perspective on labor migration's role within the world economy. It apprehends this role within a complex, hierarchical world system structured through and along axes of uneven development in a way that narrower focuses on "triple-wins," or the quantity of remittance flows, cannot. It roots the locus of this extractive operation in the geographical distancing of social reproduction from the site of productive labor, across state borders and so securing the labor-power of the migrant without the attendant costs of reproducing domestic labor. Expanded extractivism itself is incomplete as an approach to the export of labor-power, no matter how politically determinant that particular export is within national economies. Rather, it is necessary to situate the export of labor-power within wider transnational processes of uneven development as well to understand how these processes unfold in the reproduction of labor-power as commodity within the sending state itself.

Part IV

CONCLUSION

Chapter Ten

Conclusion and New Directions

Jeffery R. Webber

The main objective of this edited collection has been straightforward: to reintroduce the category of labor into the heart of the literature on extractive economic sectors in contemporary Latin American societies using the framework advanced in Charles Bergquist's classic book *Labor in Latin America* as a shared point of departure. Bergquist insisted that Chilean nitrate and copper workers, Argentine meat and wheat workers, Venezuelan oil workers, and Colombian coffee workers played a fundamental role in shaping the social, political, and economic trajectories of their respective countries in the twentieth century, and that the varied political orientations and patterns of struggle assumed by the labor movements within these respective export sectors were significantly determined by differences between their predominant structures of production and patterns of ownership. The myriad perspectives and generative tensions on display across the different chapters of this collection suggest the fecundity of wrestling once again with Bergquist's framework, at least as an initial entry into the ongoing project of collectively regenerating social scientific and political attentiveness to the question of labor within capitalist extractivism in Latin America.

AXIOMATIC PREMISES

In the introduction to the volume, the editors focus specifically on value-productive labor, conceived of as all labor that directly creates value in the Marxist sense, and which is therefore distinct from social reproductive labor and general human labor. That priority is then integrated theoretically into a framework of triadic dialectics as originally advanced by Fernando Coronil, in which capital, labor, and land/nature each receive the attention they warrant. The main point of triadic dialectics is to better enable a true grasp of the nature-society relation under capitalism, or the "metabolic interaction" between nature and society, where nature and society are understood as distinct but unified. Whereas Coronil turned to triadic dialectics in response to the limits of the dual dialectical focus on merely capital and labor that reigned in much Marxist political economy at the time of his research, the editors of this volume respond to a differently malignant dualism, that of capital-nature, which is preponderant in the (mostly non-Marxist) extant literature on Latin American extractivism.

If the missing category identified by Coronil was nature, the missing category the editors identify is labor, and, more specifically, productive labor. The introduction's focus on productive labor is then associated with the distinction between workers' structural and associational power, concepts first elaborated by Erik Olin Wright. The emphasis in this regard is the structural power productive workers enjoy due to their position within the economic system, a structural power to disrupt accumulation that, if it is to be acted upon, requires adequate associational power on the part of these same workers, that is their collective organization. Finally, the editors suggest that, appropriately modified to take into account the changes wrought to economies and labor markets over recent decades, the seven factors first identified by Charles Bergquist in the 1980s to explain variation in patterns of economic development and labor-movement formation within Latin American societies might still prove to be a fruitful point of departure for inquiry into productive labor in contemporary capitalist extractivism in Latin America. These factors are geographic location and climatic conditions, nationality and concentration of ownership, capital intensiveness and technological sophistication, degree of vulnerability to seasonal cycles and/or world market fluctuation, reservoir of surplus labor,ethnic composition and citizenship status of the workforce, and nationalism. Bergquist's underlying expectation was that export sectors characterized by foreign ownership and concentrated production would tend to produce more culturally autonomous, class-conscious, and anti-capitalist labor movements, whereas export sectors characterized by national ownership, low capital necessities, and differentiated production would tend to produce weaker, more fractured, and ideologically co-opted labor movements.

REVISITING THE CLASSIC CASES

The chapters constituting part II of the volume revisit the classical cases explored in Bergquist's seminal book—Argentina, Chile, Colombia, and Venezuela—sometimes in comparative perspective. Ruth Felder and Viviana

Patroni engage critically with Bergquist's historical treatment of the Argentine case as a way of launching a novel interpretation of the strengths and weaknesses of the contemporary Argentine labor movement, particularly the organizing dynamics of informal and precarious workers in the wake of neoliberal restructuring over the 1990s. They take Bergquist to task for what they understand to be his one-sided interpretation of organized labor's alignment with Peronism historically. Whereas Bergquist understood classical Peronism to have been essentially characterized by the reactionary containment of the Argentine labor movement, Felder and Patroni emphasize its internal contradictions, ideological heterogeneity, and transformations over distinct historical periods (with the rise of left-wing factions at key moments in the 1960s and 1970s).

What attracted workers to Peronism, they argue, were the real material and legal gains experienced by the industrial working class during Perón's first presidency (1946–1952), and even if the material limits of the aspired capital-labor compromise had tilted much further toward capital by Perón's second term (1973–1974), for Felder and Patroni, "Peronism gave the working class a new political identity that would stand the test of time, allowing it to become a central political actor over the critical twenty years after the downfall of Perón in 1955 as the country confronted an increasingly violent deadlock." Through an examination of the Confederación de Trabajadores de la Economía Popular (Confederation of Popular Economy Workers), they develop their key argument that although precarious workers lack structural power (at least in the sense proposed by the editors in the introduction to this volume), their potential transformative power needs to be evaluated in relation to the surprising ability they have demonstrated to organize despite the tremendous obstacles they face, and their potential to contribute to the political unification of an increasingly fragmented and heterogenous working class, not least through their focus on social reproductive labor. Theoretically and politically, therefore, Felder and Patroni stress the necessity of combining analyses of productive and social reproductive labor, as well as their gendered components.

Whereas Bergquist's framework would seem to suggest that the relatively fragmented and individualized productive structure characteristic of Argentina's neoliberal "popular economy" would result in organizationally and politically conservative expressions of class struggle, Felder and Patroni stress that the truly innovative character of organizations like Confederación de Trabajadores de la Economía Popular is their "political conceptualization as the social space where workers who have lost the connection to a workplace and to the rights other workers enjoy, can find common grounds for their struggles and unity." Nonetheless, Felder and Patroni are not blind to the potential limits of organizations such as Confederación de Trabajadores de la Economía Popular, emphasizing that, because they lack structural power, for their genuine successes at association to be sustainable in the medium to longer term they need to be linked to broader political projects of unity with wider layers of the working class. In the absence of this, "rather than radicalize workers, working in the popular economy may constitute a form of managing and containing the potentially disruptive effects of widespread precarity and poverty." Interestingly, then, Felder and Patroni also mount a more implicit critique of a certain structural-determinacy in Bergquist's framework, at least with respect to the idea that fragmented productive structures are more likely than not to lead to conservative outcomes in associated labor movements, whereas later chapters by Andrea Marston and Phillip Hough, on the Bolivian and Colombian cases, respectively, seem to lend more support to Bergquist's theoretical expectations in this regard.

The chapter on the classical case of Venezuela, by Kristin Ciupa, traces the fate of Venezuela's labor movement and the Marxist left since 1980, focusing on the country's oil dependency, and against this backdrop the evolving relationship between the Venezuelan state, oil companies, and union organizing. Ciupa divides her analysis into periods of neoliberalism (1980–1999), the Pink Tide (2000–2014), and the post–Pink Tide (2015–present). Methodologically, Ciupa borrows from Bergquist's framework an attentiveness to the relationship between patterns of economic development in the oil sector and processes of labor movement formation therein, foreign/domestic ownership and degree of concentration of ownership, and the mediating influence of nationalism. To these three axes, Ciupa adds an analysis of state-corporate-labor relations, the cyclical dynamics of oil prices and rentier social relations, and the impact of an oil-dominated economy on labor organizing beyond the oil sector itself.

Ciupa shares Bergquist's basic axiom that class struggle, unfolding within the moving constraints of the oil economy, has had a tremendous impact on the social and political development of Venezuela. She traces the specific mechanisms and channels through which oil rents have helped to shape the Venezuelan state form and attendant relations between the state (including the party system) and unions and oil companies, as well as the distinctive potentialities for labor organizing in periods of capitalist expansion (the Pink Tide era) and contraction (the neoliberal and post–Pink Tide eras), and within formal and informal labor markets. Ciupa's chapter investigates not only the structural constraints molding labor movement formation, but also the contingent social and political struggles within the labor movement itself that forged particular paths at different moments, within the ostensible parameters of the possible (at times changing those parameters themselves in the process).

A key insight of Ciupa's chapter is that the nature of Venezuela's rentier state form activates a gravitational pull on the class struggle, from above and below, toward state capture, and thus access to oil rents. Within this dynamic, labor unions have tended to align themselves strategically with mainstream or oppositional political parties, a factor that is underdeveloped in Bergquist's original analysis. Tendential bureaucratization of labor unions in Venezuela has placed constraints on both the associational and structural powers of the country's working class, with labor unions shifting between active support for, and anemic opposition to, neoliberal policy at different junctures in recent history. One major phenomenon in the Venezuelan labor market in recent decades has been the accelerated expansion of informal labor. Whereas others have highlighted the associational possibilities of organizing among informal workers in Venezuela in descriptive terms, Ciupa's originality is to uncover previously hidden structural powers in this sector, precisely due to their indirect integration into (rather than marginalization or exclusion from) the rentier oil economy. The concealed but real structural integration of informal workers into the oil economy broadly conceived provides the theoretical and political basis for potential united social and political action between formal and informal workers, rooted in overlapping interests "formed by conditions of oil export and the global oil market, as well as by the political projects and distribution networks of particular governments." Although Ciupa's conclusion on the hidden structural power of informal workers is distinct from Felder and Patroni's findings in the Argentine case, where informal workers are said to lack structural power in the traditional sense, there are nonetheless overlaps between the two chapters with regard to the necessity and plausibility of informal and formal layers of the working class organizing together for shared political projects based on a number of shared class interests.

Colombia is the next of Bergquist's classic cases addressed in this volume. Whereas Bergquist focused on the politically consequential conservatism of Colombia's coffee farmers for much of the twentieth century, Phillip Hough's chapter maps the declining significance of this rural labor force in the opening decades of the twenty-first century, as cocaine eclipsed coffee as the country's leading export. Counterintuitively, rather than signifying the fading utility of Bergquist's framework, the underlying continuities in productive export structures and ownership patterns between coffee and cocaine in Colombia have made his core analytic more pertinent than ever to understanding the country's political economy. If the laborers in the coffee export sector contributed centrally to the development of Colombia's twentieth-century social and political institutions, coca growers producing cocaine for export are doing the same for the opening years of the twenty-first. The

cocaine economy, Hough points out, like the coffee economy a century earlier, "has absorbed surplus labor, stimulated domestic processes of economic
growth, and ultimately facilitated Colombia's re-insertion into the global
economy of the twenty-first century."

Paradoxically, as Hough demonstrates, the cocaine market intervention in
the 1980s, 1990s, and 2000s by the Revolutionary Armed Forces of Colombia (FARC), despite their self-identification as Marxist-Leninists, assumed
a form comparable to that of the National Federation of Coffee Growers
(Fedecafé) at the midpoint of the twentieth century. As long as the FARC
maintained its presence in large swathes of the Colombian countryside,
bolstered indirectly by the cocaine economy, the Colombian ruling classes'
efforts in the 1980s and 1990s to open the rural parts of the country to neoliberal extractivism were significantly impeded. The war-making initiatives
of President Álvaro Uribe in the opening decades of the twenty-first century
eventually undid this scenario by militarily defeating the FARC, and the new
balance of forces that has opened the countryside to capital-intensive and
labor-repulsive cattle-ranching, mining, and energy extraction found its formal expression in the peace accord reached between Uribe's successor, Juan
Manel Santos, and the FARC in 2016. While Hough builds his analysis on
the pillars established by Bergquist, he also extends Bergquist's analysis in
the spirit of the introduction to this volume, drawing expressly on Fernando
Coronil's "triadic dialectic" of capital-labor-nature.

In his chapter, Omar Manky places the classic case of Chile in comparison
with neighboring Peru. He finds strong support for Bergquist's conclusions
that the geographic isolation, structure and nationality of ownership, labor-
force demographics, and technicalities of the labor process in the Chilean
nitrate and copper industries of the late nineteenth and early twentieth centuries helped to produce a radically anti-capitalist labor movement with significant long-term impacts on social, political, and economic development in
the country as a whole. As in Chile, Manky shows, the export of minerals has
long been central to Peruvian capitalist development. In partial confirmation
of Bergquist's analytical framework, the mining sector in Peru was also the
locale for the country's most radical labor struggles relative to other sectors
of the labor movement. At the same time, the radicalism of mine workers in
Peru never approached that of Chile (or another neighbor of both countries,
Bolivia, for that matter), revealing the structuralist limits of the Bergquistian
point of departure.

The main thrust of Manky's chapter examines the theoretical strengths
and limits of Bergquist's hypotheses for understanding both the Chilean and
Peruvian cases since the onset of neoliberal restructuring in the late twentieth century and the concomitant transformations in labor markets and labor

organizing in the key export sectors of both countries. While most of the contemporary literature on the mining sector in each country ignores the contemporary significance of labor struggles, Manky insists that labor struggles in the mining export sectors continue to play a critical role in shaping the general dynamics of the Chilean and Peruvian labor movements, but that the struggles of mine workers are carried out in radically transformed structures of production. In sympathetic dialogue with Bergquist, and in a similar manner to Ciupa, Manky aims to extend and refine Bergquist's framework for the present rather than to challenge it frontally or abandon it entirely. In the process he seeks to explain how different structural points of departure created a weaker and less radical labor movement in Peru than in Chile in both the early to mid-twentieth-century period examined by Bergquist, as well as the late twentieth and early twenty-first centuries.

Manky's extension and refinement of Bergquist's perspective involves three analytical moves. The first is to integrate a historical sociology of state formation into Bergquist's toolkit, a missing feature acknowledged by Bergquist himself. A process of weak-repressive-oligarchic state formation in the Peruvian case allowed for fewer openings to radical labor than the comparatively democratic and strong process of Chilean state formation. The Peruvian ruling class maintained greater direct control of the comparatively weaker Peruvian state than did their Chilean counterparts and were able to repress labor and delay or prevent unionization in the mines. According to Manky, this basic dynamic of ruling-class-state relations characteristic of early Peruvian state formation continues to characterize the country's present.

The second analytical maneuver is to elaborate and make explicit the theoretical importance of space, scale, and social mobility (the geography of labor) in the making of labor movements in Latin American export sectors, a factor that is present at times but undertheorized in Bergquist's seminal book. In the process of analyzing the distinct geographies of labor in the two cases Manky also argues (in contrast to the discussion in the introduction to this volume) that the differences between them are explicable only with an account of the differentiated patterns in each of productive and social reproductive labor considered together. In Peru, unlike in Chile, there has been "continuous interaction between productive spaces and social reproduction spaces," resulting in "a proletarianization that is not only lengthy but complex and nuanced, and . . . almost incomplete when compared to the Chilean case."

The third element in Manky's effort to extend and refine Bergquist is the stress he places on the importance of the relationship between political activists and export workers in any explanation of the specificities and variations in labor movement formation. Although he does not tackle the issue of structural and associational power directly, the spirit of this third variable is essentially similar to the discussion of structure and association found in the introduction to this volume. Manky is stressing the elements of political contingency and human agency involved in labor movement formation (in other words, associational power), that may or may not result in workers effectively utilizing the potentiality inherent in their available structural power. Put simply, in the Peruvian case, left-wing political activists attempting to organize mine workers made more crucial political errors in their efforts to respond to the structural conditions in which they found themselves than did their Chilean counterparts.

FOUNDATIONAL CRITIQUE

In the last chapter of part II, Guido Starosta and Fernando Javier Cazón offer what is without doubt the most far-reaching and careful theoretical and empirical challenge to the foundational pillars of the Bergquistian analytic, as developed in *Labor in Latin America*. This is also a challenge, indirectly, therefore, to at least some of the premises of the introduction to this volume, as well as the overarching thrust of many of the other chapters of the collection. Their chapter makes an essential contribution to the volume as a whole, sharpening the terms of debate and elevating its rigor and theoretical seriousness. Given the far-reaching character of Starosta and Cazón's critique of some of the axiomatic premises of the rest of the collection, and precisely as a measure of the seriousness and scope of their critique, a critical response is necessary to develop as part of this conclusion.

Starosta and Cazón recognize the merit of Bergquist's emphasis on "Latin American societies derived from the essentially global dynamics of the capital accumulation process and the resulting forms of the international division of labor and uneven development." In their view, however, these promising elements of Bergquist's book are ultimately undermined by at least two major theoretical failings. The first is Bergquist's "utterly extrinsic" theoretical understanding of the relationship between "the economic" and "the political," which lead him both toward excessively voluntaristic political interpretation as well as to merely descriptive assessment of the outward, immediate, and empirical dimensions of the Latin American labor movements he studies (especially their ideologies and political organizations), as distinct from their immanent contents and fundamental determinants. The second theoretical problem in Bergquist's framework, in this account, is that his "characterization of the 'economic structure' of Latin American societies in terms of the particular configuration of the 'export sector' of each country, falls short of a rigorous explanation of the specific form of this region's national processes of capital accumulation and their role in the international division of labor." Theoretically, the alternative approach advanced by Starosta and Cazón pivots on two axes: (a) the class struggle "is the necessary political mode of realization of the contradictory economic content of capitalist social relations," and (b) "an abundant extraordinary mass of social wealth, in the social form of ground-rent, has systematically complemented the surplus-value extracted from the domestic working class to the point of marking the very specificity of the accumulation process in Latin American countries."

The critique of Bergquist advanced by Starosta and Cazón is itself mainly extrinsic rather than immanent insofar as it demands, on the one hand, a much higher level of abstraction at a theoretical level than the one operative in Bergquist's book (Bergquist is expressly skeptical of such an exercise), and, on the other hand, proceeds in terms of empirical analysis with an entirely different metric of "success" regarding the outcomes of specific labor movements. Theoretically, for Starosta and Cazón, the only way to understand the qualitative specificity of Latin American societies is through "a particular 'systematic-dialectical' approach to the Marxian critique of political economy, which grasps working class struggles as 'form-determined' by the 'law of value.'" After such systematic development, it will become obvious that the class struggle is "the necessary political form that mediates the contradictory establishment of the material unity between the productive and consumptive requirements of the reproduction of total social capital."

A key failing in Bergquist, from this perspective, is his representation of different Latin American labor movements as being at once externally conditioned by economic factors, and, at the same time, autonomously developed as self-moving political factors. This autonomous development as self-moving political factors then has a reverberating impact back upon, and thus externally conditions, the differentiated economic development of capitalism in each country. Instead, Starosta and Cazón contend, class struggle ought to be understood as "the most general direct social relation between collective personifications of commodities (thereby differentiated as a political form of social relations), which mediates the unfolding of the essentially indirect relations of capitalist production through the generalized commodity-form (hence distinguished as the economic form of social relations)," or, as "the necessary political form that mediates the contradictory establishment of the material unity between the productive and consumptive requirements of the reproduction of the total social capital." The class struggle, then, does not enjoy "autonomy" as a self-moving political factor, being instead, "the necessary political mode of realization of the contradictory economic content of capitalist social relations."

On the question of workers' agency, they insist that "it goes without saying that this does not imply the denial of the transformative powers of human practice personified by workers," but that "whatever transformative powers the political action of workers might have—whether capital-reproducing or capital-transcending political action—must be an immanent determination begotten by the movement of capital accumulation and not external to it." In practice, this theoretical foundation tends to mean that as they shift their focus—without, it seems to me, sufficient development of the necessary mediations—to the concrete analysis of Argentina and Chile, their account presents the actual historical development of the labor movement in each country as virtually the only one possible. At moments, their chapter therefore comes close to apology for the corporatist trade union strategies of high-Peronism, not because these are mistaken for being more militant and effective forms of trade union struggle than they were (they modestly improved the normal conditions for the reproduction of labor-power), but that they represented precisely the limit of what was possible and indeed necessary for the labor movement at the time given the conditions of capital accumulation. At the same time, on the other side of the comparison, the apparently more radical and anti-capitalist labor movement in Chile celebrated by Bergquist is depicted rather as an expression of "desperate resistance" (desperate because only reformist ends were possible given the reigning economic content of capital accumulation in the given period), which had the deleterious effect of simply delaying "the universalization of unionization levels and the crystallization of effective legally sanctioned recognition of labor rights until significantly later."

In sharp contradistinction to Bergquist's analysis, counterfactual historical inquiry—questions like, What might have happened if a particular labor movement had developed in a different political direction at crucial historical turning points?—is more or less ruled out in Starosta and Cazón's analytic, or at least it is difficult to discern what part such questions could play in their framework. As a result, the importance of workers' political strategy (and the possibility of error) is similarly reduced in importance. Instead, the form of class struggle that was in fact historically assumed over the long run was the necessary (and therefore only possible?) political form assumed by the class struggle given the contradictory movement of capital accumulation in that historical period within the national space in question. Counterfactual inquiry, however seriously and restrictively conducted, on what might have been done differently in terms of political strategy and organization, to produce better, more far-reaching results for a particular labor movement, is too easily dismissed as voluntarism in this framework, or at a higher level of abstraction waived away as missing the dialectical unity of the economic and the political.

In terms of selection of different metrics to measure "success" or "strength" of a particular labor movement, Starosta and Cazón argue that Bergquist is mistaken in his emphases on the ideology, political organization, and strategy of struggle assumed by different labor movements at different historical junctures as part of a measure of their "strength." But, of course, these ideological, organizational, and strategic factors are only deemed important by Bergquist in relation to the potential structural power that the workers he investigated enjoyed because of their strategic economic position within key export sectors. Their political orientation is only important to Bergquist because of their potential to disrupt capital accumulation. That is, ideology, political organization, and strategy become important for Bergquist, not as metrics of "success" or "strength" in and of themselves (the politics, ideology, and organization of nonstrategic export workers does not feature at all in his work), but because the adoption of one strategy rather than another, or one form of class struggle vis-à-vis the state, instead of another, had an impact on whether the latent potential structural power, enjoyed by these particular workers who are rooted in key export sectors, was realized to its fullest, or partially, or not at all. For Bergquist, this does not imply that any and all ideological, political, and organizational options are available for workers to choose from in any given historical scenario (i.e., voluntarism). It is only to insist that structural potential power is not realized automatically and that different strategic political approaches will lead to different outcomes of potential significance, within limits.

Interestingly, while Starosta and Cazón offer a critique of the ostensible politicism of Bergquist's account, for Manky, as noted earlier, Bergquist's framework is insufficiently political, insofar as it downplays the importance of political activists and the differentiated level of success they enjoyed in organizing workers similarly structured in comparable export sectors. To investigate political, organizational, and strategic questions to the extent Bergquist does is, for Starosta and Cazón, to assume an extrinsic perspective on the relationship between "the economic" and "the political," and to assume the autonomy, or relative autonomy, of ideology, organization, and strategy. And yet their alternative to such "voluntarism" seems to be to minimize quite radically the interventionist possibilities of class struggle (except as a necessary political expression of a given economic content). Strategic, political, and ideological elements of labor struggle become explicable only as the "necessary" political forms assumed by the contradictory rhythms of capitalist accumulation within a given national space.

For Starosta and Cazón, the "'measure' of the objective (progressive) transformative potentiality of a certain historical expression of the labor movement does not simply boil down to those ideological forms. Instead, it is objectively manifested in the extent to which it manages to improve the conditions of productive consumption and reproduction of labor-power in a relatively universal or undifferentiated manner across the different organs of the working class." The real metric to determine the strength of a labor movement within capitalist develpoment is to assess its ability to improve the "conditions of normal reproduction of labor-power." Operationally, in order to get at this metric, they turn to data on the comparative purchasing power of economy-wide real wages in Chile and Argentina from 1940 to 1982, as well data on economy-wide real wages in Argentina alone between 1900 and 1982. In the context of twentieth-century Latin America, strength or weakness of labor movements on this measure are, in turn, determined by the potentiality of the process of capital accumulation in a given Latin American country to "develop through a broader and deeper [import-substitution industrializa- tion] ISI process," that if realized will create the need for "the generation and reproduction of a working class that embodies more complex productive capacities (and also of their expanded absorption as active 'industrial army,' i.e., through rising manufacturing employment)." For these reasons, countries that attained more thoroughgoing processes of ISI exhibited "an overall ten- dency for an average higher value of labor power of the respective national fragment of the working class" and a "stronger labor movement in its conflict against the bourgeoisie."

Bergquist's celebration of the apparently radical, conflictual, and Marxist character of the Chilean labor movement, and his criticism of the apparently conservative and co-opted Peronist character of its Argentine counterpart, makes little sense when seen through Starosta and Cazón's alternative theo- retical framework. For them, Bergquist confuses ideological and political appearance with the actual content of labor movement strength or weakness as measured by its ability to improve the conditions of the normal reproduc- tion of labor-power. On the latter metric, Bergquist's central conclusions on the respective strength and weakness of Argentine and Chilean labor movements would need to be reversed, given that Argentina's more thor- oughgoing ISI produced a stronger labor movement (despite apparent ideo- logical conservatism), while Chile's shallower ISI produced a weaker labor movement (despite apparent ideological radicalism). The more conflictual, class-struggle-based unionism—or, in their words, "desperate resistance"— found in Chilean history and admired by Bergquist is of little import when considered alongside Chile's relatively weaker concrete improvements in the normal conditions of the reproduction of labor-power over a comparable period in Argentina.

In sum, Starosta and Cazón's account is an internally consistent, theo- retically sophisticated, and empirically rigorous challenge to the Bergquistian framework that underpins—if not uncritically—the intended analytical purpose and initiative represented by this volume as a whole. The disproportionate attention their chapter has received in this conclusion is exactly a measure of the seriousness with which I take their contribution to the debate the editors intended to introduce with this volume, a debate I hope continues to be developed and refined elsewhere.

STRETCHING THE FRAMEWORK

Part III of the book moves beyond discussion of the cases studied by Bergquist himself, in an effort to consider the possibilities of critically extending elements of his framework beyond what he was able to do on his own. The chapter by Anna Zalik and Aleida Hernández Cervantes focuses on Mexico, beginning with Bergquist, but also moving beyond him into new theoretical terrain. Bergquist's *Labor in Latin America* offers some provocative and insightful, but also fleeting and undeveloped, ideas about how one might extend the underlying heuristic of his book to the concentrated and particular study of Mexican history. Zalik and Hernández Cervantes take up and refine this mantle. Adhering not merely to the heuristic model presented by Bergquist in the introductory and concluding chapters of *Labor in Latin America*, Zalik and Hernández Cervantes are also attentive to the spirit with which Bergquist developed the detailed, painstaking narratives of his four national case studies, paying special attention as Zalik and Hernández Cervantes do to the historical singularities and complexities of the Mexican case. Zalik and Hernández Cervantes move systematically through the 1917 Mexican Revolution, the oil expropriation and nationalization of 1938 during the presidency of Lázaro Cárdenas, and subsequent consolidation of a system of corporatist state-labor relations. They then go on to chart the unraveling of both this national control over oil and its attendant corporatist labor system during the neoliberal restructuring of the 1980s, 1990s, and 2000s. Associated with this neoliberal turn, they highlight the expansion of gendered labor exploitation in the maquila sector that accelerated in the wake of the North American Free Trade Agreement in 1994, as well as its successor, the US-Mexico-Canada Agreement in 2020. They point out that greater labor transnationalism and independent trade-unionism emerged in response to the changing material realities introduced by these initiatives.

Throughout their chapter, Zalik and Hernández Cervantes frame their historical narrative analytically through the thematic prisms of extractivism, labor-nature, and productive/reproductive labor. Indeed, one of the features that partially distinguishes this chapter from the framework advanced in the introduction to this volume is its insistence on both the historical and analytical inseparability of categories like human society and nonhuman nature, as well as productive and social reproductive labor. Likewise, they depart from the restrictive definition of extractivism advanced in the introduction, including (in an interesting parallel to the chapter by Christopher Little) the export of labor itself through migration (and not simply transborder migration, but internal migration within Mexico itself toward the maquila sector in the north) as part of their understanding of capitalist extraction in the neoliberal period. In a final methodological innovation, they call for the transcendence of the comparative-national analytical lens of labor movements developed by Bergquist (if always, for him, understood as developing within an international division of labor) toward a more transnational framework, in order to better comprehend processes such as the labor solidarities that developed between Mexican, American, and Canadian workers for and against agreements such as the North American Free Trade Agreement and the US-Mexico-Canada Agreement.

Substantively, Zalik and Hernández Cervantes find broad confirmation of the connection Berquist draws between foreign ownership in extractive sectors and the development of radically anti-imperialist labor movements in their analysis of the role of export laborers in both the Mexican Revolution and the subsequent expropriation and nationalization of foreign oil companies. Likewise, they take it to be a confirmation of Berquist's framework that once this externally uniting force of foreign ownership was extinguished through nationalization of oil, the labor movement gradually lost much of its class independence and radicalism, as corporatist state-labor relations were consolidated. Finally, Bergquist's framework on foreign ownership and anti-imperialism is also useful, they argue, for understanding the substantive (if never formalized) processes of denationalization and privatization of Mexico's oil sector, beginning as early as the 1970s, but accelerating from the 1990s forward. The crushing of corporatist labor unions and the reintroduction of foreign firms were necessary elements of this restructuring and they spurred, as Bergquist's framework would expect, a reignition of more autonomous forms of labor organizing, with an anti-imperial sensibility. The gains that this reignited labor militancy would eventually achieve found formal expression in the labor reforms embedded in the US-Mexico-Canada Agreement and associated domestic Mexican legislation under the presidency of Manuel López Obrador. Nonetheless, such gains can only be fully understood, according to Zallik and Hernández Cervantes, by moving beyond Bergquist's focus on national labor movements toward an understanding of labor internationalism between workers in Mexico, the United States, and Canada. Similarly, for Zalik and Hernández Cervantes, the limits of what has been achieved by the reignition of autonomous labor struggles thus far in terms of gender also requires an analysis that exceeds the parameters laid out by Bergquist. Specifically, they argue, the gendered dynamics of both productive and reproductive labor must be taken into account.

Bolivia, a neighboring country of two of Bergquist's classic cases—Chile and Argentina—is the subject of Andrea Marston's chapter. In particular, Marston examines the historical fragmentation of the labor movement in the mining sector, documenting a decisive, prolonged shift—involving long stretches of gradualism, punctuated by years of great intensity—from radical *sindicalismo* (trade unionism) to much more conservative *cooperativismo* (cooperativism) between 1960 and the present, with the fundamental acceleration of the cooperative sector beginning with the collapse of the tin industry and the onset of radical neoliberal restructuring in the mid-1980s. Bergquist's portrayal of culturally autonomous, class-conscious, and anti-capitalist nitrate and copper workers in late nineteenth and early twentieth-century Chile finds a close echo in Marston's characterization of mid-twentieth-century Bolivian labor struggles in the tin mining sector. However, the productive structure undergirding this radicalism was fundamentally undermined in the neoliberal era, with lasting implications to the present. In the mid-1980s, a significant proportion of the labor-power embodied by workers formerly employed in the state mining sector was absorbed through "cooperativization," mainly in abandoned deposits of tin, as well as of other metals. Here, these newly consecrated cooperativistas used their past union experiences in the state-owned tin sector to organize and struggle on behalf of their evolving material interests, finding themselves as they did within a radically distinct productive structure and pattern of ownership.

In a fascinating interpretation of Bergquist, one that parallels crucial elements of Hough's findings vis-à-vis contemporary coca growers in the Colombian case, Marston argues that the cooperativization of Bolivian mining labor had the paradoxical result of transforming the sector from one closely resembling the paradigmatic productive structure and political orientation of Bergquist's most radical example of labor movement formation—Chilean nitrate and copper workers—to one closely resembling his most conservative case—mid-twentieth-century Colombian coffee growers. In Bolivia, the mid-twentieth-century, state-owned tin industry was "capital intensive and technologically sophisticated," with mostly national Bolivian workers concentrated in "a handful of geographically isolated mining towns." This scenario helped to produce a "stridently anti-imperialist" labor movement that "sought workers' control over mining operations."

Following the shift to cooperativism, the productive structure has been characterized by geographically dispersed areas of extraction, relatively low capital requirements using mainly existing technologies, and cooperative miners themselves assuming the helm of mining operations. The associated shift in political orientation is expressed in the typical demands of cooperativistas: "more work areas, lower taxes, and reduced regulatory oversight." Over the last two decades, Marston shows, a global commodity boom has driven large numbers of workers into the labor-intensive cooperative sector "at the same moment that a newly leftist government was refocusing its efforts on natural gas production, which has comparatively low labor requirements." Successful agitation on the part of cooperativistas influenced the policy of state subsidization of mining cooperatives under that leftist government of Evo Morales. If Marston's conclusions on cooperativistas mirror patterns found in the Colombian case of coca growers explored by Hough, Marston also arrives at a similar conclusion to Ciupa on informal Venezuelan workers when Marston argues that Bolivian cooperativistas have been able to translate a lasting and effective associational power into material gains and supportive governmental policies by mobilizing in expressly political forms, rather than traditional economic strikes (given that these are no longer structurally available to them).

In the final chapter of part III, Christopher Little takes Bergquist's "methodological and theoretical prioritization of the structurally bounded agency of labor" as the point of departure for an investigation of "circuits of labor migration as a form of extractivism," elaborating upon a range of theoretical issues that are then grounded in the concrete dynamics of contemporary migrant labor-power extraction from El Salvador, Guatemala, and Honduras. Of all the chapters in the collection, Little's chapter presents perhaps the most daring speculative exploration of the limits to which Bergquist's broad theoretical membrane can be stretched and adapted to novel methodological premises and analytical presuppositions without tearing, and while preserving its most essential characteristics. The first analytical move is, of course, to shift attention to the export of extracted labor-power itself from Bergquist's original purpose of studying labor within extractive export sectors. Drawing on dominant strands of the latest literature on Latin American extractivism, and in contradistinction to the narrower view of extractivism defended in the introduction to this volume, Little's second innovation is to re-read Bergquist through the interpretive lens of a broad schema of extractivism, "whereby the extractive logic operating in the utilization of natural resources under capitalism also extends into other spheres of accumulation," including, most pertinently, migration. A third and final stretching occurs through a shift from Bergquist's focus on productive labor to an explicit theorization of social reproductive labor, because, according to Little, "it is ultimately in this realm that the process of extracting migrant labor-power takes place."

Little's primary contention is that the export of labor-power ought to be understood as extractivism, "when it takes place under certain combined conditions of uneven development, accumulation by dispossession . . . and the externalization of the costs of social reproduction by the receiving states." What is at stake, theoretically and politically, is the analytical exposure of the essence of labor migration as a central basis for the reproduction "of an uneven, hierarchical international system that distributes wealth upwards, reinforcing the relative positions of richer and poorer states alike," even as it assumes the immediate appearance as virtuous driver of meaningful development in impoverished countries. The conditions under which migrant labor-power is extracted in the current order of global capitalism, "reflects the subordination of workers' agency and structural power to the demands of the world economy." As an underlying heuristic set of premises, Little finds inspiration in Bergquist's careful dialectical and processual treatment of both the world-economic structural forces that condition the limits of labor's agency at the periphery of the world-system, as well as the ever-present potentiality of labor to act upon the structural power at its disposal, and in so doing to redefine the limits of possibility set out by world-systemic structures. If, for Bergquist, workers in export production should constitute the principal subject area of Latin American labor history in the early twentieth century, for Little, "one of the primary objects of contemporary Latin American labor studies should be migrant works and the export of labor-power."

REFLECTIONS

At a minimum, this volume has succeeded in exposing an enormous gap regarding the question of labor in the existing literature on capitalist extractivism in Latin America. It has also intended to move beyond mere exposure of this absence by collecting a range of chapters by leading specialists from a variety of disciplines with the aim of formulating the beginning of an effective response, as well as the bases and stimuli for further debate. While there are significant differences among the contributors regarding the utility of Bergquist's heuristic framework as a whole—or select parts of that whole—for understanding labor within contemporary Latin American extractivism, the elevated level of the discussion provoked by the exercise has itself been a tribute to Bergquist's memory shortly after his death, as well as to his particular contributions to radical Latin American social history, especially his most important and relatively neglected text, *Labor in Latin America*, which remains lamentably out of print at the time of writing.

The combining in the introduction by the editors of Bergquist's analytical framework with Coronil's triadic dialectic of capital-labor-nature, as well as Wright's associational and structural powers, finds sympathetic echo across a number of the chapters collected here. At the same time, there is clearly much less agreement among the contributors regarding the editors' insistence on a restrictive definition of extractivism, and their argument for clear analytical distinctions between general human labor, productive labor, and social reproductive labor, as well as between human society and nonhuman nature. Likewise, unresolved issues abound across the chapters regarding the associational and structural potentialities for workers' struggle in both informal and formal sectors under conditions of extractive capitalism, as well as the possibilities for forging working-class unity across these apparent divides. Both the implicit and explicit tensions revealed by the different contributions to this volume surrounding these themes suggest the need for further elaboration and debate.

Nor are these debates merely scholasticism. There is no longer any reasonable doubt surrounding the monumental ecological and social destruction engendered by the expansion of capitalist extractivism around the world generally, and in Latin America in particular. It is also evident that capitalist extractivism is bound to extend and deepen its grip on the region—with horrific consequence for the region and the world—if popular classes and oppressed peoples of the region prove unable to develop a sufficiently powerful and articulated opposition and alternative. If Bergquist was correct that strategically located export workers sometimes became the pivotal force behind wider political labor movements of a radically anti-capitalist nature in modern Latin American history, might they not do the same today? How did they do so then? In alliance with whom? How might they do so today? In alliance with whom? It is hardly an exaggeration to suggest that our future—in Latin America, certainly, but also in many ways the world more generally—may depend on the answers to these questions.

Bibliography

Abreu, Wladimir. 2020. "Informal Economy and Quarantine, a Bad Match." *Venezuelanalysis*, May 28, https://venezuelanalysis.com/analysis/14889.

Acosta, Alberto, and John Cajas-Guijarro. 2022. "Mariátegui and Dependency Theory: Reviewing a Powerful Inheritance in Latin American Thought." *Latin American Perspectives* 49, no. 1: 199–217.

Aggio, Alberto. 2008. "La Cultura Política del Radicalismo Chileno en Clave de Revolución Pasiva." *Ayer* no. 70: 141–68.

Almaraz Paz, Sergio. 1980. *El poder y la caida: El estaño en la historia de Bolivia.* La Paz: Los Amigos del Libro.

Alonso-Fradejas, Alberto. 2012. "Land Control-Grabbing in Guatemala: The Political Economy of Contemporary Agrarian Change." *Canadian Journal of Development Studies* 33 (4): 509–28. https://doi.org/10.1080/02255189.2012.743455.

Alonso-Fradejas, Alberto. 2015. "Anything but a Story Foretold: Multiple Politics of Resistance to the Agrarian Extractivist Project in Guatemala." *Journal of Peasant Studies* 42: 489–515.

Alonso-Fradejas, Alberto. 2021. "Life Purging Agrarian Extractivism in Guatemala: Towards a Renewable but Unlivable Future?" In *Agrarian Extractivism in Latin America*, edited by Ben M. McKay, Alberto Alonso-Fradejas, and Arturo Ezquerro-Cañete, chapter 7. New York: Routledge.

Altamirano, Carlos. 2001. *Bajo el signo de las masas (1943–1973).* Buenos Aires: Ariel.

Alzaga, Oscar. 2018. "Huelgas, sindicatos y luchas sociales en la historia de Mexico." *Alegatos* 99 (May/August).

Amat y Leon, Patricia. 2015. *Transitando caminos: Mujeres y minería: Voces y textos sobre los comités de amas de casa mineros (1982–1992).* Lima: Filomena Tomaira Pacsi.

Andía, Juan Javier Rivera, and Cecilie Vindal Ødegaard. 2019. "Introduction: Indigenous Peoples, Extractivism, and Turbulences in South America." In *Indigenous*

Life Projects and Extractivism Ethnographies from South America, edited by Juan Javier Andía and Cecilie Vindal Ødegaard. New York: Palgrave Macmillan.

Angenendt, Steffen. 2014. "Triple Win Migration—Challenges and Opportunities." Framework paper, Migration Strategy Group on Global Competitiveness, https://www.bosch-stiftung.de/sites/default/files/publications/pdf/2019-01/MSG_policy_brief_Angenendt.pdf.

Angotti, Tom, ed. 2017. *Urban Latin America: Inequalities and Neoliberal Reforms*. Lanham, MD: Rowman & Littlefield Publishers.

Antonio Menedez, G. 1958. *Doheny El Cruel: Episodios de la Sangrienta Lucha por el Petroleo Mexicano*. Mexico: Bolsa Mexicano del Libro.

Antunes de Oliveira, Felipe. 2022. "Lost and Found: Bourgeois Dependency Theory and the Forgotten Roots of Neodevelopmentalism." *Latin American Perspectives* 49, no. 1: 36–56.

Aravena, Antonio, and Daniel Núñez. 2009. *El renacer de la huelga obrera en Chile*. Santiago de Chile: Ocho Libros.

Arboleda, Martín. 2016. "Spaces of Extraction, Metropolitan Explosions: Planetary Urbanization and the Commodity Boom in Latin America." *International Journal of Urban and Regional Research* 40, no. 1: 96–112.

Arboleda, Martín. 2020. *Planetary Mine: Territories of Extraction under Late Capitalism*. London: Verso.

Aricó, José. 1999. "La hipótesis de Justo. Escritos sobre el socialismo en América Latina." *Editorial Sudamericana*. Buenos Aires, Argentina.

Arroyo, Michelle, and Anna Zalik. 2016. "Displacement and Denationalisation: The Mexican Gulf 75 Years After the Expropriation." *Area* 48, no. 2: 134–41.

Arruzza, Cinzia. 2014. "Remarks on Gender." *Viewpoint Magazine*, September 2, https://www.viewpointmag.com/2014/09/02/remarks-on-gender/.

Arruzza, Cinzia. 2015. "Functionalist, Determinist, Reductionist: Social Reproduction Feminism and Its Critics." *Science and Society* 80, no. 1: 9–30.

Atabaki, Touraj, Elisabeth Bini, and Kaveh Ehsani. 2018. *Working for Oil: Comparative Social Histories of Labor in the Global Oil Industry*. New York: Springer.

Auty, Richard M. 2001. "The Political Economy of Resource-Driven Growth." *European Economic Review* 45, no. 4: 839–46.

Azzellini, Dario. 2018. *Communes and Workers' Control in Venezuela: Building 21st Century Socialism from Below*. Chicago: Haymarket Books.

Baglioni, Elena, Liam Campling, Neil M. Coe, and Adrian Smith, eds. 2022. *Labor Regimes and Global Production*. Newcastle upon Tyne: Agenda Publishing.

Bair, Jennifer, and Phillip A. Hough. 2012. "The Legacies of Partial Possession: From Agrarian Struggle to Neoliberal Restructuring in Mexico and Colombia." *International Journal of Comparative Sociology* 53, no. 5–6: 345–66.

Bakker, Isabella, and Stephen Gill. 2019. "Rethinking Power, Production, and Social Reproduction: Toward Variegated Social Reproduction." *Capital & Class* 43, no. 4: 503–23. https://doi.org/10.1177/0309816819880783.

Balbi, Carmen Rosa. 1980. *El partido comunista y el APRA en la crisis revolucionaria de los años treinta*. Lima: G. Herrera.

Banaji, Jairus. 2003. "The Fictions of Free Labor: Contract, Coercion, and So-Called Unfree Labor." *Historical Materialism* 11, no. 3: 69–95. https://doi.org/10.1163/1 56920603770678319.

Barbosa, Fernando. 2003. *El petroleo en los Hoyos de Dona.* Mexico City: Miguel Angel Porrua/UNAM.

Barragán Romano, Rossana. 2017. "Los K'ajchas* y los proyectos de industria y mación en Bolivia (1935-1940)." *Revista Mundos do Trabalho* 9 (18): 25–48.

Barrios, Pablo Artaza, Sergio González Miranda, and Susana Jiles Castillo. 2009. *A cien años de la Masacre de Santa María de Iquique.* Santiago, Chile: LOM Ediciones.

Barrios de Chungara, Domitila. 1978. *"Si me permiten hablar . . ." Testimonio de Domitila, una mujer de las minas de Bolivia.* Buenos Aires: Siglo XXI Editores.

Bascuas, Maisa, Ruth Felder, Ana Logiudice, and Viviana Patroni. 2021. "Rethinking Working-class Politics: Organising Informal Workers in Argentina." *Global Labour Journal* 12, no. 3: 244–66.

Basualdo, Eduardo, Pablo Manzanelli, María José Castells, and Mariano Barrera. 2019. *Informe de coyuntura N° 32.* Buenos Aires: Centro de Investigación y Formación de la República Argentina. http://www.centrocifra.org.ar/docs/32.pdf.

Bebbington, Anthony, Abdul-Gafaru Abdulai, Denise Humphreys Bebbington, Marja Hinfelaar, and Cynthia Sanborn. 2018. *Governing Extractive Industries: Politics, Histories, Ideas,* illustrated edition. Oxford, UK: Oxford University Press.

Bebbington, Anthony, and Jeffrey Bury, eds. 2013. *Subterranean Struggles: New Dynamics of Mining, Oil, and Gas in Latin America.* Austin: University of Texas Press.

Bebbington, Anthony. 2012a. *Social Conflict, Economic Development and Extractive Industry: Evidence from South America.* Abingdon, Oxfordshire: Routledge.

Bebbington, Anthony. 2012b. "Extractive Industries, Socio-Environmental Conflicts and Political Economic Transformations in Andean America." In *Extractive Industries, Social Conflict and Economic Development: Evidence Form South America,* edited by Anthony Bebbington. London: Routledge.

Bell, Lee, Dave Evers, and Mark Burton. 2021. "La exposición al mercurio de las mujeres en cuatro países Latinoamericanos productores de oro." Red Internacional de Eliminación de Contaminantes (IPEN). https://ipen.org/sites/default/files/documents/ipen-lac-hg-hair-sampling-four-countries-v1_9bw-es.pdf.

Benitez, Fernando. 1984. "La expropriacion petrolera." In *Lazaro Cardenas y la Revolucion Mexicana.* Mexico: Biblioteca Joven/Fondo de Cultura Economica.

Bergquist, Charles. 1978. *Coffee and Conflict in Colombia, 1886–1910.* Durham, NC: Duke University Press.

Bergquist, Charles. 1984. *Labor in the Capitalist World Economy.* Beverly Hills: Sage Publications.

Bergquist, Charles 1986. *Labor in Latin America: Comparative Essays on Chile, Argentina, Venezuela, and Colombia.* Stanford: Stanford University Press.

Bergquist, Charles. 1990. "Latin American Labor History in Comparative Perspective: Notes on the Insidiousness of Cultural Imperialism." *Labor/Le Travailleur* 25: 189–98.

Bergquist, Charles. 1996. *Labor and the Course of American Democracy: US History in Latin American Perspective*. London: Verso.

Bergquist, Charles. 2001. "Waging War and Negotiating Peace: The Contemporary Crisis in Historical Perspective." In *Violence in Colombia, 1990–2000: Waging War and Negotiating Peace*. Wilmington, DE: Scholarly Resources, Inc.

Bergquist, Charles, Ricardo Peñaranda, and Gonzalo Sánchez, eds. 1992. *Violence in Colombia: The Contemporary Crisis in Historical Perspective*. Wilmington, DE: Scholarly Resources, Inc.

Bernstein, Henry. 2000. "Colonialism, Capitalism, Development." In *Poverty and Development Into the 21st Century*, edited by Tim Allen and Alan Thomas. Oxford: Oxford University Press.

Bertranou, Fabio, Luis Casanova, and Marianela Sarabia. 2013. "How, Why and in What Sectors Employment Informality Decreased in Argentina from 2003 to 2012." Paper presented at the Third Regulating for Decent Work Conference, "Regulating for Equitable and Job-Rich Growth." Geneva, July 3–5. http://dx.doi.org/10.2139/ssrn.2276034.

Bhattacharya, Tithi. 2015. "How Not To Skip Class: Social Reproduction of Labor and the Global Working Class." *Viewpoint Magazine*. https://www.viewpoint-mag.com/2015/10/31/how-not-to-skip-class-social-reproduction-of-labor -and-the-global-working-class/.

Bisio, Rubén, Osvaldo Battistini, and Juan Montes Cató. 1999. "Transformaciones de la negociación colectiva durante la vigencia de gobeiernos constitucionales a partir de 1973." In *Política y Relaciones Laborales en la Transición Democrática Argentina*, edited by Arturo Fernández and Raúl Bisio, 135–79. Buenos Aires: Editorial Lumen/Humanitas.

Bonilla, Heraclio. 1974. *El minero de los Andes: Una aproximación a su estudio*. Instituto de Estudios Peruanos.

Bouzas Ortíz, Alfonso. 2022. *Economic Growth and Income Distribution*. Welfare and Public Policies, Mexico City, IIEc-UNAM.

Braga, Ruy. 2012. *A politica do precariado: Do populismo à hegemonia Lulista*. São Paulo: Boitempo.

Breman, Jan. 1994. *Wage Hunters and Gatherers: Search for Work in the Urban and Rural Economy of South Gujarat*. Oxford: Oxford University Press.

Brown, Jonathan. 1985. "Why Foreign Oil Companies Shifted their Production from Mexico to Venezuela during the 1920s." *The American Historical Review* 90, no. 2: 362–85.

Brown, Jonathan. 1993/2022. *Oil and Revolution in Mexico*. San Francisco: University of California Press.

Brown, Jonathan, and Alan Knight. 1992. *The Mexican Petroleum Industry in the Twentieth Century*. Austin: University of Texas Press.

Burawoy, Michael. 2010. "From Polanyi to Pollyanna: The False Optimism of Global Labour Studies." *Global Labour Journal* 1, no. 2: 301–13.

Burawoy, Michael. 1976. "The Functions and Reproduction of Migrant Labor: Comparative Material from Southern Africa and the United States." *American Journal of Sociology* 81, no. 5: 1050–87.

Burchardt, Hans-Jürgen, and Kristina Dietz. 2014. "(Neo-)Extractivism—A New Challenge for Development Theory from Latin America." *Third World Quarterly* 35, no. 3: 468–86. https://doi.org/10.1080/01436597.2014.893488.

Burke, Melvin. 1987. "The Corporación Minera de Bolivia (Comibol) and the Triangular Plan: A Case Study in Dependency." *Latin American Issues* 4. http://sites .allegheny.edu/latinamericanstudies/latin-american-issues/volume-4/.

Burt, Jo-Marie. 2007. *Political Violence and the Authoritarian State in Peru.* New York: Palgrave Macmillan.

Buxton, Julia. 2020. "Continuity and Change in Venezuela's Bolivarian Revolution." *Third World Quarterly* 41, no. 8: 1371–87.

Caligaris, Gastón, Alejandro Fitzsimons, Sebastián Guevara, and Guido Starosta. 2022. "A Missing Link in the Agrarian Question: The Role of Ground-Rent and Landed Property in Capital Accumulation. The Case of Argentina (1993-2019)." *Journal of Peasant Studies* 50, no. 5: 1709–34.

Caligaris, Gastón, Alejandro Fitzsimons, and Guido Starosta. 2024. *Value, Money and Capital. The Critique of Political Economy and Contemporary Capitalism.* London: Routledge.

Campling, Liam, and Alejandro Colas. 2021. *Capitalism and the Sea: The Maritime Factor in the Making of the Modern World.* London: Verso.

Campling, Liam, Satoshi Miyamura, Jonathan Pattenden, and Benjamin Selwyn. 2016. "Class Dynamics of Development: A Methodological Note." *Third World Quarterly* 37, no. 10: 1745–67. https://doi.org/10.1080/01436597.2016.1200440.

Canelas Orellana, Amada. 1981. *¿Quiebra de la minería estatal Boliviana?* La Paz/ Cochabamba: Los Amigos del Libro.

Carr, Barry. 2002. Globalization from Below: Labour Internationalism under NAFTA. *International Social Science Journal* 51, no. 159: 49–59.

Caruso, German, Lautaro Chittaro, Maria Emilia Cucagna, and Luis Pedro Espana. 2021. "From Bad to Worse: The Economic Impact of COVID-19 in Developing Countries. Evidence from Venezuela." *Latin American Economic Review* 30: 1–22.

Castells, Manuel. 1996. *The Rise of the Network Society.* Malden, MA: Blackwell Publishers.

Castles, Stephen, and Raúl Delgado Wise. 2012. "Notes for a Strategic Vision on Development, Migration and Human Rights." *Migración y Desarrollo* 10 (March): 173–78.

Castro, Laura Rodriquez. 2021. "Extractivism and Territorial Dispossession in Rural Colombia: A Decolonial Commitment to Campesinas' Politics of Place." *Feminist Review* 128, no. 1: 44–61. https://doi.org/10.1177%2F01417789211015269.

Cazón, Fernando. 2015. "Las características de la acción sindical en la acumulación de capital Argentina entre 1940 y 1955." XV Jornadas Interescuelas/Departamentos de Historia. Comodoro Rivadavia, Argentina.

Cazón, Fernando. 2019. "La institucionalización y regulación de la acción sindical en el proceso de acumulación de capital en Argentina: Un análisis del decreto 23852/45." XIII Jornadas de Sociología. Buenos Aires, Argentina.

Cazón, Fernando. 2021. "Las etapas de la legislación laboral en tanto expresión de la reproducción de la fuerza de trabajo en el proceso de acumulación de capital en Argentina." *XIV Jornadas de Sociología*. Buenos Aires, Argentina.

Cerda, René. 2014. *La masacre de El Salvador*. Santiago: Cerda Editor.

CETYD (Capacitación y Estudios sobre Trabajo y Desarrollo: Seguimiento de la Situación Laboral). 2019. Sguimiento Permanente de la Situación Laboral Actualización #17, December. http://www.cetyd.unsam.edu.ar/documentos/situacion-laboral/segiumient_completo.pdf (accessed 20 June 2020).

Chagnon, Christopher W., Francesco Durante, Barry K. Gills, Sophia E. Hagolani-Albov, Saana Hokkanen, Sohvi M. J. Kangasluoma, Heidi Konttinen, et al. 2022. "From Extractivism to Global Extractivism: The Evolution of an Organizing Concept." *The Journal of Peasant Studies* 49 (4): 1–33. https://doi.org/10.1080/03066 150.2022.2069015.

Chartrand, Tyler, and Leah F. Vosko. 2021. "Canada's Temporary Foreign Worker and International Mobility Programs: Charting Change and Continuity Among Source Countries." *International Migration* 59 (2): 89–109. https://doi.org/10.1111/imig.12762.

Chiasson-LeBel, Thomas. 2016. "Neo-Extractivism in Venezuela and Ecuador: A Weapon of Class Conflict." *The Extractive Industries and Society* 3, no. 4: 888–901. https://doi.org/10.1016/j.exis.2016.10.006.

Chilcote, Ronald H., and Joana Salém Vasconcelos. 2022. "Introduction: Whither Development Theory?" *Latin American Perspectives* 49, no. 1: 4–17.

Chomsky, Aviva. 2019. "In Colombia, 'Without Life, There Are No Jobs.'" *NACLA* 51, no. 3: 293. http://dx.doi.org/10.1080/10714839.2019.1650510.

Chomsky, Aviva, and Steve Striffler. 2014. "Empire, Labor, and Environment: Coal Mining and Anticapitalist Environmentalism in the Americas." *International Labour and Working-Class History*, no. 85: 194–200. https://doi.org/10.1017/S0147547913000525.

Ciccariello-Maher, George. 2013. *We Created Chavez: A People's History of the Venezuelan Revolution*. Durham: Duke University Press.

Clemente, Dario. 2022. "From Lula to Bolsonaro: The Crisis of Neodevelopmentalism in Brazil." *Latin American Perspectives* 49, no. 2: 87–103.

Coalition Against the Mining Pandemic. 2022. *No Reprieve. For Life and Territory: COVID-19 and Resistance to the Mining Pandemic*. Ottawa: MiningWatch Canada. https://miningwatch.ca/sites/default/files/lat-am_covid_report_english.pdf.

Coker, Trudie. 2001. "Globalization and Corporatism: The Growth and Decay of Organized Labor in Venezuela, 1900–1998." *International Labour and Working-Class History* 60: 180–202.

Collier, Ruth, and David Collier. 1991. *Shaping the Political Arena: Critical Junctures, the Labor Movement, and Regime Dynamics in Latin America*. Princeton: Princeton University Press.

Compa, Lance, and T. Brooks. 2019. *NAFTA and NAALC: Twenty-Five Years of North American Trade-Labor Linkage*. Alphen aan den Rijn, Zuid-Holland, Netherlands: Kluwer Law International BV.

Coronil, Fernando. 1997. *The Magical State: Nature, Money, and Modernity in Venezuela*. Chicago: University of Chicago Press.

Cotler, Julio. 2005. *Clases, estado y nación en el Perú*. Lima: Instituto de Estudios Peruanos.

Cypher, James. 2014. "Energy Privatized: The Ultimate Neoliberal Triumph." *NACLA Report on the Americas* 47, no. 1: 27–31.

Cypher, James M. 2018. "From Structuralism to Neoliberal Depredation and Beyond: Economic Transformations and Labor Policies in Latin America, 1950-2016." *Latin American Perspectives* 45, no. 1: 24–46.

Dale, Gareth. 1999. "Capitalism and Migrant Labor." In *The European Union and Migrant Labor*, edited by Gareth Dale and Mike Cole. Oxford: Berg.

Da Silva, Olivia. 2018. "South American Silver Granted US$28 Million in Malku Khota Dispute." *Investing News*, November 25. https://investingnews.com/daily/resource-investing/precious-metals-investing/silver-investing/south-american-silver-malku-khota-dispute/.

Davis, Charles L. 2014. *Working-Class Mobilization and Political Control: Venezuela and Mexico*. Lexington: University Press of Kentucky.

De Genova, Nicholas. 2010. "The Queer Politics of Migration: Reflections on 'Illegality' and Incorrigibility." *Studies in Social Justice* 4, no. 2: 101–26. https://doi.org/10.26522/ssj.v4i2.997.

De Genova, Nicholas, and Sandro Mezzadra. 2020. "Migration and the Question of New Political Possibilities: Nicholas De Genova and Sandro Mezzadra—In Dialogue." *Political Anthropological Research on International Social Sciences (PARISS)* 1, no. 2: 337–74. https://doi.org/10.1163/25903276-BJA10010.

De La Garza Toledo, Enrique. 1993. *Restructuracion productiva y respuesta sindical*. Mexico: Institute for Economic Research, UNAM.

De la Garza Toledo, Enrique. 2007. "The Crisis of the Maquiladora Model in Mexico." *Work and Occupations* 34, no. 4: 399–429.

Del Campo, Hugo. 2012. *Sindicalismo y peronismo, los comienzos de un vínculo perdurable*. Buenos Aires: Siglo XXI.

Delgado Wise, Raúl. 2015. "Migration and Labor under Neoliberal Globalization: Key Issues and Challenges." In *Migration, Precarity, and Global Governance: Challenges and Opportunities for Labor*, edited by Carl-Ulrik Schierup, Ronaldo Munck, Branka Likic-Brboric, and Anders Neergaard. Oxford: Oxford University Press. https://doi.org/10.1093/acprof:oso/9780198728863.003.0002.

Delgado Wise, Raúl. 2022a. "Imperialism, Unequal Exchange, and Labor Export." In *The Oxford Handbook of Economic Imperialism*, edited by Zak Cope and Immanuel Ness, 251–65. Oxford: Oxford University Press. https://global.oup.com/academic/product/the-oxford-handbook-of-economic-imperialism-9780197527085?cc=us&lang=en.

Delgado Wise, Raúl. 2022b. "The Migration and Development Question for the 21 St Century: Imperialism and the Export of Labor Power." ResearchGate. https://www.researchgate.net/publication/362530732_The_Migration_and_Development_question_for_the_21_st_century_Imperialism_and_the_Export_of_Labour_Power

Denning, M. 2010. "Wageless Life." *New Left Review* 66: 79–97.

Departamento Administrativo Nacional de Estadística. 2004. *Statistical Yearbook.* Bogotá, Colombia: Departamento Administrativo Nacional de Estadística.

Diamond, Alex. 2018. "Murder in Colombia's Peace Laboratory/ Homicidio En El Laboratorio de Paz Colombiano." *NACLA*, July 19.

Di Caro, G., and Laura MacDonald. 2022. "CUSMA's labor mechanisms a testing ground for protecting North American workers: Will the Canada-U.S.-Mexico trade agreement usher in a new era for labor protections in North America?" *The Monitor*, July.

Dobson, P. 2021. "Venezuela Trade Unions, Left Parties Blast 'Pyrrhic' May 1 Wage Increase." Venezuelanalysis, May 3, 2021. https://venezuelanalysis.com/new/15193.

Donoso, Sofia. 2013. "Reconstructing Collective Action in the Neoliberal Era: The Emergence and Political Impact of Social Movements in Chile since 1990." PhD thesis, University of Oxford, Oxford.

Doyon, Louise. 1977. "Conflictos obreros durante el régimen peronista (1946–1955)." *Desarrollo Económico* 17 (67): 437–73.

Drinot, Paulo. 2011. *The Allure of Labor: Workers, Race, and the Making of the Peruvian State.* Durham, NC: Duke University Press

Dunkerley, James. 1984. *Rebellion in the Veins: Political Struggle in Bolivia, 1952–1982.* London: Verso.

Durand, Anahí. 2010. "De mineros a indígenas. Cambios en la organización social y la identidad de los trabajadores mineros de la Sierrra Central." In *Jorge del Prado y Los Mineros de la Sierra Central*, 187–212. Lima: Fondo Editorial del Congreso del Perú.

Duran-Palma, Fernando. 2011. "Union Strategies in the Era of Globalisation: Case Studies from Chile's Large-Scale Copper Mining Sector." Tesis de Doctorado en Employment Relations, Loughborough University, London.

Dwyer, John J. 2008. *The Agrarian Dispute: The Expropriation of American-owned Rural Land in Postrevolutionary Mexico.* Durham, NC: Duke University Press.

Economic Commission for Latin America and the Caribbean (ECLAC). 2011. "The 'China Effect' on Commodity Prices and Latin American Export Earnings." April. https://www.cepal.org/en/publications/11471-china-effect-commodity-prices-and-latin-american-export-earnings.

Economic Commission for Latin America and the Caribbean (ECLAC). 2022a. "Pressure on Natural Resources in Latin America and the Caribbean: A Statistical Approach." September 1. https://www.cepal.org/en/notes/pressure-natural-resources-latin-america-and-caribbean-statistical-approach.

Economic Commission for Latin America and the Caribbean (ECLAC). 2022b. "Developments in the Prices of Natural Resources for Export in Latin America and the Caribbean." April 29. https://www.cepal.org/en/insights/developments-prices-natural-resources-export-latin-america-and-caribbean.

Edwards, Bob, and Patrick Gillham. 2013. "Resource Mobilization Theory." In *The Wiley-Blackwell Encyclopedia of Social and Political Movements*, edited by David Snow, 1–6. Hoboken, NJ: Wiley.

Ellner, Steve. 1993. *Organized Labor in Venezuela 1958–1991: Behavior and Concerns in a Democratic Setting*. Wilmington: SR Books.

Ellner, Steve, ed. 2020. *Latin American Extractivism: Dependency, Resource Nationalism, and Resistance in Broad Perspective*. Lanham, MD: Rowman & Littlefield.

Ellner, Steve, and Miguel Tinker Salas. 2005. "Introduction: The Venezuelan Exceptionalism Thesis: Separating Myth from Reality." *Latin American Perspectives* 32, no. 5: 5–19.

Espino, Alma, and Soledad Salvador. 2013. *El sistema nacional de cuidados: Una apuesta al bienestar, la igualdad y el desarrollo*. Uruguay: Friedrich Ebert Stiftung, Análisis.

Espinoza, Jorge. 2013. "Minería estatal: Una historia de fracasos?" In *De vuelta al estado minero?* edited by Henry Oporto, 49–126. La Paz, Bolivia: Fundación Vicente Pazos Kanki.

Exitosa Noticias. 2022. "Trabajadores de Las Bambas: 'Han usado a los pobladores para anunciar esto.'" https://www.youtube.com/watch?v=8Uy1qttCX3E.

Fajardo, Darío. 2014. *Las guerras de la agricultura Colombiana, 1980–2010*. Bogotá, Colombia: Instituto Latinoamericano para una Sociedad y un Derecho Alternativos.

Farmsworth-Alvear, Ann. 2000. *Dulcinea in the Factory: Myths, Morals, Men, and Women in Colombia's Industrial Experiment, 1905–1960*. Durham, NC: Duke University Press.

Felder, Ruth. 2013. "Neoliberal Reforms, Crisis and Recovery in Argentina (1990s-2000s)." PhD dissertation, York University, Toronto, Canada.

Felder, Ruth, and Viviana Patroni. 2011. "Austerity and its Aftermath: Neoliberalism and Labor in Argentina." *Journal of Socialist Studies* 7, no. 1: 259–81.

Felder, Ruth, and Viviana Patroni. 2018a. "Precarious Work in Recession and Growth: A New Structural Feature of Labor Markets in Argentina?" *Radical Review of Political Economics* 50, no. 1: 44–65.

Felder, Ruth, and Viviana Patroni. 2018b. "Organizing the 'Unorganisable': The Case of popular economy workers in Argentina." *Journal of Labour and Society* 21, no. 2: 121–36.

Felder, Ruth, and Viviana Patroni. 2021. "Informal Workers and the Politics of Working-Class Transformation in the Americas." *Global Labour Journal* 12, no. 3. https://doi.org/10.15173/glj.v12i3.4897.

Felix, Gil. 2022. "On the Concept of the Reserve Army of Labor in Ruy Mauro Marini." *Latin American Perspectives* 49, no. 1: 75–90.

Ferguson, Susan. 2019. *Women and Work: Feminism, Labor, and Social Reproduction*. London: Pluto Press.

Ferguson, Susan, and David McNally. 2015. "Precarious Migrants: Gender, Race and the Social Reproduction of a Global Working Class." *Socialist Register* 51. https://socialistregister.com/index.php/srv/article/view/22092.

Fernández-Álvarez, María Inés. 2019. "'Having a Name of One's Own, Being a Part of History': Temporalities of Precarity and Political Subjectivities of Popular Economy Workers in Argentina." *Dialectical Anthropology* 43, no. 1: 61–76.

Ferre, Juan Cruz. 2020. "Precarious Work in Argentina, 2003–2017." *Latin American Perspectives* 48, no. 241: 143–59.

Field, Thomas C., Jr. 2014. *From Development to Dictatorship: Bolivia and the Alliance for Progress in the Kennedy Era.* Ithaca: Cornell University Press.

Finn, Janet L. 1998. *Tracing the Veins: Of Copper, Culture, and Community from Butte to Chuquicamata.* Berkeley/Los Angeles: University of California Press.

Fiscalía General. 2019. *Fiscalía Logra Histórico Esclarecimiento de Homicidios.* Bogotá, Colombia: Fiscalía General de la Nación.

Fischer, Brodwyn, Bryan McCann, and Javier Auyero, eds. 2014. *Cities From Scratch: Poverty and Informality in Urban Latin America.* Durham: Duke University Press.

Fitzsimons, Alejandro and Guido Starosta. 2018. "Rethinking the Determination of the Value of Labor Power." *Review of Radical Political Economics* 50(1): 99–115.

Flichman, Guillermo. 1985. "The State and Capital Accumulation in Argentina." In *The State and Capital Accumulation in Latin America*, edited by Christian Anglade and Carlos Fortín, 1–31. Pittsburgh: University of Pittsburgh Press.

Flores Bordais, Lourdes Eddy. 2015. "Mariátegui, los comunistas y el movimiento sindical minero en el Perú (1928–1931)." Tesis de Licenciatura en Ciencia Política y Sociología, Universidad Federal da Integração Latino-Americana.

Flores Galindo, Alberto. 1974. *Los mineros de la Cerro de Pasco, 1900–1930.* Lima: Pontificia Universidad Católica del Perú.

Flores Galindo, Alberto. 1974a. *La agonía de Mariátegui: La polémica con la Komintern.* Lima: Desco.

Flores Galindo, Alberto. 1974b. *Los mineros de la Cerro de Pasco, 1900–1930.* Lima: Pontificia Universidad Católica del Perú.

Flores Galindo, Alberto, and Jorge Del Prado. 2010. *Jorge del Prado y los mineros de la Sierra Central. Testimonio sobre la Masacre de Malpaso.* Lima: Fondo Editorial del Congreso del Perú. https://www2.congreso.gob.pe/sicr/dgp/Didp_con.nsf/3CB E22761FACB84E05257895006ADDF6/$FILE/103942.PDF.

Flores, Mauricio E. Muñóz. 2014. "El conflicto como unidad de asociación, antagonismo y síntesis." *Sociedad y Discurso* 25.

Fox-Hodess, Katy. 2019. "Worker Power, Trade Union Strategy, and International Connections: Dockworker Unionism in Colombia and Chile." *Latin American Politics and Society* 61, no. 3: 29–54. http://dx.doi.org/10.1017/lap.2019.4.

Fox-Hodess, Katy, and Camilo Santibáñez Rebolledo. 2020. "The Social Foundations of Structural Power: Strategic Position, Worker Unity and External Alliances in the Making of the Chilean Dockworker Movement." *Global Labour Journal* 11, no. 3. https://doi.org/10.15173/glj.v11i3.4236.

Francescone, Kirsten. 2015. "Cooperative Miners and the Politics of Abandonment in Bolivia." *The Extractive Industries and Society* 2, no. 4: 746–55.

Francescone, Kirsten, and Vladimir Díaz. 2013. "Cooperativas Mineras: Entre Socios, Patrones y Peones." *Petropress* 30, no. 1: 32–41.

Fraser, Nancy. 2014. "Behind Marx's Hidden Abode." *New Left Review* 86, no. 86: 55–72.

Fundación Ideas para la Paz. 2018. *¿En Qué Va La Sustitución de Cultivos Ilícitos? Balance Del 2017 y Lo Que Viene En 2018. 03.* Bogotá, Colombia: Fundación Ideas para la Paz.

Fundación Ideas para la Paz. 2020. *Informe de Gestión 2019.* Bogotá, Colombia: Fundación Ideas para la Paz.

Gago, Verónica. 2015. "Financialization of Popular Life and the Extractive Operations of Capital: A Perspective from Argentina." *South Atlantic Quarterly* 114, no. 1: 11–28. https://doi.org/10.1215/00382876-2831257.

Gago, Verónica. 2021. "Extractivism." In *The SAGE Handbook of Marxism*, edited by Beverley Skeggs, Sara R. Farris, Alberto Toscano, and Svenja Bromberg, first edition, 662–82. Thousand Oaks: SAGE Inc.

Gago, Verónica, and Sandro Mezzadra. 2017. "A Critique of the Extractive Operations of Capital: Toward an Expanded Concept of Extractivism." *Rethinking Marxism* 29 (4): 574–91. https://doi.org/10.1080/08935696.2017.1417087.

Galeano, Eduardo. 1997. Ope*n Veins of Latin America: Five Centuries of the Pillage of a Continent.* New York: NYU Press.

Gálvez Olaechea, Alberto. 2020. *Chimbote en la memoria. Las luchas de 1973.* Lima: Fauno Ediciones.

Gálvez Olaechea, A. 2021. *Entre Guerras. Militancia y activismo sindical minero en las décadas 70 y 80.* Lima: Fauno Ediciones.

Ganz, Marshall. 2000. "Resources and Resourcefulness: Strategic Capacity in the Unionization of California Agriculture." *American Journal of Sociology* 105, no. 4: 1003–62.

Garces, Cecilia. 2012. "Bolivia's Mine Nationalization of South American Silver in Mallku Khota." *Socialist Project's The Bullet*, July 17. https://socialistproject.ca/2012/07/b666/.

Gaudichaud, Franck, Massimo Modonesi, and Jeffery R. Webber. 2022. *The Impasse of the Latin American Left.* Durham: Duke University Press.

Gaudio, Ricardo, and Jorge Pilone. 1984. "Estado y relaciones laborales en el periodo previo al surgimiento del Peronismo, 1935–1943." *Desarrollo Económico* 24, no. 94: 235–73.

Gilbert, Chris, and Cira Pascual Marquina. 2020. *Venezuela, The Present as Struggle.* New York: Monthly Review Press.

Gill, Lesley. 1997. "Relocating Class: Ex-Miners and Neoliberalism in Bolivia." *Critique of Anthropology* 17, no. 3: 293–312.

Gill, Lesley. 2016. *A Century of Violence in a Red City: Popular Struggle, Counterinsurgency, and Human Rights in Colombia.* Durham, NC: Duke University Press.

Gindin, Jonah. 2005. "Made in Venezuela: The Struggle to Reinvent Venezuelan Labor." *Monthly Review* 74. https://monthlyreview.org/2005/06/01/made-in-venezuela-the-struggle-to-reinvent-venezuelan-labor/.

Gómez-Barris, Macarena. 2017. *The Extractive Zone: Social Ecologies and Decolonial Perspectives.* Durham: Duke University Press Books.

Gordon, Todd. 2019. "Capitalism, Neoliberalism, and Unfree Labor." *Critical Sociology* 45, no. 6: 921–39. https://doi.org/10.1177/0896920518763936.

Gordon, Todd, and Jeffery R. Webber. 2016. *Blood of Extraction: Canadian Imperialism in Latin America*. Halifax: Fernwood.

Gordon, Todd, and Jeffery R. Webber. 2020. "Complex Stratification in the World System: Capitalist Totality and Geopolitical Fragmentation." *Science & Society* 84, no. 1: 95–125. https://doi.org/10.1521/siso.2020.84.1.95.

Gowan, Peter. 1999. *The Global Gamble: Washington's Faustian Bid for World Dominance*. New York: Verso.

Granados, Oscar. 2014. "Bankers, Entrepreneurs, and Bolivian Tin in the International Economy, 1900-1932." In *Tin and Global Capitalism, 1850-2000: A History of "the Devil's Metal,"* edited by Mats Ingulstad, Andrew Perchard, and Espen Storli, 46–73. New York: Routledge.

Grayson, George. 1988. *Oil and Mexican Foreign Policy*. Pittsburgh: University of Pittsburgh Press.

Green, Duncan. 2003. *Silent Revolution: The Rise and Crisis of Market Economics in Latin America*. New York: Monthly Review Press.

Grinberg, Nicolás. 2022. "From Populism to Neoliberalism. The Political Economy of Latin American Import- Substitution Industrialization: Argentina, Brazil, Mexico and Colombia in Comparative Perspective." *Latin American Perspectives* 49, no. 2: 1–24.

Grinberg, Nicolás, and Guido Starosta. 2009. "The Limits of Studies in Comparative Development of East Asia and Latin America: The Case of Land Reform and Agrarian Policies." *Third World Quarterly* 30, no. 4: 761–77.

Grinberg, Nicolás, and Guido Starosta. 2015. "From Global Capital Accumulation to Varieties of Centre-Leftism in South America." In *Crisis and Contradiction: Marxist Perspectives on Latin American in the Global Economy*, edited by Susan Spronk and Jeffery Webber, 236–72. Leiden: Brill.

Grinspun, Ricardo, and M.A. Cameron, eds. 1993. *The Political Economy of North American Free Trade*. New York: Springer.

Grinspun, Ricardo, and Yasmine Shamsie, eds. 2007. *Whose Canada?: Continental Integration, Fortress North America, and the Corporate Agenda*. Montreal: McGill-Queen's Press-MQUP.

Gudynas, Eduardo. 2009. "Diez Tesis Urgentes Sobre el Nuevo Extractivismo: Contextos y Demandas Bajo el Progressismo Sudamericano Actual." In *Extractivismo, Política y Sociedad*, 187–225. Quito: Centro Andino de Acción Popular and Centro Latinoamericano de Ecología Social.

Gudynas, Eduardo. 2012. "Estado Compensador y Nuevos Extractivismos: Las Ambivalencias del Progresismo Sudamericano." *Nueva Sociedad* 237 (January-February): 128–46.

Gudynas, Eduardo. 2015. *Extractivismos: Ecología, economía y política de un modo de entender el desarrollo la naturaleza*. Cochabamba: CEDIB.

Gudynas, Eduardo. 2018a. "Extractivisms: Tendencies and Consequences." In *Reframing Latin American Development*, edited by Ronaldo Munck and Raúl Delgado Wise, 61–76. London: Routledge. https://doi.org/10.4324/9781315170084-4.

Gudynas, Eduardo. 2018b. *Naturaleza, extractivismo y corrupción*. Cochabamba: CEDIB.

Gudynas, Eduardo. 2021. *Extractivisms: Politics, Economy and Ecology*. Halifax: Fernwood.

Guillaudat, Patrick. 2019. "Quien dirige Venezuela? Casta o boliburguesia?" Viento Sur.

Gustafson, Bret. 2020. *Bolivia in the Age of Gas*. Durham: Duke University Press Books.

Hamilton, Nora. 1982/2014. *The Limits of State Autonomy: Post-Revolutionary Mexico*. Princeton: Princeton University Press.

Hanieh, Adam. 2018. *Money, Markets, and Monarchies: The Gulf Cooperation Council and the Political Economy of the Contemporary Middle East*. Cambridge: Cambridge University Press.

Hanieh, Adam. 2019. "The Contradictions of Global Migration." *Socialist Register* 55.

Harvey, David. 2003. *The New Imperialism*. Oxford: Oxford University Press.

Helfgott, Federico. 2013. "Transformations in Labor, Land and Community: Mining and Society in Pasco, Peru, 20th Century to the Present." Tesis de Doctorado en Antropología e Historia, University of Michigan. https://deepblue.lib.umich.edu/handle/2027.42/99793.

Helfgott, Federico. 2017. "La persistencia de lo social: Los convenios laborales y los convenios comunidadempresa en las zonas mineras de la Sierra Central." In *Trabajo y sociedad. Estudios sobre el mundo del trabajo en el Perú*, edited by Omar Manky, 84–103. Lima: Centro de Investigaciones Sociológicas, Económicas, Políticas y Antropológicas de la Pontificia Universidad Católica del Perú

Helwege, Ann. 2015. "Challenges with Resolving Mining Conflicts in Latin America." *The Extractive Industries and Society* 2, no. 1: 73–84. https://doi.org/10.1016/j.exis.2014.10.003.

Hernández Cervantes, Aleida. 2018. *Entre la globalización y el trabajo. Los derechos en entredicho*. Aguascalientes-San Luis Potosí, CENEJUS-UASLP, México.

Hernández Cervantes, Aleida. 2021. *T-MEC, reforma laboral e igualdad de género: Apuesta por el adelanto de las trabajadoras*. Mexico: Red de Mujeres Sindicalistas.

Hernández Cervantes, Aleida, and Anna Zalik. 2018. "Canadian Capital and the Denationalization of the Mexican Energy Sector." *Journal of Latin America Geography* 17, no. 3: 42–72.

Herod, Andrew. 2001. *Labor Geographies: Workers and the Landscapes of Capitalism*. New York: Guilford Press.

Hite, Amy, and Jocelyn S Viterna. 2005. "Gendering Class in Latin America: How Women Effect and Experience Change in the Class Structure." *Latin American Research Review* 40, no. 2: 50–82. https://doi.org/10.1353/lar.2005.0023.

Horowicz, Alejandro. 2007. *Los cuatro Peronismos*. Buenos Aires: Edhasa.

Hough, Phillip A. 2010. "Hegemonic Projects and the Social Reproduction of the Peasantry: Fedecafé, Fedegán, and the FARC in Comparative Historical Perspective." *Review (Fernand Braudel Center)* 33, no. 1: 25–67.

Hough, Phillip A. 2011. "Guerrilla Insurgency as Organized Crime: Explaining the So-Called 'Political Involution' of the Revolutionary Armed Forces of Colombia." *Politics & Society* 39, no. 3: 379–414.

Hough, Phillip A. 2019. "The Winding Paths of Peripheral Proletarianization: Local Labor, World Hegemonies, and Crisis in Rural Colombia." *Journal of Agrarian Change* 19, no. 3: 506–27. https://doi.org/10.1111/joac.12303.

Hough, Phillip A. 2022. *At the Margins of the Global Market: Making Commodities, Workers, and Crisis in Rural Colombia.* London: Cambridge University Press.

Howard, April, and Benjamin Dangl. 2006. "Tin War in Bolivia: Conflict Between Miners Leaves 17 Dead." *Upside Down World*, October 10.

Hristov, Jasmin. 2009. *Blood and Capital: The Paramilitarization of Colombia.* Athens: Ohio University Press.

Huber, Matthew T. 2022. *Climate Change as Class War: Building Socialism on a Warming Planet.* London: Verso.

Human Rights Watch. 2010. *World Report 2010.* New York, NY: Human Rights Watch.

Human Rights Watch. 2020. "Colombia: Seek Ex-Paramilitary Commander's Extradition." August 15.

Hylton, Forrest, and Catherine C. LeGrand. 2021. "Charles W. Bergquist (1942–2020)." *Hispanic American Historical Review* 101, no. 3: 491–96. https://doi.org/10.1215/00182168-9051846.

Iñigo Carrera, Juan. 2007. *La formación económica de la sociedad Argentina.* Volume 1. Buenos Aires: Imago Mundi.

Iñigo Carrera, Juan. 2008. *El capital: Razón histórica, sujeto revolucionario y conciencia.* Buenos Aires: Imago Mundi.

Iñigo Carrera, Juan. 2018. "Precios, productividad y renta de la tierra agraria: ni «términos de intercambio deteriorados», ni «intercambio desigual» *Realidad Económica* 47, no. 317: 41–78.

Iñigo Carrera, Juan. 2022. *La formación económica de la sociedad Argentina.* Volume 2. Buenos Aires: Imago Mundi.

Iñigo Carrera, Nicolás. 2019. *Estrategias de la clase obrera en los orígenes del Peronismo.* Mar del Plata, Argentina: EUDEM.

International Organization for Migration. 2008. *Managing Labor Mobility in the Evolving Global Economy.* Geneva: International Organization for Migration .

Issa, Daniela. 2017a. "Modern Slavery and Human Trafficking in Latin America." *Latin American Perspectives* 44, no. 6: 4–15. https://doi.org/10.1177/0094582x17725488.

Issa, Daniela. 2017b. "Reification and the Human Commodity: Theorizing Modern Slavery in Brazil." *Latin American Perspectives* 44, no. 6: 90–106. https://doi.org/10.1177/0094582X17727480.

Jaffe, Aaron. 2020. *Social Reproduction Theory and the Socialist Horizon: Work, Power and Political Strategy.* London: Pluto Press.

James, Daniel. 1988. *Resistance and Integration: Peronism and the Argentine Working Class, 1946-1976.* Cambridge: Cambridge University Press.

Jaramillo, Carlos Felipe. 1998. *Liberalization, Crisis, and Change in Colombian Agriculture.* Boulder, CO: Westview Press.

Javier, Eduardo, and Aguilar Santur. 2017. "Los profesores contra Velasco: La oposición de los maestros al proyecto de reforma educativa presentado por el gobierno revolucionario de las fuerzas armadas en 1972." Tesis de Licenciatura en

Historia, Pontificia Universidad Católica del Perú. http://tesis.pucp.edu.pe/repositorio/handle/20.500.12404/9864.

Jeydel, Alana S. 2000. "Social Movements, Political Elites and Political Opportunity Structures: The Case of the Woman Suffrage Movement from 1890-1920." *Congress & the Presidency: A Journal of Capital Studies* 27: 15–40.

Jonakin, Jon. 2009. "Labour and Its Discontents: The Consequences of Orthodox Reform in Venezuela and Mexico." *Journal of Development Studies* 45 (8): 1284–306.

Jongkind, Fred. 1993. "Venezuelan Industry under the New Conditions of the 1989 Economic Policy." *European Review of Latin American and Caribbean Studies* 54: 65–93.

Johnson, Richard L. 2021. "Reversing Channels and Unsettling Binaries: Rethinking Migration and Agrarian Change under Expanded Border and Immigration Enforcement." *Land* 10 (3): 228. https://doi.org/10.3390/land10030228.

Kabat, Marina, Agustina Desalvo, and Julia Egan. 2017. "The Tip of the Iceberg: Media Coverage of 'Slave Labor' in Argentina." *Latin American Perspectives* 44, no. 6: 50–62. https://doi.org/10.1177/0094582X17699909.

Karl, Terry Lynn. 1997. *The Paradox of Plenty: Oil Booms and Petro-States*. Oakland: University of California Press.

Katz, Cindy. 2001. "Vagabound Capitalism and the Necessity of Social Reproduction." *Antipode* 33, no. 4: 709–28.

Katz, Claudio. 2015. "Dualities of Latin America." *Latin American Perspectives* 42, no. 4: 10–42. https://doi.org/10.1177/0094582X15574714.

Katz, Claudio. 2022. "The Cycle of Dependency 50 Years Later." *Latin American Perspectives* 49, no. 2: 8–23.

Kaup, Brent Z. 2010. "A Neoliberal Nationalization?" *Latin American Perspectives* 37, no. 3: 123–38.

Kay, Cristóbal. 2015. "The Agrarian Question and the Neoliberal Rural Transformation in Latin America." *European Review of Latin American and Caribbean Studies* 100: 73–83. https://doi.org/10.18352/erlacs.10123.

Kellogg, Paul. 2015. "The Political Economy of Oil and Democracy in Venezuela and Alberta." In *Alberta Oil and the Decline of Democracy in Canada*, edited by Meenal Shrivastava and Lorna Stefanick, 139–70. Athabasca: Athabasca University Press.

Killoran-McKibbin, Sonja, and Anna Zalik. 2016. "Rethinking the Extractive/Productive Bnary under Neoliberalism." In *Handbook of Neoliberalism*, edited by Kean Birch, Simon Spring, and Julie Macleavy, 565–76. London: Routledge.

Klubock, Thomas Miller. 1998. *Contested Communities: Class, Gender, and Politics in Chile's El Teniente Copper Mine, 1904-1948*. Durham, NC: Duke University Press.

Knight, Alan. 1990. *The Mexican Revolution: Counter-Revolution and Reconstruction*. Lincoln: University of Nebraska Press.

Kohl, Benjamin, and Linda Farthing. 2012. "Material Constraints to Popular Imaginaries: The Extractive Economy and Resource Nationalism in Bolivia." *Political Geography* 31, no. 4: 225–35.

Kruijt, Dirk, and Menno Vellinga. 1979. *Labor Relations and Multinational Corporations: The Cerro de Pasco Corporation in Peru.* Amsterdam: Van Gorcum. http:// www.refworks.com/refworks2/?r=references|MainLayout::init#

Kurtz, Marcus J. 2013. *Latin American State Building in Comparative Perspective: Social Foundations of Institutional Order.* Cambridge: Cambridge University Press.

Lakhani, Nina. 2019. "Living without Water: The Crisis Pushing People out of El Salvador." *The Guardian,* July 30. https://www.theguardian.com/global-development/2019/jul/30/el-salvador-water-crisis-privatization-gangs-corruption.

La Nación. 2016. "El senado convirtió en ley por unanimidad el proyecto de emergencia social." November 18. https://www.lanacion.com.ar/politica/el-senado-convirtio-en-ley-por-unanimidad-el-proyecto-de-emergencia-social-nid1966970/.

Lander, Edgardo, and Luis A. Fierro. 1996. "The Impact of Neoliberal Adjustment in Venezuela, 1989-1993." *Latin American Perspectives* 23, no. 3: 50–73.

Leary, J. P. 2007. "Untying the Knot of Venezuela's Informal Economy." *NACLA.* https://nacla.org/news/untying-knot-venezuela's-informal-economy

Lebowitz, Michael A. 2008. "Building Twenty-First Century Socialism." *Canadian Dimension,* September 6. https://canadiandimension.com/articles/view/building-twenty-first-century-socialism.

Le Gouill, Claude. 2016. "Imaginaires Miniers et Conflits Sociaux en Bolivie: Une Approche Multiniveaux du Conflit de Mallku Khota." *Cahiers des Amériques Latines* 82: 49–69.

Levins, Richard, and Richard Lewontin. 1985. *The Dialectical Biologist.* Cambridge, MA: Harvard University Press.

Li, Tania. 2017. "After Development: Surplus Population and the Politics of Entitlement." *Development and Change* 48, no. 6: 1247–61.

Logiúdice, Ana. 2022. *Metamorfosis de la asistencia Argentina: Continuidades y rupturas de la política social asistencial en la Argentina de la postconvertibilidad (2002–2012).* Buenos Aires: El Colectivo and Instituto de Estudios de América Latina y el Caribe.

Lomnitz, Claudio. 2014. *The Return of Comrade Ricardo Flores Magón.* New York: Zone Books.

López, C., Sara Raquel, Mirtha Maldonado, and Miguel H. López. 2022. "El sindicalismo y su lucha dentro del modelo extractivista." In *Defensa del territorio, la cultura y la vida ante el avance extractivista: Una perspectiva desde América Latina,* 95–109. Buenos Aires: CLACSO.

López, Sinesio. 1978. "El estado oligárquico en el Perú: Un ensayo de unterpretación." *Revista Mexicana de Sociología* 991–1007.

Lora, Guillermo. 1977. *A History of the Bolivian Labour Movement 1848-1971,* translated by Christine Whitehead. Cambridge, UK: Cambridge University Press.

Lowenthal, Abraham F. 2023. "Venezuela in 2023 and Beyond: Charting a New Course." Latin America Program, Wilson Center.

Lunn, Ben, and Paul Dobson. 2020. "A New Revolutionary Alternative for the People of Venezuela." *Venezuelanalysis.* https://venezuelanalysis.com/analysis/15030.

MacDonald, Laura. 2002. "Globalization and Social Movements: Comparing Women's Movements Responses to NAFTA in Mexico, the USA and Canada." *International Feminist Journal of Politics* 4, no. 2: 151–72.

Macdonald, Laura. 2020. "Stronger Together? Canada-Mexico Relations and the NAFTA Re-negotiations." *Canadian Foreign Policy Journal* 26, no. 2: 152–66.

Machado Bichir, Maíra. 2022. "Fascism and Dependency in Latin America in the Thinking of Theotônio dos Santos." *Latin American Perspectives* 49, no. 1: 107–22.

Makki, Fouad. 2015. "Reframing Development Theory: The Significance of the Idea of Uneven and Combined Development." *Theory and Society* 44, no. 5: 471–97. https://doi.org/10.1007/s11186-015-9252-9.

Mallon, Florencia. 2003. *Campesino y nación: La construcción de México y Perú poscoloniales*. Mexico: CIESAS.

Mallory, I. A. 1990. "Conduct Unbecoming: The Collapse of the International Tin Agreement." *American University National Law Review* 5, no. 3: 835–92.

Malm, Andreas. 2016. *Fossil Capital: The Rise of Steam Power and the Roots of Global Warming*, illustrated edition. London: Verso.

Malm, Andreas. 2018. *The Progress of This Storm: On the Dialectics of Society and Nature in a Warming World*. London: Verso.

Månberger, André. 2021. "Renewable Energy Transition, and Demand for Metals and Resource Curse Effects." In *Handbook of Sustainable Politics and Economics of Natural Resources*, edited by Stella Tsani and Indra Overland, 30–40. Cheltenham, UK: Edward Elgar Publishing Limited.

Manky, Omar. 2011. "El día después del tsunami. Notas para comprender a los sindicatos obreros Peruanos en las últimas décadas del siglo XX." *Debates en Sociología* 36: 107–34.

Manky, Omar. 2017. "From Towns to Hotels: Changes in Mining Accommodation Regimes and Their Effects on Labour Union Strategies." *British Journal of Industrial Relations* 55, no. 2. doi:10.1111/bjir.12202.

Manky, Omar. 2018. "Resource Mobilisation and Precarious Workers' Organisations: An Analysis of the Chilean Subcontracted Mineworkers' Unions." *Work, Employment and Society* 32, no. 3: 581–98.

Manky, Omar. 2019a. "Liderazgos precarios: Organización y lideres sindicales en perspectiva comparada." *Latin American Research Review* 54, no. 4. https://doi.org/10.25222/larr.160.

Manky, Omar. 2019b. "¿Los límites del clasismo?: Identidad y vínculos entre trabajadores regulares y precarios." *Revista Internacional de Sociología* 77, no. 2: 125.

Manky, Omar. 2020a. "The End of Mining Labor Struggles? The Changing Dynamics of Labor in Latin America." *The Extractive Industries and Society* 7: 1121–27.

Manky, Omar. 2020b. "Mineros en movimiento: Patrones residenciales y cultura sindical en perspectiva comparada." *Debates en Sociología* 49: 81–102.

Manrique, Hernán, and Cynthia Sanborn. 2021. *La minería en el Perú: Balance y perspectivas de cinco décadas de investigación*. Lima: Universidad del Pacífico.

Marini, Ruy Mauro. 2002. *The Dialectics of Dependency*. New York: Monthly Review Press.

Mariobo Moreno, Pedro. 2007. *El cooperativismo minero: Solución, engaño o solución?* La Paz: CEPROMIN.

Marquina, Cira Pascual. 2020. "A Flawed Case: A Conversation with Iracara Chirinos." *Venezuelanalysis*, June 12. https://venezuelanalysis.com/interviews/14903.

Marquina, Cira Pascual. 2021. "The Working Class in Its Labyrinth: A Conversation with Eduaro Sánchez." *Venezuelanalysis*, April 16. https://venezuelanalysis.com/interviews/15175.

Marston, Andrea. 2020. "Vertical Farming: Tin Mining and Agro-Mineros in Bolivia." *The Journal of Peasant Studies* 47 (4): 820–40.

Martins, Carlos Eduardo. 2022. "The Longue Durée of the Marxist Theory of Dependency and the Twenty-First Century." *Latin American Perspectives* 49, no. 1: 18–35.

Marx, Karl. 1867/1976. *Capital.* Volume One, translated by B. Fawkes. Harmondsworth: Penguin.

Marx, Karl. 1977. *Capital: Volume One.* New York: Vintage.

Marx, Karl. 1992. "Economic and Philosophical Manuscripts." In *Early Writings.* London: Penguin.

Matsushita, Hiroshi. 2014. *Movimiento obrero Argentino 1930–1945.* Buenos Aires, Argentina: Ediciones RyR.

Mazzeo, Miguel, and Fernando Stratta. 2021. "Pensar la economía popular. Pequeño ensayo a modo de introducción." In *¿Qué es la economía popular? Experiencias, voces y debates*, edited by M. Mazzeo and F. Stratta, 15–72. Buenos Aires: Editorial El Colectivo.

McKay, Ben M., Alberto Alonso-Fradejas, and Arturo Ezquerro-Cañete. 2021. *Agrarian Extractivism in Latin America.* London: Routledge.

Medina, Andrea, and Peña Dafne. 2020. *Discriminación y violencia laboral contra las mujeres en México. Elementos para el debate y propuestas de armonización legislativa y de acceso a la justicia.* Mexico: Red de Mujeres Sindicalistas.

Medina, Jose Carlos. 2019. "Desencuentros por la izquierda durante el Velasquismo: La Matanza de Cobriza." *Revista Argumentos* 13, no. 2: 49–54.

Melgar Bao, Ricardo. 2020. "Izquierdas y cultura militante en el frente minero: Perú 1928–1930." *Avances del Cesor* 17, no. 22: 127–48.

Mendez Garzón, Fernando, and István Valánszki. 2019. "Repercussions in the Landscape of Colombian Amazonas (Caquetá and Putumayo Region) Caused by Deforestation and Illicit Crops During the Internal Armed Conflict; a Review." *Proceedings of the Fábos Conference on Landscape and Greenway Planning* 6, no. 1.

Meyer, Lorenzo. 1972. *Mexico and the United States in the Oil Controversy 1917–42.* Austin: University of Texas Press/El Colegio de Mexico.

Meyer, Lorenzo, and Isidro Morales. 1990. *Petróleo y nación: La política petrolera en México, 1900–1987.* Mexico: Colegio de Mexico.

Mezzadra, Sandro, and Brett Neilson. 2019. *The Politics of Operations: Excavating Contemporary Capitalism.* Durham, NC: Duke University Press.

Ministerio de Minería y Metalurgia. 2021. *Anuario Estadístico Minero 2020.* La Paz: Bolivia.

Mitchell, Timothy. 2011. *Carbon Democracy: Political Power in the Age of Oil*. New York: Verso.

Mitre, Antonio. 1993. *Bajo un cielo de estaño: Fulgor y ocaso del metal en Bolivia*. La Paz: Asociación Nacional de Mineros Medianos.

Molina, Luis Bonilla. 2021. "The Popular Revolutionary Alternative and the Current Situation." *Fourth International*, April 7. https://www.fourth.international/en/latin-america/354.

Mommer, B. 2003. "Subversive Oil." In *Venezuelan Politics in the Chavez Era: Class, Polarization, and Conflict*, edited by S. Ellner and D. Hellinger, 131–146. Boulder, Colorado: Lynne Rienner Publishers.

Moody, Kim. 2014. *In Solidarity: Essays on Working-Class Organization and Strategy in the United States*. Chicago: Haymarket.

Moore, Jason W. 2015. *Capitalism in the Web of Life: Ecology and the Accumulation of Capital*. New York: Verso.

Moreno, Andrade, and Saul Horacio. 2007. *Dilemas Petroleros: Cultura, Poder y Trabajo en el Golfo de México*. Mexico: Ciesas.

Morton, Adam David. 2010. "Reflections on Uneven Development: Mexican Revolution, Primitive Accumulation, Passive Revolution." *Latin American Perspectives* 37, no. 1: 7–34.

Muñoz, Mauricio. 2017. *Identidad en movimiento. El proceso de construcción identitaria en los trabajadores subcontratados de la gran minería del cobre en Chile*. El Colegio de México.

Murmis, Miguel, and Juan Carlos Portantiero. 1971. *Estudios sobre los orígenes del Peronismo*. Buenos Aires: Siglo Veintiuno.

Naím, Moises. 1993. *Paper Tigers and Minotaurs: The Politics of Venezuela's Economic Reforms*. Washington: The Carnegie Endowment for International Peace.

Narancio, Constanza, ed. 2022. *Feminismo y ambiente: Un campo emergente en los estudios feministas de América Latina y el Caribe*. Buenos Aires: CLACSO.

Nash, June. 1979. *We Eat the Mines and the Mines Eat Us: Dependency and Exploitation in Bolivian Tin Mines*. New York: Columbia University Press.

Nore, Petter, and Terisa Turner. 1980. *Oil and Class Struggle*. London: Zed Books.

North, Liisa L. 2021. "The Historical and Contemporary Causes of 'Survival Migration.' From Central America's Northern Triangle." *Revista de Estudios Globales. Análisis Histórico y Cambio Social* 1, no. 1: 43–70. https://doi.org/10.6018/reg.497751.

North, Liisa L., and Ricardo Grinspun. 2016. "Neo-Extractivism and the New Latin American Developmentalism: The Missing Piece of Rural Transformation." *Third World Quarterly* 37, no. 8: 1483–504. https://doi.org/10.1080/01436597.2016.1159508.

Noticias Fides. 2012. "Mineros cooperativistas y sindicalizados se enfrentan en mina Colquiri." Agencia de Noticias Fides, 31 May. https://www.noticiasfides.com/nacional/sociedad/mineros-cooperativistas-y-sindicalizados-se-enfrentan-en-mina-colquiri-318515-318502.

Novick, Marta, Miguel Lengyel, and Marianela Sarabia. 2009. "From Social Protection to Vulnerability: Argentina's Neo-Liberal Reforms of the 1990s." *International Labor Review* 148, no. 3: 235–52.

Nuñez, Daniel. 2009. "El movimiento de los trabajadores contratistas de CODELCO." In *El renacer de la huelga obrera en Chile*, edited by Daniel Nuñez and A. Aravena, 37–74. Santiago: LOM.

Ødegaard, Cecilie Vindal, and Juan Javier Rivera Andía, eds. 2019. *Indigenous Life Projects and Extractivism: Ethnographies from South America*. New York: Palgrave Macmillan.

Office of the United Nations High Commissioner for Human Rights. 2021. "Situation of Human Rights and Technical Assistance in the Bolivarian Republic of Venezuela – Report of the United Nations High Commissioner for Human Rights (A/HRC/48/19)." Geneva.

Ollman, Bertell. 1977. *Alienation: Marx's Conception of Man in a Capitalist Society*, second edition. Cambridge: Cambridge University Press.

Olvera, Claudia. 2022. *Diagnóstico sobre la situación actual de la población trabajadora en México: Derechos humanos laborales ante la firma del T-MEC y su Capítulo 23*. Mexico: Red de Mujeres Sindicalistas.

Organisation for Economic Co-operation and Development. 2017. *La lucha por la igualdad de género: Una batalla cuesta arriba*. Mexico: OECD.

Organization of the Petroleum Exporting Countries. 2020. "Annual Report 2020." https://www.opec.org/opec_web/en/publications/337.htm.

Organization of the Petroleum Exporting Countries. 2023. "Monthly Oil Market Report, March 2023." https://www.opec.org/opec_web/en/publications/7107.htm.

Oporto Ordóñez, Luis. 2007. *Uncía y llallagua: Empresa minera capitalista y estrategias de apropiación real del espacio (1900–1935)*. La Paz: IFEA/Plural Editores.

Organic Hydrocarbons Law. 2001. *Ley Orgánica de Hidrocarburos*. Caracas: Gaceta Oficial de la República Bolivariana de Venezuela N. 37323.

Organic Labour Law. 2012. *Ley Orgánica del Trabajo, Los Trabajadores y Las Trabajadoras*. Caracas: Gaceta Oficial de la República Bolivariana de Venezuela N. 6.076.

Osorio, Jaime. 2022. "Assessing a Proposal for Updating the Marxist Theory of Dependency." *Latin American Perspectives* 49, no. 1: 153–65.

Palomino, Héctor. 2010. "La instalación de un nuevo régimen de empleo en Argentina." In *La nueva dinámica de las relaciones laborales en la Argentina*, edited by H. Palomino et al, 179–206. Buenos Aires: Jorge Baudino Ediciones.

Panfichi, Aldo, and Omar Coronel. 2010. "Cambio entre los vínculos entre la sociedad civil y el estado en el Perú: 1968–2008." *Cambios sociales en el Perú*.

Panigo, Demián, and Julio Neffa. 2009. "El mercado de trabajo Argentino en el nuevo modelo de desarrollo." Dirección Nacional de Programación Macroeconómica, Dirección de Modelos y Proyecciones, Ministerio de Economía, República Argentina.

Paredes, Maritza. 2016. "The Glocalization of Mining Conflict: Cases from Peru." *The Extractive Industries and Society* 3, no. 4: 1046–57.

Patroni, Viviana. 2000. "Democracy and Organized Labor in Argentina: Challenges and New Alternatives?" In *Economic Liberalization, Democratization and Civil*

Society in the Developing World, edited by Remonda Bensabat-Kleinberg and Janine A. Clark, 241–62. London: Macmillan Press.

Patroni, Viviana. 2018a. "Historical Overview." In *Labor Politics in Latin America: Democracy and Worker Organization in the Neoliberal Era*, edited by Paul Posner, Viviana Patroni, and Jean Francois Mayer, 12–38. Gainesville: University Press of Florida.

Patroni, Viviana. 2018b. "Uncertain Transitions: Labor and the Politics of Reform in Argentina." In *Labor Politics in Latin America: Democracy and Worker Organization in the Neoliberal Era*, edited by Paul Posner, Viviana Patroni, and Jean Francois Mayer, 102–34. Gainesville: University Press of Florida.

Pereira, Hugo, Eraldo da Silva Ramos Filho, and Angelina Herrera, eds. 2022. *Defensa del territorio, la cultura y la vida ante el avance extractivista: Una perspectiva desde América Latina*. Buenos Aires: CLACSO.

Perreault, Thomas. 2006. "From the Guerra Del Agua to the Guerra Del Gas: Resource Governance, Neoliberalism and Popular Protest in Bolivia." *Antipode* 38, no. 1: 150–72.

Petras, James, and Henry Veltmeyer, eds. 2014. *The New Extractivism: A Post-Neoliberal Development Model or Imperialism of the Twenty-First Century*. London: Zed Books.

Phillips, Nicola. 2009. "Migration as Development Strategy? The New Political Economy of Dispossession and Inequality in the Americas." *Review of International Political Economy* 16, no. 2: 231–59. https://doi.org/10.1080/09692290802402744.

Portes, Alejandro, and Kelly Hoffman. 2003. "Latin American Class Structures: Their Composition and Change during the Neoliberal Era." *Latin American Research Review* 38, no. 1: 41–82.

Poveda Ávila, Pablo. 2014. *Formas de producción de las cooperativas mineras en Bolivia*. La Paz: CEDLA.

Poveda Ávila, Pablo. 2021. "Explotación y comercialización de oro en Bolivia." *CEDLA: Reporte Anual de Industrias Extractivistas* 6 (April): 65–117.

Purcell, Thomas. 2013. "The Political Economy of Social Production Companies." *Latin American Perspectives* 40, no. 3: 146–68.

Quijada, José Alejandro, and José David Sierra. 2019. "Understanding Undocumented Migration from Honduras." *International Migration* 57 (4): 3–20. https://doi.org/10.1111/imig.12429.

Rahim, Afaf, Glenn Rayph, and Ilse Ruyssend. 2021. "Towards a Triple Win: Transforming Circular Migration into Circular Skill Mobility Schemes." Policy Brief, G20 Insights. https://www.g20-insights.org/policy_briefs/towards-a-triple-win-transforming-circular-migration-into-circular-skill-mobility-schemes/.

Ramdoo, Isabelle. 2020. *The Impact of COVID-19 on Employment in Mining*. Ottawa: International Instituted for Sustainable Development. https://www.iisd.org/publications/brief/impact-covid-19-employment-mining.

Raposo, Bruna Ferraz, Niemeyer Almeida Filho, and Marisa Silva Amaral. 2022. "The Pattern of Capital Reproduction in Dependent and Financialized Capitalism." *Latin American Perspectives* 49, no. 1: 166–81.

Renique, José Luis. 1989. "EEUU y los obreros de la cerro en 1930. Mueran los gringos . . . viva la huelga." *Márgenes: Encuentro y Debate* 5/6: 240–65.

Revista Theomai. 2015. "No. 32." https://www.redalyc.org/revista.oa?id=124&tipo=coleccion.

Revista Theomai. 2012. "No. 26." https://www.redalyc.org/revista.oa?id=124&tipo=coleccion.

Richani, Nazih. 2002. *Systems of Violence: The Political Economy of War and Peace in Colombia.* Albany, NY: SUNY Press.

Riofrancos, Thea. 2020. *Resource Radicals: From Petro-Nationalism to Post-Extractivism in Ecuador.* Durham: Duke University Press Books.

Rivas Castro, Gabriel. 2022. "Renta de la tierra y valorización de capital a través de la lucha de clases en Chile 1940–2017." Unpublished PhD dissertation, University of Buenos Aires, Argentina.

Rivera Cusicanqui, Silvia. 1987. *"Oppressed but not Defeated": Peasant Struggles among the Aymara and Qhechwa in Bolivia, 1900-1980.* Geneva, Switzerland: United Nations Research Institute for Social Development.

Roberts, Kenneth M. 2003. "Social Correlates of Party System Demise and Populist Resurgence in Venezuela." *Latin American Politics and Society* 45, no. 3: 35–57.

Robinson, William. 2006. "'Aqui estamos y no nos vamos!' Global Capital and Immigrant Rights." *Race & Class* 48, no. 2: 77–91. https://doi.org/10.1177/0306396806069525.

Robinson, William I. 2008. *Latin America and Global Capitalism: A Critical Globalization Perspective*, first edition. Baltimore: Johns Hopkins University Press.

Rodríguez, Francisco. 2023. "How Sanctions Contributed to Venezuela's Economic Collapse." *Global Americans*, February 9. https://theglobalamericans.org/2023/01/how-sanctions-contributed-to-venezuelas-economic-collapse/

Rodríguez, Santiago. 2016. "Agenda común contra el ajuste." *Página 12*, Buenos Aires, September 8.

Rodríguez Porras, Simon, and Miguel Sorans. 2018. *Why Did Chavismo Fail?* Buenos Aires: Centro de Estudios Humanos y Sociales.

Rodriguez Weber, Javier. 2014. "La economía política de la desigualdad de ingreso en Chile, 1850–2009." Unpublished PhD dissertation, University of the Republic, Montevideo, Uruguay.

Ros, Jaime, and Carlos Monsiváis. 1987. *El auge petrolero: De la euforia al desencanto.* Mexico: UNAM.

Rougier, Marcelo, and Martín Schorr. 2012. *La industria en los cuatro Peronismos.* Buenos Aires: Capital Intelectual.

Ruiz Arrieta, Adriana Gloria. 2012. "Tramas de sentidos y significaciones durante las nacionalizaciones mineras de Huanuni y Colquiri en Bolivia." *Revista Latinoamerica de Antropología del Trabajo* 2, no. 3: 1–25.

Sablich, Lucas, ed. 2022. *Ambiente, cambio climático y buen vivir en América Latina y el Caribe.* Buenos Aires: CLACSO.

Sánchez, Eduardo. 2021. "The Working Class in Its Labyrinth: A Conversation with Eduardo Sánchez." April 16. https://venezuelanalysis.com/interviews/15175.

Sankey, Kyla. 2018. "Extractive Capital, Imperialism, and the Colombian State." *Latin American Perspectives* 45, no. 5: 52–70.

Santiago, Myrna. 2006. *The Ecology of Oil: Environment, Labor and the Mexican Revolution 1900-1938*. Cambridge: Cambridge University Press.

Santiago, Myrna. 2009. "Women of the Mexican Oil Fields: Class, Nationality, Economy, Culture, 1900–1938." *Journal of Women's History* 21, no. 1: 87–110.

Santiago, Ramon. 2008. "On the Anniversary of Black Friday: Venezuela's Devaluation and Inflation Debacle from 1983 to 1998." *Axis of Logic*. http://www.axisoflogic.com/artman/publish/Article_26069.shtml.

Sassen, Saskia. 1990. *The Mobility of Labor and Capital*. Cambridge: Cambridge University Press. https://ideas.repec.org/b/cup/cbooks/9780521386722.html.

Saunders, Olivia. 2016. "Preserving the Status Quo: Britain, the United States, and Bolivian Tin, 1946–56." *The International History Review* 38, no. 3: 551–72.

Saxe-Fernández, John. 2016. *La compraventa de México. Una interpretación histórica y estratégica de las relaciones México-Estados Unidos, Colección El Mundo Actual: Situación y Alternativas*. Mexico: CIESAS.

Schvarzer, Jorge. 1998. *Implantación de un modelo económico: La experiencia Argentina entre 1975 y el 2000*. Buenos Aires: A-Z Editora.

Selwyn, Benjamin. 2014. *The Global Development Crisis*, first edition. Cambridge, UK: Polity.

Seoane, José, Emilio Taddei, and Clara Algranati. 2013. *Extractivismo, despojo y crisis climático: Desafíos para los movimientos sociales y los proyectos emancipatorios de Nuestra América*. Buenos Aires: Herramienta.

Shields, David. 2003. *Pemex: Un Futuro incierto*. Mexico: Editorial Planeta Mexicana.

Sigal, Silvia, and Ezequiel Gallo. 1963. "La formación de los partidos políticos contemporaneos. La Unión Cívica Radical (1890–1916)." *Desarrollo Económico* 3, no. 1/2: 173–230.

Silva Herzog, Jesus. 1964/2010. *Historia de la expropiación petrolera*. México: El Colegio Nacional.

Silver, Beverly J. 2003. *Forces of Labor: Workers' Movements and Globalization Since 1870*. Cambridge: Cambridge University Press.

SINCHI. 2000. *Caquetá: Dinamica de un proceso*, edited by L. M. Mantilla Cardenas. Bogotá, Colombia: Instituto Amazónico de Investigaciones Científicas.

Smale, Robert L. 2010. *I Sweat the Flavor of Tin: Labor Activism in Early Twentieth-Century Bolivia*. Pittsburgh: University of Pittsburgh Press.

Smart, Sebastian. 2020. "The Political Economy of Latin American Conflicts over Mining Extractivism." *The Extractive Industries and Society* 7, no. 2: 767–79. https://doi.org/10.1016/j.exis.2020.02.004.

Smilde, David. 2008. "The Social Structure of Hugo Chávez." *Contexts* 7 (1): 38–43.

Smith, William 1989. *Authoritarianism and the Crisis of the Argentine Political Economy*. Stanford: Stanford University Press.

Snow, David, Sarah Soule, and Hanspeter Kriesi. 2004. *The Blackwell Companion to Social Movements*. Oxford: Blackwell Publishing.

Starosta, Guido. 2015. *Marx's Capital, Method and Revolutionary Subjectivity*. Leiden: Brill.

Starosta, Guido. 2019. "Global Capital Accumulation and the Specificity of Latin America." In *The Oxford Handbook of Karl Marx*, edited by Matt Vidal, Tony Smith, and Thomas Rotta, 661–78. Oxford: Oxford University Press.

Sulmont, Denis. 1980. *Historia del movimiento obrero minero metalurgico (hasta 1970)*. Lima: Tarea.

Sulmont, Denis. 1985. "El frende sindical minero." *Cuadernos Laborales* 28 (May).

Sutherland, Manuel. 2018. "La ruina de Venezuela no se debe al 'socialismo' ni a la 'revolución.'" *NUSO N* 274 (Marzo–Abril).

Svampa, Maristella. 2013. "'Consenso de los commodities' y lenguajes de valoración en América Latina." *Nueva Sociedad* 244: 30–46.

Svampa, Maristella. 2017a. *Debates Latinoamericanos: Indianismo, desarrollo, dependencia y populismo*. Buenos Aires: Edhasa.

Svampa, Maristella. 2017b. *Del cambio de época al fin de ciclo: Gobiernos progresistas, extractivismo y movimientos sociales en América Latina*. Buenos Aires: Edhasa.

Svampa, Maristella. 2019. *Neo-Extractivism in Latin America: Socio-Environmental Conflicts, the Territorial Turn, and New Political Narratives, Elements in Politics and Society in Latin America*. Cambridge: Cambridge University Press. https://doi.org/10.1017/9781108752589.

Tandeter, Enrique. 1992. *Coacción y mercado: La minería de la plata en el Potosí colonial, 1692–1826*. Buenos Aires: Editorial Sudamericana.

Tate, Winifred. 2015. *Drugs, Thugs, and Diplomats: U.S. Policymaking in Colombia*. Stanford, CA: Stanford University Press.

Taylor, Marcus. 2014. *The Political Ecology of Climate Change Adaptation: Livelihoods, Agrarian Change and the Conflicts of Development*, first edition. London: Routledge.

Taylor, Marcus, and Sébastien Rioux. 2017. *Global Labor Studies*, first edition. Malen, MA: Polity.

TeleSUR. 2016. "Venezuela's Caracazo: State Repression and Neoliberal Misrule." March 1. https://venezuelanalysis.com/analysis/11868

The Economist. 2010. "The Weakening of the 'Strong Bolivar.'" January 14. https://www.economist.com/the-americas/2010/01/14/the-weakening-of-the-strong-bolivar.

Thomson, Sinclair, Rossana Barragán, Xavier Albó, Seemin Qayum, and Mark Goodale, eds. 2018. *The Bolivia Reader: History, Culture, Politics*. Durham, NC: Duke University Press.

Thorp, Rosemary, and Geoffrey Bertram. 1978. *Peru, 1890–1977: Growth and Policy in an Open Economy*. New York: Columbia University Press.

Tinker Salas, Miguel. 2009. *The Enduring Legacy: Oil, Culture and Society in Venezuela*. Durham: Duke University Press.

Toro Pérez, Catalina, Julio Fierro Morales, Sergio Coronado Delgado, and Tatiana Roa Avendaño, eds. 2012. *Minería, territorio y conflicto en Colombia*. Bogotá: CENSAT, Universidad Nacional de Colombia.

Torre, Juan Carlos. 2014. *La vieja guardia sindical y Perón*. Buenos Aires, Argentina: Ediciones RyR.

Torrijos Rivera, Rafael. 2019. *Cifras de Contexto Ganadero Caquetá 2019*. Florencia, Caquetá, Colombia: Comité Departamental de Ganadero del Caquetá.

Toscano, Alberto. 2018. "Antiphysis/Antipraxis: Universal Exhaustion and the Tragedy of Materiality." *Mediations* 31, no. 2. https://mediationsjournal.org/articles/antiphysis-antipraxis.

Treacy, Mariano. 2022. "Dependency Theory and the Critique of Neodevelopmentalism in Latin America." *Latin American Perspectives* 49, no. 1: 218–36.

Tribuna Popular. 2018. "Unitary Agreement Between PSUV and PCV." https://prensapcv.wordpress.com/2018/03/02/unitary-agreement-between-psuv-and-pcv/.

Trujillo, Jorge León, and Susan Spronk. 2018. "Socialism Without Workers? Trade Unions and the New Left in Bolivia and Ecuador." In *Reshaping the Political Arena in Latin America: From Resisting Neoliberalism to the Second Incorporation*, edited by Eduardo Silva and Federico M. Rossi, 129–56. Pittsburgh: University of Pittsburgh Press.

UN High Commissioner for Refugees. 2023. "Venezuela Situation Fact Sheet." https://reporting.unhcr.org/document/4450.

UN High Office of Drug Control. 2019. *Colombia: Monitoreo de Territorios Afectados Por Cultivos Ilícitos, 2018*. Vienna: UN Office on Drugs and Crime.

UN Network on Migration. n.d. "Triple Win Programme." https://migrationnetwork.un.org/projects/triple-win-programme.

UN Verification Mission in Colombia. 2019. *UN Verification Mission in Colombia Condemns Assassination of Former FARC Combatant in Reintegration Area*. Bogotá, Colombia: UN Verification Mission in Colombia.

Unidad de Planeación Minero Energética. 2006. *Colombia: País Minero*. Bogotá, Colombia: Unidad de Planeación Minero Energética.

United Nations. 2019. *Venezuela: An Overview of Priority Humanitarian Needs*. Geneva.

Uribe Iniesta, Rodolfo. 2008. "Privatización solapada y reforma energética inexistente: La cuestión de la superficie petrolera." *Topodrilo* 14–19.

US Geological Survey. 2013. *Metal Prices in the United States Through 2010*. Reston, Virginia: US Geological Survey.

Valenzuela, Hernán Cuevas, Jorge Budrovich Sáez, and Claudia Cerda Becker. 2021. "Neoliberal Economic, Social, and Spatial Restructuring: Valparaíso and Its Agricultural Hinterland." *Urban Planning* 6, no. 3: 69–89. https://doi.org/10.17645/up.v6i3.4242.

Vales, Laura. 2020. "Quiénes son y qué hacen las 500 mil personas que ya se anotaron como trabajadores de la 'Economía Popular.'" *Página 12 Buenos Aires*, August 21.

Vergara-Camus, Leandro. 2014. "Sugarcane Ethanol: The Hen of the Golden Eggs? Agribusiness and the State in Lula's Brazil." In *Crisis and Contradiction: Marxist Perspectives on Latin America in the Global Political Economy*, edited by Susan Spronk and Jeffery R. Webber, 211–35. Leiden: Brill Academic Publishers.

Vergara-Camus, Leandro, and Cristóbal Kay. 2017. "Agribusiness, Peasants, Left-Wing Governments, and the State in Latin America: An Overview and Theoreti-

cal Reflections." *Journal of Agrarian Change* 17, no. 2: 239–57. https://doi-org
.libproxy.uregina.ca/10.1111/joac.12215.

Vergara-Camus, Leandro and Cristóbal Kay. 2017. "The Agrarian Political Economy
of Left-Wing Governments in Latin America: Agribusiness, Peasants, and the Limits of Neo-Developmentalism." *Journal of Agrarian Change* 17, No. 2: 415–437.

Vergès, Francois. 2019. "Capitalocene, Waste, Race, and Gender." *E-flux Journal*,
100. http://worker01.e-flux.com/pdf/article_269165.pdf.

Viceministerio de Cooperativas Mineras. 2021. *Q'ujta: Boletín Informativo Institu-
cional del Viceministerio de Cooperativas Mineras (No. 11)*. La Paz: Bolivia.

Villar, Leonardo, and Pilar Esguerra. 2007. "El comercio exterior Colombiano en el
siglo XX." In *Economia Colombiana del siglo XX: Un analisis cuantitativo*. Bogotá,
Colombia: Banco de la Republica.

Villegas Flores, Karla, Sergio Sandoval Camponovo, Richard Zenteno, and Juan José
Salmon. 2021. *Mercurio en la pequeña minería aurífera de Bolivia*. La Paz: Plural
Editores.

Vosko, Leah F. 2019. *Disrupting Deportability: Transnational Workers Organize*.
Ithaca, NY: Cornell University Press.

Warnecke-Berger, Hannes. 2020. "Remittances, the Rescaling of Social Conflicts,
and the Stasis of Elite Rule in El Salvador." *Latin American Perspectives* 47, no.
3: 202–20. https://doi.org/10.1177/0094582X19898502.

Webber, Jeffery. 2011. "Venezuela Under Chavez: Prospects and Limitations for
Socialism." In *21st Century Socialism: Reinventing the Project*, edited by Henry
Veltmeyer, 175–203. London: Merlin Press.

Webber, Jeffery R. 2017. *The Last Day of Oppression, and the First Day of the Same:
The Politics and Economics of the New Latin American Left*. Chicago: Haymarket.

Webber, Jeffery. 2019. "State, Bureaucracy, and Rentier Capital." *Dissent*. https://
www.dissentmagazine.org/online_articles/state-bureaucracy-rentier-capital
-maduro-venezuela-crisis.

Weisbrot, Mark. 2023. "Omitting the Evidence: What the IMF Gets Wrong about
Venezuela." Center for Economic and Policy Research, Washington. https://www
.cepr.net/omitting-the-evidence-what-the-imf-gets-wrong-about-venezuela/.

Weisbrot, Mark, Rebecca Ray, and Luis Sandoval. 2009. "The Chavez Administration at 10 Years: The Economy and Social Indicators." Center for Economic and
Policy Research, Washington.

Weisbrot, Mark, and Jeffrey Sachs. 2019. "Economic Sanctions as Collective Punish-
ment: The Case of Venezuela." Center for Economic and Policy Research, Washington. https://cepr.net/images/stories/reports/venezuela-sanctions-2019-04.pdf.

Wood, Ellen Meiksins. 2017. *The Origin of Capitalism: A Longer View*. New York:
Verso.

World Bank. 2022. "Commodity Price Data (The Pink Sheet)." September 2. https://
www.worldbank.org/en/research/commodity-markets.

World Bank. 2023a. "Personal Remittances, Received (% of GDP)." https://data
.worldbank.org/indicator/BX.TRF.PWKR.DT.GD.ZS.

World Bank. 2023b. "Total Natural Resources Rents (% of GDP)." https://data
.worldbank.org/indicator/NY.GDP.TOTL.RT.ZS.

Wrathall, David J. 2012. "Migration amidst Social-Ecological Regime Shift: The Search for Stability in Garifuna Villages of Northern Honduras." *Human Ecology* 40, no. 4: 583–96.

Wright, Erik Olin. 2000. "Working-Class Power, Capitalist-Class Interests, and Class Compromise." *American Journal of Sociology* 105, no. 4: 957–1002.

Wright, Melissa. 2006. *Disposable Women and Other Myths of Global Capitalism.* London: Routledge.

Ye, Jingzhong, Jan Douwe van der Ploeg, Sergio Schneider, and Teodor Shanin. 2020. "The Incursions of Extractivism: Moving from Dispersed Places to Global Capitalism." *The Journal of Peasant Studies* 47, no. 1: 155–83. https://doi.org/10.1080/03066150.2018.1559834.

Zaconeta, Alfredo. 2022. "Reactivación minera entre despidos y empleos precarios." *CEDLA: Alerta Laboral* 90 (April): 18–20.

Zalik, Anna. 2006. "Re-regulating the Mexican Gulf." Working Paper 15, Centre for Latin American Studies, University of California at Berkeley.

Zapata, Antonio, and Marcos Garfias. 2014. *Apuntes de una historia de organización y lucha.* Lima: FNTMMP

Zapata, Francisco. 2002. "Los mineros como actores sociales y políticos en Bolivia, Chile y Perú durante el siglo XX." *Estudios Atacameños* 22: 91–103.

Zavaleta Mercado, René. 1986. *Lo nacional popular en Bolivia.* México: Siglo XXI Editores.

Index

About the Contributors

Fernando Cazón holds a degree in sociology from the University of Buenos Aires, where he is currently undertaking a PhD in social sciences. He is a member of the Centre for Research as Practical Criticism. His research interests are in the conditions of reproduction of labor power and the changing forms of the class struggle in Argentina throughout the twentieth century.

Kristin Ciupa is an assistant professor in the Department of Sociology and Social Studies at the University of Regina. Her research focuses on the political economy of oil, extractivism, and regionalism in Latin America. Her publications include articles in *Globalizations*, *Extractive Industries and Society*, and *Critical Sociology*. She is author of the book *The Political Economy of Oil in Venezuela: Class Conflict, the State, and the World Market* (forthcoming).

Ruth Felder is member of the Political Science Program at the Faculty of Social Science and Humanities, Ontario Tech University. Her research focuses on the political economy of Latin America with a focus on Argentina, and she has conducted research on the role of the state in neoliberal reforms and on the transformation of labor markets, the rise of precarious and informal work, and the forms of collective action of precarious workers.

Aleida Hernández Cervantes is a researcher at the Center for Interdisciplinary Research in Sciences and Humanities and a professor in the Division of Postgraduate Studies of the Faculty of Law at the Universidad Nacional Autónoma de México. She has several publications on theory, legal epistemology, gender, social security, and work.

Phillip A. Hough is a Colombian-American sociologist and associate professor at Florida Atlantic University, Boca Raton. He is the author of *At the Margins of the Global Market: Making Commodities, Workers, and Crisis in Rural Colombia* (2022). He received a Fulbright US Global Scholar Award (2022–2024) that is financing rounds of fieldwork in Colombia, Kenya, and Vietnam, and that will be the basis of his next book, *Post-Neoliberal Possibilities: Production, Livelihoods, and Development across the Global Coffee Belt.*

Christopher Little is a PhD candidate in the Department of Politics at York University, Toronto. He researches the political economy of labor migration, agriculture, and uneven development, with a focus on the experience of workers within the structural constraints of the world economy, how agency is exercised amid these forces, and the social reproduction of labor-power. His PhD thesis is focused on agrarian labor migration flows between Guatemala and Ontario, Canada, and their relationship to transnational processes of agrarian change during the era of neoliberal capitalism.

Omar Manky is an associate professor of sociology at Universidad del Pacífico in Lima, Peru. His research focuses on labor movements, social conflicts, and extractive industries in Latin America. He has published widely on these topics in journals such as *British Journal of Industrial Relations* and *Latin American Perspectives.*

Andrea Marston is an assistant professor in the Geography Department at Rutgers University. Her research focuses on the political economy and material politics of resource extraction in Latin America, with a focus on small-scale mining in Bolivia. Her publications include articles in *Journal of Peasant Studies*, *Latin American Perspectives*, *Political Geography*, and *Annals of the Association of American Geographers*. Her book, *Subterranean Matters: Cooperative Mining and Resource Nationalism in Plurinational Bolivia*, is forthcoming.

Viviana Patroni is a member of the Department of Social Science at York University, where she teaches in the International Development Studies program. Her research focuses on the political economy of Latin America, the dramatic changes in the world of work in this region since the 1980s, the centrality of labor struggles in shaping patterns of development, and the transformation of labor markets in Argentina since the 1990s. Her most recent work includes an interest on the rise of organizations of informal workers and their challenge to prevalent views within labor movements about their understanding of work and working class.

Guido Starosta is professor in the history of economic thought at the National University of Quilmes and a member of the National Council of Scientific and Technical Research in Argentina. He is also a member of the Centre for Science as Practical Criticism. His research interests are in the critique of political economy and political economy of development.

Jeffery R. Webber is a professor of politics at York University, Toronto. He is author of a number of books on the political economy of Latin America. Most recently, he is co-author of *The Impasse of the Latin American Left* (2022).

Anna Zalik is an associate professor in the Faculty of Environmental Studies at York University, Toronto, where she teaches in the area of global environmental politics and critical development studies. Her scholarly articles have appeared in *International Social Science Journal, Journal of Latin American Geography, Extractive Industries and Society,* and *Environment and Planning A*, among other journals. Her research, in conjunction with colleagues and community organizations, examines and critiques the political ecology and political economy of industrial extraction, with a focus on the merging of corporate security and social welfare interventions in strategic exporters.